A Future and a Hope

Contents

Foreword

Canon Dr. Michael Bourdeaux

One would think—at first glance—that the collapse of the Soviet Union in 1991 offered the Protestant churches in Russia, Ukraine and new countries of the Former Soviet Union an unprecedented opportunity not only to cast off the shackles, but to evangelize freely and be rid of the legacy of persecution once and for all. As *A Future and a Hope* illustrates, in conclusions based on varied and deep personal experience, this has failed to come about.

Concentrating mainly on Ukraine, where Mykhailo N. Cherenkov grew up and where Joshua T. Searle has worked, but also alluding freely to Russia, the co-authors emphasise the legacy of *homo sovieticus* (the "new Soviet man" which the Soviet system signally failed to introduce to society). In one of the most telling passages of the book, they interpret the limitation on the gains made by the Protestant churches over the past quarter of a century as a result of the persistence of a Soviet mentality. "*Homo sovieticus,*" the authors claim, "is a Dostoevskian caricature of a degraded humanity which is paralyzed by the existential tension arising from the tragicomic situation of being, on the one hand, created for freedom, but, on the other, being too weak to embrace the risk, responsibility and vulnerability that freedom brings." By contrast, in Ukraine there is now a new spirit of freedom in 2014, born of the demonstrations on Maidan Square in Kyiv, but affecting large sections of the population in places other than the Ukrainian capital.

Let it not be thought, however, that this is primarily a political book. It is only partly so, while its main characteristic is the fact that at all points it draws deeply on the gospel. Herein lies the hope that underlies the pessimism expressed on many pages.

Is the Orthodox Church forever to be the bedrock of Russian culture? In my first book, *Opium of the People* (1965), spending a year as an exchange student at Moscow State University, I posed the question: "If I had a Russian friend who was a potential convert to Christianity, would I introduce him first to the Orthodox Church or to the Baptist?" After setting out two sides of an argument at some length, I concluded: "In most instances, taking everything into consideration, I would probably advise a potential convert to go to the Baptist church." This remark called forth widespread opprobrium and I later revised this opinion. However, now—almost fifty years later—I would opt for a preference for my original thoughts and perhaps express them more strongly.

The Russian Orthodox Church has lost most of its moral authority, due primarily to the practical concept of *symfonia* between Church and State. This is a doctrine, inherited from Byzantium a millennium ago, that the two work in concert, the Church providing the moral authority, the State the political, for the just governance of the people. This might once have worked satisfactorily, though fraught with danger, when the "duumvirate" really did have corresponding ideals. However, the concept was shattered for all time by the imposition of an atheist authority under the Bolsheviks after 1917. The attempts of the Orthodox Church to re-establish it during an era of persecution reeked of compromise, one for which there has been scarcely a note of repentance. Since the collapse of communism in 1991, the *symfonia* has resounded with ever more glaring political orchestration. President Putin and Patriarch Kirill, since his election in 2009, have clearly envisaged the same objective: a Russia spiritually and politically strong, quickly regaining the powerful status in the world which the USSR formerly enjoyed. Recent developments in the Ukrainian crisis may well have caused tensions between the two (the jurisdiction of the Moscow Patriarchate in Ukraine is now deeply divided between pro- and anti-Moscow activists), but the basic united vision of a strong Russia remains unscathed. Furthermore, the "Slavic brotherhood," so ardently proclaimed by both Patriarch Kirill and President Putin, has been ruptured by Moscow's clodhopping interventions in Ukraine's affairs, dating at least back to Putin's earlier visits to Kyiv to influence Ukrainian elections. Ukrainians have become much more collectively aware than they were of the way in which the Bolsheviks suppressed the short-lived Ukrainian independence after 1917 and the *holodomor* (death by starvation), the artificially induced famine of the 1930s, when Russia stole Ukrainian grain and caused the millions to perish as a result.

The authors have some harsh words about this current issue: "Putin and his fellow mobsters in the Kremlin are trying to turn Ukraine into its own image: an authoritarian failed state controlled by the mafia, in which the organs of state power become instruments for racketeering, repression and corruption." The Kremlin wants Ukraine to become another Belarus, part of Russia's fiefdom.

This bold statement, although justified, is not a main theme of the book, which, in the main, puts directly political issues into the middle distance. Much more central is a detailed study of foreign Protestant mission to Ukraine and its overall failure. These missionaries, typically though not exclusively from America, have failed to consolidate their initial impact because of lack of sensitivity and cultural acclimatisation to Ukrainian conditions. After all, Ukraine has been Christian for 1025 years, a historical perspective scarcely shared by the United States!

Western fundamentalist evangelical missionaries, as the authors tell us, have inherited an "impoverished understanding of mission" and it is tragic that this has been grafted on to Ukraine from the outside. This has led, in its turn, to a widespread resistant conservatism, which treats as suspect anything which local pastors fear might be contaminated by "liberal" or "ecumenical" theology in the West.

In the Soviet period religious education was in general banned at all levels, the exceptions being three theological seminaries and two academies for the Orthodox and one with a tiny intake for Lithuanian Catholics. For Protestants there was no residential seminary, though occasionally pastors were permitted to study abroad. It was an achievement of the Baptist-Evangelical administration in Moscow that in later years the authorities permitted the establishment of a non-residential correspondence course. Now this has been reversed and there are numerous Protestant seminaries throughout the Former Soviet Union. However, according to the authors, they both suffer an enrolment shortfall, which, in its turn, limits the scope of the education on offer.

However, the book ends on an optimistic note: the promise of "the flowering of evangelical ecumenism in action." Not only those sympathetic to the Christian cause in the former Soviet Union, but especially those in the West who remain faithful to the vision of Christian unity in the future, will have cause to rejoice in the publication of this book.

Michael Bourdeaux
Oxford, September 2014

Preface

The aim of this book is to offer an overview of some of the challenges and opportunities for evangelical theological education and mission in the Former Soviet Union (hereafter FSU). The Church in this huge region has now reached a crucial phase in its historical development. Pastors and academic leaders are seeking the kind of visions and values that will be needed to navigate a new course into an uncertain but exhilarating future. These reflections have arisen out of the authors' experience of serving alongside those who are working to build the Kingdom of God through targeted initiatives of mission and transformative theological education in the FSU. We hope that this book will raise awareness among English-speaking readers of evangelical communities in the former USSR. Our main aim, however, is to make a small but significant contribution to the raising up of a new generation of Christian leaders who will build the Kingdom of God in this fascinating—but very troubled—part of the world.

In the interests of brevity, clarity and focus, the analysis will be focused mainly on Ukraine. However, the challenges and opportunities described in this book are not confined to Ukraine or even to the nations of the FSU. Although missiological challenges and opportunities are always shaped by specific local factors, they can be meaningfully addressed only by a creative application of timeless biblical principles and imperatives, such as compassion, justice and reconciliation, which require careful, sensitive and creative application to specific contexts. It is hoped, therefore, that the issues raised here will be meaningful and relevant for any church or theological institution, particularly in the FSU, that is grappling with the issue of how to train and equip the next generation of Christian leaders for service in the Church and society.

This book is the product of a deep friendship between two authors, one in his 20s, and the other in his 30s, whose lives and vocations have converged in remarkable ways. The reflections contained in this work have arisen out of a profound commitment to the Great Commission, an overriding allegiance to the gospel of hope and an ardent desire for the Church to rediscover its prophetic voice and become a major factor in the positive transformation of post-Soviet society. The idea for this book emerged in the autumn of 2012 when the authors, who were colleagues at Donetsk Christian University, perceived the need to map out the contours of a vision of hope that would serve the Church and the Kingdom of God in this region. At the time, both authors realized the inadequacy of stale antinomies (e.g. academy vs. church; lay vs. ordained; conservative vs. liberal; faith vs. evidence; divine revelation vs. human experience, and so on) that had been imported from Western theology. These dichotomies were alien to the natural inclinations of the Eastern Slavic mindsets, which were more inclined to identify commonalities in phenomena than to dissect and analyze in terms of sharp polarities. We perceived the conspicuous deficiencies of many of the models of theological education, imported from other contexts, and how they were enervating the life and witness of evangelical communities in the FSU, leaving pastors ill-equipped for ministry and mission in this region.

Since moving away from Donetsk, both authors have engaged in an extended dialogue of shared discussion and mutual critique. This work is, therefore, a genuinely collaborative endeavor and the experience of co-authoring this book has been enriching and has broadened our horizons in ways that we hope will add to the rigor, depth and significance of our reflections. If our analysis seems at times unduly critical and pessimistic, we remind readers that this book has arisen out of a deep commitment to the Church and an overriding hope that evangelical Christian communities in the former USSR can not merely survive, but can thrive and flourish and even play a significant role in helping post-Soviet society jettison the burden of its Soviet past. The inspiration that has led us to write this book is the hope that our generation will be able to witness and experience a new movement of the Holy Spirit that will sweep through the nations of the FSU bringing new life, redemption, reconciliation, renewal and compassion in its wake.

Joshua T. Searle and Mykhailo N. Cherenkov
Kyiv and London, 2014

Acknowledgments

We dedicate this book to our many friends and partners in mission who have supported and encouraged us over the past few years. Belonging to the Baptist tradition and endeavoring to offer new proposals concerning its development, we convey our appreciation to all its best representatives whose wisdom and faithfulness have made it visible and influential. We express a special word of gratitude to our fathers, Roy Searle and Nikolai Cherenkov, whose fine example of faithful service inspires us to look to the future with hope.

We gratefully acknowledge the support of the Keston Institute, which funded our post-doctoral fellowships, thus enabling both authors to visit the Keston Archive at Baylor University, Texas, for extended periods of research. We are very grateful to the staff at the Keston Centre at Baylor, particularly to Larisa Seago, who directed us towards crucial sources and gave generously of her time and archival expertise to ensure that we were able to make the most of our time in the magnificent Keston Archive. Many of the insights contained in this work are based on original sources that we unearthed during the time we spent burrowing through the voluminous materials stored in this historical and theological treasure trove. We both owe a profound debt of gratitude to the President of the Keston Institute, Michael Bourdeaux, and to the Chairperson, Xenia Dennen, for their encouragement and inspiration. To our long-term friend and esteemed colleague, Sergey Rakhuba, President of Mission Eurasia (formerly known as Peter Deyneka Russian Ministries), we convey our warmest thanks and appreciation for the wisdom, experience and support he has given us and for the ways he has encouraged us in the process of writing this book. We are grateful to Denys Baranov for the editorial work he did to prepare the book for publication and to Rachel Ruvarac for her judicious corrections to the text. We also extend our thanks to the *European Journal of Theology* for allowing us to include chapter 7, which is largely based on an article published in that journal in 2014.

Joshua is indebted to his gifted and dedicated colleagues at Spurgeon's College for their support and friendship. He is particularly grateful to the College Principal, Roger Standing, who has been an abundant source of wise counsel and encouragement through his personal example and his expertise in the field of missiology. Most of all Joshua acknowledges his gratitude to his wife and soulmate, Varduyi Rosa. Although she may not think of herself as a "professional" theologian or missiologist, Varduyi is an indispensible partner in Joshua's ministry. Her constant companionship, generosity and kindness have inspired many of the better thoughts contained in this volume that Joshua might have been able to contribute. Mykhailo expresses his deepest thanks to his wife, Nina, to whom he will be forever grateful for the sacrifices she has made and the patience she has shown. Mykhailo gratefully acknowledges Nina's constant dedication to their children, which enabled him to spend many long hours in the study and to be away while conducting research for this book.

Introduction

Looking to the Future with Hope

The future and the hope of post-Soviet churches are connected with recovering the vital organic link between the life of the Church, missional practice, Christian formation and theological education. Unfortunately, for many evangelicals these areas remain separated and their picture of the world is fragmented. This book provides an analysis and outlook on the ministry of the post-Soviet Church that embraces the integrity, oneness, and interconnectedness of theology, mission, education, and ministry.

Another aspect of these reflections is their focus on the future at a time when post-Soviet churches are characteristically oriented to times past and constantly looking back at their historical experience, particularly those dating to Soviet times. In an atmosphere when the Church is contemplating the past, the picture of the world in which it lives, and its thoughts about that world are fragmented, self-critical theology and theological education may seem superfluous. Critical theological reflection has not been prominent among post-Soviet evangelicals, many of whom find it difficult to integrate the insights of academic theology into the day-to-day routine of sheltered church life. Yet our key contention is that it is precisely theology and a theological education that might serve as the catalyst of change for the Church and its mission.

There are at least three reasons why some find it awkward and of little benefit to talk and write about the Church, its mission, theology and education in today's post-Soviet context. Firstly, most of the hopes and expectations that emerged after the collapse of the USSR were not realized, and the euphoria of those days gave way to fatigue and frustration. The tendency is to avoid painful issues, to scroll past the pages of misfortune and setbacks. Secondly, an objective discussion of the religious processes underway in a post-Soviet space is increasingly risky in light of Russia's anti-Western stance. Thirdly, post-Soviet churches, missions and schools are rarely open to self-criticism, so any attempts at analysis usually boil down to simply asking, "Who can we blame?" All three of these will result in serious consequences if they are ignored. We must make our way through the experience of fatigue and disillusionment, through the temptation of a convenient anti-Westernism, and through the anxiety caused by contentious topics, criticisms and responsibilities.

We need to open up to different voices, including the voices of the tired and disillusioned, and those outside of the Church, as well as those on its margins. Not long ago, a certain Ukrainian pastor, a teacher of theology, admitted ruefully that, "The past 20 years of the ministry have proved to be a disappointing endeavor. My church has not grown, and my students have not become active, successful leaders." Similar sentiments can be heard from church leaders: "Where are the results of our sowing? Where is the long-awaited transformation of society? Where is the reformation of the Church?" We echo the prophet's lament that we seem to have sown so much, but reaped so little.[1]

The same lament sounds from the society towards the Church. These were the concerns of the people involved in the protests on the Maidan in central Kyiv. The protesters were disillusioned with the corruption and lawlessness of society, and with the indifference and irresponsibility of the Church. Instead of demonstrating solidarity with those social agents campaigning for social justice (which is an unambiguous biblical imperative), the response of the Church to pressing issues that emerge from the public sphere is often devoid of a theological basis and sometimes directly contradicts fundamental biblical-theological principles. The Church seems not always to have recognized that "the needs of the world, not the concerns of the Church, are primary to an understanding of effective evangelism," and that, "the Church is most true to its calling when its people are mobilized to look beyond themselves and out into the world."[2] Thus, although we encounter loyalty to the State, rarely do we demonstrate solidarity with

1. Hag 1:6.
2. Drane, *Faith in a Changing Culture*, 71–72.

society. We see the justification of simplicity, but rarely do we witness the active encouragement of intellectual development.

It is easy to justify the marginalization of the Church, and equally easy to justify its social passivity and unwillingness to take responsibility for the public sphere. In lieu of theological answers, leaders of evangelical Churches substitute outside ideas. Thus Russian Baptists like to refer to articles by the American fundamentalist, Pat Buchanan, about "Putin, the Defender of Christianity." In these ill-informed contributions to public debates, we see how convenient pseudo-theological notions are pronounced concerning the death of Christianity in the West and the special spiritual vitality of the Slavs. Dubious theses are persistently reiterated about the dangers of "Western" theology and the allegedly "superfluous" education of those purportedly enticing the Church away from the simplicity of the gospel with their arcane theories and sophisticated theology.

Another focus of the present work is an analysis of how religious and theological processes are inextricably connected with socio-political processes. The main discernable tendency can be understood as a gradual emancipation from the Soviet legacy, which takes the form of de-sovietization (as in Ukraine) or neo-sovietization (as in Russia). Even in the rhetoric of church leaders, it is easy to see that the Church, and its image of itself and its mission, invariably fits into a social context. Therefore, a discussion of this context is unavoidable. The discussion needs to be nuanced and aware of the complexities of the Church's engagement with culture. It is important not to be confined to sociological straightjackets of "Christ against Culture" or "Christ of Culture." Instead, the Church should seek to exercise proper discernment concerning which social trends are consistent with the vision of the Kingdom of God. As Miroslav Volf contends, "The proper stance of Christians toward the larger culture cannot be that of unmitigated opposition or whole-scale transformation. A much more complex attitude is required—that of accepting, rejecting, learning from, transforming, and subverting or putting to better use various elements of an internally differentiated and rapidly changing culture."[3] In order to fulfill its prophetic role, the Church needs to be clear about where it should adjust to the context, where it should contest it, and where it should engage in conflict with it. Antoine Arjakovsky rightly maintains that, "The Church . . . believes that all power in heaven *and on earth* has been given by God the Father to Jesus Christ, as stated in the Gospel of Matthew (28:18). Consequently, the

3. Volf, *Public Faith*, xvi.

Church must relativize the role of the State while orienting it towards the responsibility they hold in common: to make the Kingdom of God come on earth."[4] Accordingly, we will focus on the future of the Church, its mission, theology and theological education in their inextricable interconnectedness. This book will also focus on the Church's prospects, taking into account the socio-political context.

While drawing liberally on a wide range of relevant scholarship, including theology, missiology, philosophy, history, psychology, and the social sciences, this work is intended not only for professional academics or experts in missiology; rather the analysis and reflection that follows are offered as a challenge and encouragement to anyone who is interested in how the good news of the gospel can become a meaningful and empowering message of hope for the wholesale transformation of society. It is hoped that this study will be of particular interest to those who would like to understand the contribution that theological education could make towards the elucidation and realization of a truly contextual theology that will equip both "professional Christians" and "Christian professionals" to address the challenges of contemporary post-Soviet culture with a "proper confidence"[5] that is rooted in the light of Christ and the hope of the gospel. This work is written in the conviction that theological education has a role akin to that of a midwife of the future; that is, education can facilitate the birth of new missional churches throughout Ukraine and the nations of the FSU, which in turn will have a positive leavening effect on the wider post-Soviet society.

The recurring thesis of what follows is that the challenges confronting theological education and mission in Ukraine can best be addressed not merely by developing new strategies or even by dreaming new visions; rather, what is needed above all is a renewed focus on the central component of the mission of Jesus as depicted in the gospels: *compassion* (Greek: ἀγάπη).[6] Visions and aspirations come and go, but gospel values endure. Visions and grand strategies must be sustained by a clear set of values derived from gospel principles that are lived out in the context of a community (κοινωνία) that is characterized by service (διακονία) and mutual love (ἀγάπη).

This argument is simple and may even sound naïve and not particularly "academic" or "scientific," but in the flurry of missionary enthusiasm that followed the downfall of communism and the so-called triumph of

4. Arjakovsky, "The Role of the Churches in the Ukrainian Revolution."
5. This term is borrowed from Newbigin, *Proper Confidence.*
6. Matt 9:36; 14:14; Mark 6:34; Luke 7:13; 10:33; 15:20.

the West,[7] it was easy to lose focus on the simple message of Jesus's compassion. It has been noted that the early evangelical Protestant missionary movement in the FSU placed too much focus on planning and executing programs. Thus instead of responding with compassion and building the Kingdom of God in contextualized ways, many Western missionaries created what Johannes Reimer disparagingly calls an "evangelism industry."[8] According to some critics, considerable missionary energy was expended on obtaining outcomes that were important to Western funding organizations, but which had little positive impact on the local populations of believers.

If the evangelical churches in this region are to offset the trend of decline and deterioration, they must learn from the mistakes of the churches in Western Europe, and develop radically new ways of living missionally in the rapidly changing cultural context. Part of the analysis will be directed towards the elucidation of a contextual theology that connects with the spiritual, social and economic realities of the communities within which evangelicals live and work. One of the most persistent laments in recent scholarship in this area has been over the failure of post-Soviet evangelicals to develop a genuinely contextual missiology that would equip the churches of the FSU.[9] During a study trip to a large North American theological college, Mykhailo bewailed the fact that, amid the wealth of diverse missiological research contained in the college library from Africa, Japan, India, China, Papua New Guinea, and various other regions throughout the world, he found almost nothing on the churches in the FSU.[10]

Addressing this lack of a contextual post-Soviet missiology, theological education should, accordingly, be directed towards equipping people to relate effectively to the hopes, fears, anxieties and aspirations of the local people whom they serve. This will involve the formation of a contextual theology that seeks to impart the gospel "in the light of the respondent's worldview and then adapting the message, encoding it in such a way that

7. Walter Sawatsky argues that it is possible that no other event in the history of missions had generated as much hope and excitement among evangelicals as the collapse of the Soviet Union; see Sawatsky, "Return of Mission," 94–119.

8. Reimer, "Mission," 16–39.

9. Cherenkov, "Postsovetskiye yevangel'skiye tserkvi v poiskakh," 7–16.

10. Cherenkov, "Post-Soviet Churches Struggle." Alexander Negrov and Miriam Charter similarly lamented the failure of Russian Protestants to develop a contextual theology and offered several convincing explanations; see Negrov and Charter, "Why Is There No Russian 'Protestant' Theology in Russia?"

it can become meaningful to the respondent."[11] Post-Soviet evangelical communities require a new missional paradigm that responds to the needs and questions of people beyond the walls of the Church. Moreover, this paradigm must be able to serve as a "matrix for appropriate theologies" and "bring together the inner world of the church and outer world of culture, overcoming the spiritual and social dichotomy."[12] It is now clear that the development of a missional paradigm that can refract the real lived experiences and hopes and fears of the people and nations of the post-Soviet society is one of the most urgent tasks of evangelical theology in Slavic contexts today.

The quest for an appropriate missional paradigm is vitally connected to what Walter Rauschenbusch called "the essential purpose of Christianity," which, he affirmed, is "to transform human society into the Kingdom of God by regenerating all human relations and reconstituting them with the will of God."[13] This is the task that confronts the worldwide Church, including the churches scattered throughout the vast territory of the FSU. In working towards the fulfillment of this task, we must remember the tremendously high stakes involved: if the churches fail to develop an adequate social philosophy that can connect meaningfully with contemporary cultural realities, then the nations of the FSU could be plunged into a new dark age of moral depravity, spiritual decadence and political corruption and instability. If, on the other hand, the Ukrainian churches can fulfill their vocation by becoming a transformative presence for the renewal of culture, then the evangelical community could lead the way towards building the Kingdom of God throughout Eastern Europe, Russia and Central Asia.

Clarifying the Key Terms

Before proceeding, we need to make a few clarifications and stipulations regarding terms and limitations:

On the church and the Church: Most often, when speaking of the "Church," we have in mind the community of post-Soviet evangelical churches, primarily Baptist and Pentecostal. When the word "church" is not capitalized, this refers to the church as a particular institution. But when a

---

11. Frost and Hirsch, *Shaping of Things to Come*, 83.

12. Cherenkov, *Baptism bez kavichek*.

13. Rauschenbusch, *Christianity and the Social Crisis*, xxxvii.

capital letter is used, the reference is to the unified universal Church as the Mystical Body of Christ.

On mission: In a narrow sense, "mission" is often understood as synonymous with "evangelism"; that is, as external activity by the Church to attract new people. One of the aims of this book will be to recast the meaning and significance of mission in terms of an inclusive vision of *missio Dei*. In this broader sense, the word "mission" implies not *only* the salvation of individuals from personal sin, but the wholesale transformation of society as well. Partly owing to the undue influence of Western fundamentalist evangelical missionaries in the region after the disintegration of the USSR, many evangelical churches of the FSU have inherited an impoverished understanding of mission. Mission is not primarily about engaging in evangelistic activities and programs, but is about participating in the sending of God, who is already in the process of saving the world beyond the missional activity of the Church. *Missio Dei* rather than *missio ecclesiae* is the defining essence of the Church. Mission is not restricted to verbal proclamation of propositional statements concerning God, sin, salvation and eternal life, but is rather an incarnational act that makes the gospel visible to a world which God so loved and for which he sent his only Son to die (John 3:16).

On Kingdom: The Kingdom of God refers to the sphere of God's reign in the world through which every aspect of creation and culture is redeemed, rejuvenated and transformed under the rule of Christ and the activity of the Holy Spirit. The Kingdom encompasses not only the Church, but also the whole world. Already we can see the traces and flash points of this Kingdom, but at this time we anticipate its full and final coming. The Church is not synonymous with the Kingdom, but is rightly construed as "the beachhead of the Kingdom, the place in which the reign of God begins to be made manifest here and now."[14] One of the most significant characteristics of the Kingdom of God is, as Parush Parushev notes, that it emerges "from below, subverting existing social and political arrangements at the grass-roots level."[15] The Kingdom grows like a mustard seed and acts like yeast in the dough (Matt 13:31–35). Although the coming of the Kingdom is always God's initiative, its full realization in the world requires the participation of all the people of God in order to make the Kingdom of God a visible reality in contemporary society. The Kingdom of God is therefore a vision of human fulfillment and flourishing which is made real

14. Stassen and Gushee, *Kingdom Ethics*, 230.
15. Parushev, "Kingdom of Heaven," 289.

and visible by the life and witness of the community of Jesus. This notion of the Kingdom enables us to interpret Jesus's proclamation of the Kingdom of God not only as a call to personal repentance, but also as a compassionate imperative to co-ordinate our efforts with God's call for social justice and the radical transformation of the very fabric of social life.

On the gospel: The message of the gospel cannot be reduced to narrow, pietistic conceptions of "repenting of your sins and believing in Jesus, so you can go to heaven when you die." At the heart of the gospel proclamation is a radical, inclusive and all-encompassing vision of the Kingdom of God. The gospel is a call to radical *metanoia*, to a fundamental reorientation of one's material relation towards God and towards one's fellow human beings. We maintain that the message of Christ cannot be reduced to a set of rules and dogmas passed down by traditions. Fidelity to the gospel is not a matter of being faithful to church traditions; nor is it a matter of returning to some utopian ideal supposedly represented by the early church; nor is it even simply a matter of espousing so-called sound doctrine. Rather, fidelity to the gospel means to live and believe in accordance with the vision inspired by the world-changing events that gave birth to the early Church.[16] These events, which unleashed such a powerful and world-transforming missional movement in the first few centuries of the Church, are as present now as they were at any time since then.[17] These events of the "realistic narrative"[18] of Scripture are as real and normatively binding for the faith and practice of today's church as they were for the primitive church described in the book of Acts. We are sustained by the same gospel vision and we remain faithful to the event that gave birth to Christianity not by imitation of rituals and dogma associated with tradition, but by advancing boldly into the new creation opened up by the events of incarnation, crucifixion and resurrection.

On theology: Most often, by "theology" we mean the sum of our knowledge of God, but it is worth our while to expand the scope of this concept. Theology is also a mode of thought, a system of values, a manner of relating to oneself and to the world, a way of life, and a vision involving the wholesale transformation of one's material interaction with the world. In other words, theology is a transformative enterprise that combines theory and practice, the spiritual and the social, the personal and the collective,

16. Ibid., 32.

17. Parushev, "Walking in the Dawn of the Light," 109.

18. Frei, *Eclipse of Biblical Narrative*, 16.

tradition and modernity, and the rational and the mystical. An appropriate theology recognizes that the truth of the biblical revelation cannot be encompassed by words, reduced to concepts, or comprehended in its entirety by rational analysis. Theology testifies to a truth that cannot be "reduced to intellectual affirmations or . . . objectified and dissected by experts."[19]

Already in the understanding of these concepts the impetus is toward wholeness, outside of which rigid distinctions between the Church and the Kingdom, theology and mission, theory and practice, are devoid of meaning. It is worth noting that the tendency toward wholeness coincides with the self-understanding of modern theology and a postmodern sensitivity, in which "theory no longer applies to the mental constructs that exist regardless of their incarnations in the physical, physiological and social structures of life. Theory and practice influence each other such that practice includes theory and theory can be discerned only through practice."[20] Based on the non-trivial connection between theory and practice, theology and mission, and reflection and life of the Church, we need to re-examine stereotypes about such notions as "Christian worldview," "systematic theology," and "political neutrality." Key concepts in what follows are "missiology of the Kingdom," "Kingdom formation," and "open Christianity." We hope that in light of these concepts, post-Soviet churches, while learning the lessons of history, will be able to re-envision their ministry and mission in terms of their future prospects rather than remaining trapped in the past.

19. Rollins, *Fidelity of Betrayal*, 113–14.
20. Anderson, *Shape of Practical Theology*, 21.

1

Shifting Paradigms of Mission

From Evangelical Activism to *Missio Dei*

The Church in the FSU is entering a new era. The engine of development that drives large-scale changes is missiology. For too long, post-Soviet evangelicals neglected theology, including ecclesiology, focusing on "mission" in its most basic sense as "evangelism." Before long, the needs of the mission dictated the need for missiology, and the questions of missiology came up against the need for a comprehensive theological analysis of the ties that bind Church and Kingdom, community and society, mission and education, and religion and culture. It is apparent that we are living in a time of transition. The contours of the future are still hazy; we look as through a glass darkly. Nevertheless, we can identify four stages of transition that the post-Soviet church is currently passing through and that dictate changes in its way of life and ministry.

First, we are experiencing a transition from a confessional understanding of the "mission of the Church" to a "missiology of the Kingdom." Walter Sawatsky called this a turning away from "church-centered missiology" to "God-centered missiology" where "the mission is no longer limited to the established Church, rather it signifies shalom in the Kingdom."[1] There is a gradual recognition that mission is not to be equated with evangelistic activities or outreach programs, but is much more about the whole of life.

1. Sawatsky, "Without God We Cannot," 258.

Mission is not about inviting people to religious buildings to attend religious events organized by the church. Mission is much more a matter of engaging with the world and learning to listen to God's heartbeat and discerning his purposes for particular communities in order encourage "more reflective and intelligent participation in those purposes."[2] The gospel calls us to be a missional people. As one Anglican document put it: it is not so much that the Church has a mission, but that the God of mission has a Church.[3] Mission has a theocentric, rather than an ecclesiocentric, object and point of departure. If mission, according the *missio Dei* paradigm developed by Barth[4] and Bosch[5] and others, originates in the very nature of the Triune God, then mission becomes not so much an activity in which churches engage, but a divine imperative in which the Church participates. The Kingdom of God is the object of mission. The coming of that Kingdom "on earth as in heaven" (Matt 6:10), rather than mere church growth or numerical conversions, is regarded as the true aim of mission. Mission is not about attracting people to religious services, but is concerned with the wholesale transfiguration of the kingdoms of this world into the "Kingdom of our Lord and of his Christ" (Rev 11:15).

Second, the transition from a particular understanding of the mission as the "spiritual work" of a few people empowered by the Church to the idea of a holistic mission, covering all spheres of life and mobilizing all the people of the Church to participate in the *missio Dei*, which involves an uncompromising commitment to work tirelessly in the struggle for social justice. A reconsideration of the idea of the "priesthood of all believers" provides impetus to a theological understanding of the mission as a responsibility delegated to all the people of God.[6] As Charles Spurgeon once quipped, "Every Christian is either a missionary or an imposter." Related to this is the expansion of the social base of the mission—from a ministry of professional missionaries to a movement of missional professionals. Ukraine has seen the creation of the Alliance of Christian Professional Associations.[7] Special editions of the *Desktop Gospel* are being published. If before, mission boiled down to evangelism and the planting of new churches, today it

---

2. Bevans and Schroeder, *Constants in Context*, 1.

3. Rosenthal and Erdey, *Living Communion*, 302.

4. Flett, *Witness of God*.

5. Bosch, *Transforming Mission*.

6. "Universal Priesthood," 84.

7. Dmitrenko, *Vid ponedilka*, 240.

inevitably involves campaigning for social justice, which is itself a gospel imperative.

The third trend that can be observed in connection with cultural and demographic processes is the call to revive, awaken, and reform existing church structures in order to equip the Church for mission and ministry in a changing world. The year 2013, which marked the 1025th anniversary of the Baptism of Rus,' highlighted the issue of nominal Christianity. Around eighty percent of the European regions of the FSU regard themselves as belonging to the Christian tradition. Yet only a small percentage is practicing Christians. Prayer, Bible and congregational life remain the esoteric occupations of a dwindling minority of "spiritual" people. Society is transitioning towards post-Christendom, and in many regions the Church has become a museum, a relic of a bygone era.

Fourth, a shift is taking place from the usual short-term project thinking and naive exclusivity to a meaningful partnership between traditions and regions. Thus, Peter Penner calls for dialogue and a "truly biblical partnership" in implementing "God's mission" between foreign and national movements, as well as between Evangelical and Orthodox Churches.[8] The times demand not naive globalism or Westernism. The mission of the churches will be served not by fawning and borrowing, but by mutually enriching partnerships and the creative construction of localized missiologies.

These transitions mark a more profound shift in the missiological paradigm, which is still difficult to describe, but of a magnitude suggesting that it will result in a radical rethinking of the Church and its vocation. It is no accident that these processes coincide in time with the upcoming 500th anniversary of the European Reformation. According to some, post-Soviet evangelical Christians have skipped their Reformation[9], and it is possible that this very time offers another opportunity to renew the Church and transform society.

The Missional Imperative of Compassion

We believe that in order to realize this kind of transformation, a paradigm shift in missional consciousness needs to take place at a number of levels.

---

8. Penner, "Critical Evaluation," 120–64.

9 The Ukrainian theologian Dmitry Bintsarovsky uses the term "Protestantism without a Reformation" to define the theological heritage of post-Soviet evangelicals; see Bintsarovsky, "Protestantizm," 212–29.

Firstly, the focus of evangelicals must move away from an exclusively intro-spective concern about "personal salvation" and a "personal relationship with Jesus Christ." Over the past few years, we have visited several Ukrai-nian evangelical churches and listened to hundreds of sermons. Almost without exception, the message was essentially inward looking and aimed at prompting people to repent of their sins, to believe in Jesus and be saved. The critical observation made by David Buttrick, although made in a differ-ent context, could apply just as well to the case of many Ukrainian evangeli-cal church services: "Salvation in most Protestant sermons is a happening in the heart whereby individuals are restored to God's good grace by means of a personal decision for Jesus, have psychological peace, and hope of some heavenly hereafter."[10] A false and, in our judgment, dangerous notion has crept into the preaching philosophies of many Ukrainian evangelicals. Some preachers, perhaps influenced by the teaching of certain expressions of North American fundamentalism, feel obliged to convict their hearers of sin in the hope that they will feel their guilt and turn to God in repentance. On one occasion I (Joshua) heard a Ukrainian evangelical pastor say during a sermon that, "The first and most important purpose of the gospel is to state the moral and spiritual depravity of human beings and to remind us that we all stand under the just condemnation of a righteous God." Hearing these words, I was quite disturbed and perplexed at this flagrant misreading of the gospel of hope and the blasphemous misrepresentation of good news of Jesus, who was "full of grace and truth" (John 1:14) and who came "not to condemn the world, but that the world might be saved through him" (John 3:17).

Moreover, it is very likely that many of the people sitting in this con-gregation (and countless others in Ukraine and throughout the FSU) may have had abortions, committed adultery, been divorced, taken drugs, been drunk, given or received bribes, viewed pornography or been involved in corrupt or immoral activity at some point in their lives. They already knew only too well that they were sinners. Instead of trying to convict people of their sin, the true evangelist should follow the way of Jesus in affirming the value and worth of each person as loved unconditionally by God (see, for example, John 4:1–21). This kind of approach would lead to a much greater evangelistic harvest than the kind of psychological guilt games that many preachers occasionally play with their vulnerable hearers.

---

10. Buttrick, *Preaching Jesus Christ*, 48.

The kind of change required, however, goes far beyond a revamping of current preaching practices. The necessary transformation involves a radical overhaul of the individualist modes of evangelization that were exported to Ukraine by Western missionaries in the years following the implosion of the Soviet Union and which were so unsuited to the communitarian context of post-Soviet society.[11] In the current context of widespread cultural conflict and political instability, generated by national, religious, linguistic and economic tensions, the churches need a radical vision of "Church without walls"[12] that will equip them to build communities of vulnerable, compassion-filled disciples who are able to reach out beyond the church walls and go into the "Samaria" regions and to the "ends of the earth" (Acts 1:8).

We must guard against the tendency to think about compassion in romanticized or sentimentalized terms. Too often Christian discourse about compassion has been too soft, lacking moral courage to stand up for good in the face of rampant evil. Often romanticized and sentimentalized notions of compassion have been nurtured by a distorted conception of "gentle Jesus, meek and mild," who is sometimes presented to children in Sunday school classes. In contrast to this soft, fabricated Jesus of popular Christianity, the real Savior who meets us in the Gospels is a bulldozing Jesus who confronts the powers.[13] To be compassionate in a context of corruption, injustice and the lies and fabrications of a State-controlled media means to participate in spiritual warfare by casting down strongholds through prayer and prophetic engagement with the *archai kai exousiai* (the principalities and powers), which enslave and denigrate people.[14] Deeds of mercy need to be combined with prophetic acts on behalf of justice. To paraphrase Archbishop Desmond Tutu, true Christian compassion does not just motivate us to pull bodies out of the water; it also induces us to go upstream, find out who is pushing them into the river and to resist evil in the name of Christ.

11. Chapman, "Collectivism in the Russian World View," 12–14.

12. See Searle, "Tserkov' bez sten."

13. See Wink, *The Powers That Be.*

14. See Walter Wink's "Powers Trilogy": *Naming the Powers; Unmasking the Powers; Engaging the Powers.*

Mission as Personal Salvation and Social Transformation

"Once we recognize Jesus's identification with the poor," notes David Bosch, "we cannot any longer consider our own relation to the poor as a social ethics question; it is a gospel question."[15] The Jesus of the Gospels is someone who continually demonstrates his solidarity with the poor. He acquires a bad reputation as someone who attracts sinners to himself. This Jesus is someone who lives in community and who builds the Kingdom of God through befriending and reaching out to those people who, for various social, political, religious, and economic reasons, were marginalized. This Jesus we meet in the Gospels is someone who inveighs against the religious authorities on behalf of social justice and as a result suffers and is eventually executed for treason and blasphemy. Any apparent gospel message that upholds the political and religious status quo but is not "good news to the poor" (Luke 4:18) cannot be the true gospel, regardless of how "doctrinally sound" it may seem. Historically, a passionate commitment to social justice has always been a crucial component of evangelical mission in Russia and Eastern Europe. In a keynote paper, missiologist Johannes Reimer refers to the national history of the mission and points to the example of the approaches taken by Ivan Prokhanov and Ivan Voronaev, and the importance of the social component in the success of their mission.[16] The mission-proclamation in society becomes the mission-transformation of the society in the entirety of its dimensions.

Churches that will flourish in the post-Soviet missional context will be those communities that integrate mission into their ministries of reconciliation (2 Cor 5:18) and are prepared to take risks by breaking down social barriers of race, nationality, language and even religion itself—all for the sake of the gospel. Churches that abdicate this responsibility—by maintaining an inward-looking concern with personal salvation or saving souls at the exclusion of redeeming people from social and economic injustice—will become more and more sidelined and eventually rejected as having nothing to say to the surrounding culture. The message of hope and new life in Christ should be brought out of church buildings and applied in transformative and creative ways to communities, homes, families, neighborhoods, local communities and, ultimately, to entire nations. In other words, "The theology of Evangelical churches must become an Evangelical

15. Bosch, *Transforming Mission*, 437.

16. Reimer, "Recovering the Missionary Memory," 137–49.

theology based on the Gospel as its foundation, the foremost example of a Christian way of life, thinking, and service to the world."[17]

From Attractional to Incarnational Mission

Albert Einstein is credited with having said that "insanity is doing the same thing over and over again and expecting different results." In terms of evangelization, the post-Soviet evangelical churches require a paradigm shift away from the standard focus that has governed the thinking and practice of these churches ever since the influx of Western evangelicals after *perestroika*. Since that time, many Ukrainian evangelical churches, particularly those under the strongest influence from Western missionaries, have divided the world into two zones, consisting of those who are "in" the Church and those who are "out."

According to this mentality, mission is viewed in terms of conversion and the aim of mission is regarded as trying to bring as many as possible of those who are "out" to join those who are "in." Taking their cue from these tacit Western principles, many post-Soviet evangelical Christians after 1991 operated on the assumption that the goal of their missional endeavors was to persuade their families, friends and strangers alike to attend a church service or to show up at an evangelistic rally in the hope that they would go through the standard conversion process (i.e., from conviction, to repentance, to confession, to regeneration, to sanctification).[18]

"Evangelization" and "mission" thus meant inviting people to attend religious events organized by a church, to participate in church activities and to hear the gospel message within the clearly defined confines of religious gatherings under the direction of church authorities.[19] The implicit theological assumption of this approach was that God could only truly be present in church activities and that in order for people to receive salvation, they had to "become like us" by participating in the same kind of church-related events. The missionary impulse, according to this old paradigm, is

17. Cherenkov, "Theology of Post-Soviet Evangelical Churches."

18. From our personal experience, conversionism appears to be a very prominent aspect of evangelical faith communities in Ukraine. The word for "repent," *pokayat'sya*, is often used in this regard. One of the first questions that one is asked when visiting a typical Russian-speaking Ukrainian evangelical church is, *kogda ty pokayalcya* (when did you repent)?

19. Frost, *Exiles*, 278.

essentially centripetal or inward looking; the aim of evangelism is regarded in terms of luring people into church so that they can hear the gospel, repent and be saved. While this model of mission might be able to win a few converts here and there, it will most certainly *not* generate the kind of radical transformation needed to build the Kingdom of God in post-Soviet society in this emerging generation.

Evangelical Christians should understand that the Church is the means rather than the end of mission. As Bevans and Schroeder put it in a recent landmark publication on mission: "One of the most important things Christians need to know about the church is that *the church* is not of ultimate importance." The point of the Church, they continue, is "to point beyond itself, to be a community that preaches, serves and witnesses to the reign of God."[20] In terms of *missio Dei*, it is essential that mission should have a theocentric, rather than an ecclesiocentric, focus and point of departure.[21] The ultimate aim of mission is not that the Church should grow numerically, but that the glory of God should fill the universe (1 Cor 15:28) and that "the Kingdoms of this world are become the Kingdoms of our Lord and of his Christ" (Rev 11:15).[22] On this point, we can learn from Orthodox theologians who remind us that, "The immediate goals of mission must surely follow the same line and direction as the ultimate goal; they must be the starting point and preparation for that goal. In the march of the Christian mission, our eyes must constantly be fixed on the objective, on the end, the telos, if mission is not to lose its ultimate direction."[23]

The "attractional," church-based approach to mission may have been effective, perhaps even appropriate, for Western Christendom. It may even have enjoyed some limited success in Ukraine and Russia during the early 1990s. After all, notwithstanding all the above criticism of "attractional" models, there can be no denying that after seventy years of communist repression, many things associated with "the West" (such as the free market, free speech, freedom of religion, consumerism, as well as Western types of Evangelicalism) *were* undoubtedly very attractive to many people who had grown up in the Soviet system. The trouble is that this "attractional" model of evangelism involved the imposition of cultural forms that had been imported from the West. Therefore, although many thousands of conversions

20. Bevans and Schroeder, *Constants in Context*, 7.

21. Bosch, *Transforming Mission*; Kirk, *What Is Mission?*; Schenk, *Changing Frontiers*.

22. Stamoolis, *Eastern Orthodox Mission Theology*, 51.

23. Yannoulatos, "Purpose and Motive of Mission," 5.

did result from these kind of evangelizing efforts that aimed to bring people into the fold of the Church, the long-term consequences for the post-Soviet evangelical community were, on the whole, detrimental.

By operating almost exclusively according the "attractional" model of mission, Western missionaries failed to facilitate the emergence of dedicated communities of native post-Soviet evangelicals who would be empowered to infiltrate their communities and the surrounding culture with the message of the gospel. Instead, in many cases, Western missionaries created sub-groups of "wannabe Westerners,"[24] people who were attracted not only by the message of salvation in Christ, but also by the opportunity to escape the difficult living conditions of post-Soviet society.[25] Theological education, in particular, was seen by many as a bridge between the poverty of post-Soviet society and the affluence of Western consumer society.[26] Therefore, although the early missions to the FSU did enjoy some initial success and gained several thousands of new converts, the price of such short-term gains has been a long-term disengagement of indigenous evangelicals from their local communities. This is not to say that Western missionaries who came to the FSU during and after the late 1980s did not act—for the most part, at least—with the best of intentions. Indeed, many made considerable sacrifices and served faithfully during those early years.

Instead of trying to attract people into buildings where religious events take place, the evangelical churches situated in post-Soviet societies should instead become outward-looking, boundary-pushing communities that infiltrate the surrounding population with the transformative message of the gospel. As Michael Frost and Alan Hirsch put it, churches should move towards a model of mission that involves "living out the gospel *within* its cultural context rather than perpetuating an institutional commitment *apart from* its cultural context."[27] Churches should spend their time and efforts not on developing new religious programs, but on cultivating friendships with those for whom Church and Christian faith have become irrelevant or meaningless. Instead of throwing "gospel grenades" into culture from the safety of our church citadels, we can become intentionally available and vulnerable to others by coming alongside them and journeying with them, sharing in their struggles, fears, hopes and joys. Peter exhorts us always to

24. Frost and Hirsch, *Shaping of Things to Come*, 38.

25. Markus, "Politics and Religion in Ukraine," 171.

26. Edgar, "Faculty Development," 5.

27. Frost and Hirsch, *Shaping of Things to Come*, ix.

"be prepared to give an answer to everyone who asks you to give the reason for the hope that you have. But do this with gentleness and respect" (1 Pet 3:15). Likewise, when we talk to those in our local communities who have not yet come to know about the new life and hope in Christ, we should follow the advice of Paul, who encouraged us to "be wise in the way we act towards outsiders, making the most of every opportunity. Let your conversation be always full of grace, seasoned with salt, so that you may know how to answer everyone" (Col 4:5–6).

There has been no better formulation of contextual missiology than those offered at the beginning of the twentieth century by the evangelical leader Ivan Prokhanov: "Evangelical Christians, having apprehended the principles of a Protestant understanding of Christianity, in which the principles of a free conscience and free church are fully implemented, exactly the way it was in the days of the Apostles, are trying to employ them for the benefit of their people, never ceasing to be aware that each nation should praise God according to the nature of their language, location, nationhood."[28]

Characteristics of an Appropriate Post-Soviet Missiology

An appropriate missiology in the post-Soviet context should constantly keep in view two key forces: the Soviet heritage and the Orthodox tradition. The connection with these forces is felt everywhere: in the sacralization of the State, intolerance of dissent, the myth about the particular historical destiny of the "Russian world," the special holiness and spiritual vitality of the Slavic peoples, claims to global significance, and the unity of religious faith and political power.

The peculiarities of the current post-Soviet spiritual situation are post-atheism and neo-Orthodoxy. A post-atheist condition renders it impossible to return to traditional beliefs,[29] and so Orthodoxy is possible only as a "minimal religion," very close to evangelical Christianity, or like neo-Orthodoxy, stylized after tradition with pretensions to power, and not just of the religious variety. This explains the traditional legal nihilism and the people's unprecedented alienation from government, society and State. Orthodox influence explains the "organic" nature of a State religion or of the religious State. According to Viktor Petrenko, a well-known scholar who

28. Prokhanov, "Brief Note," 24.

29. See Epstein, "Post-Atheism," 158–65.

has studied the concept of power in Orthodoxy, "Lenin proposed a Communist version of the symphony"[30] and Orthodoxy was "in the shadow of the hammer and sickle" (the title of one of the chapters in his book *The Government in the Church*).

If we consider the era of atheism in the context of Russian and Ukrainian history, we see that it dovetails with the development of Orthodoxy.[31] Atheism has proven to be the secular form of rebellion, the origins of which are found in the history of Orthodoxy. The Soviet Union proved to be a secularized form of Orthodox theocracy. Despite the vital nature of the attitude of evangelical Christians to Russian Orthodoxy, this remains one of those little-known topics of post-Soviet theology and missiology.[32] Perhaps this reflects the internal duality of post-Soviet Protestantism, located between the Western heritage of the Reformation and Orthodox spiritual culture. In 1908, speaking at the European Congress of Baptists in Berlin, Vasily Pavlov, a spokesperson for the Russian Baptists, put it this way: "The Germans outlived their Reformation more than 400 years ago, whereas it is just beginning among the Russians. The Slavic peoples, most of them, have yet to accept Christ in His pure, undistorted form, and are still under the influence of . . . the Greek-Eastern Church."[33]

For post-Soviet evangelical churches Orthodoxy is an influential cultural environment, a determining factor in politics, a deep theological tradition, but also a mission field. The missiology of evangelical churches took shape in the Orthodox religious-cultural contexts, but at the same time it looks upon this context as a sphere of its influence. And so Orthodoxy is both a factor in the formation of evangelical identity, and an object of evangelical mission. The problem is that evangelical and Orthodox churches have different ideas about the structure of the space and objectives of mission. What evangelicals see as a missionary field that is "up for grabs" or shared territory, the Orthodox regard as their own canonical territory. A post-atheist society that evangelical churches see as "not yet Christian" is deemed by Orthodox churches as "already Christian for several centuries." Accordingly, whereas evangelical missiology emphasizes the need for

30. Petrenko, *Vlast' v tserkvi*, 186.

31. See an interesting article by Andreyev and Elbakian, "Is the Law of God from God?"

32. The exception is laid out in the work of Viktor Petrenko, Andrey Murzin, and Donald Fairburn; see Murzin, *Dialogue*, 144; Petrenko, *Bogoslovie ikon*, 192; Fairbairn, *Inymi glazami*, 277.

33. Pavlov, "Načalo, razvitie," 85.

personal faith and a personal relationship with God, Orthodox missiology emphasizes the collective dimension and the general covenant concluded under Prince Vladimir during the Baptism of Rus' in 988.

Accordingly, evangelical missiology faces an issue in the theoretical justification of the specific mission concerning the Orthodox culture and Orthodox society: *to convert the nominally Orthodox into the evangelical Orthodox, and not into Baptists or Pentecostals.* In the dialogue of traditions and missiology, possibly the only genuinely indisputable unifying force is the gospel. There is absolutely no need to reject tradition in order to affirm the higher authority of Scripture. Depth and simplicity are dependent on each other, especially in theology. Evangelicalism is able to distinguish and articulate, but it lacks historicity and depth. Orthodox tradition can enrich; evangelical theology can clarify.

Protestant-Orthodox relations can develop through the comprehension of a common history, a line which passes through the writings of the Early Fathers and through the Reformation, so that what is missing from the one can be found in the other; through discussions on the privileges and temptations conferred by historicity and statehood, the connections between the dominant and subdominant forms of tradition, and the hierarchies of the titular and the marginal manifestations of ecclesiasticism. But based on the difficulty of dialogue, we must be clear: Protestants and Orthodox Christians will understand each other only when both become evangelical Christians. Neither one nor the other can return to the gospel and the apostolic church, without first putting together a map from fragments divided between the denominations. "Until we all attain to the unity of the faith" (Eph 4:13), Orthodox and Protestant are a prelude in preparation for the real Christianity. As one Ukrainian theologian put it, "You are talking about post-Christianity, about crisis and the end, but we, following after Alexander Men, believe that 'Christianity is just beginning.'"

On the map of post-Soviet religiosity, an impressive growth can be seen in the simply Orthodox and the simply Christian. A new demand for evangelical Christianity is expressed in this. Those just emerging from denominational traditions first evolve into "simply Orthodox" or "simply Protestant," and then they are "simply Christians." So not only Orthodox, but also Protestants would like to become "evangelical." In this context, the words of Prokhanov are pertinent: "Contrary to all the assurances of people who have not thought it through, evangelicals have no animosity to any of the existing religious organizations, especially to the Orthodox Church, to whom they hold the greatest respect. But they pray to God that He would restore His Church in her apostolic freedom and purity so that the light of the Gospel reform individual citizens of Russia and renew all her foundations."[34] Future post-Soviet missiology will be associated with the redefinition of relations to the Soviet legacy and the Orthodox tradition, the liberation from Soviet influence and a respectful setting and a critical, mutually enriching dialogue with Orthodoxy.

Thus, contextual missiology accepts the post-atheist and post-Orthodoxy context as the medium for its formation and its ministry, but it perceives it critically and transforms it into the light of the gospel and evangelical faith.

34. Prokhanov, "Brief Note," 25.

2

Challenges to Mission and Theological Education

The Legacy of Communism

One of the basic principles of history is that events have causes: conditions are as they are today because circumstances were as they were yesterday. Since contemporary phenomena cannot be properly explained or understood without recourse to the diverse developments in the past that created them, it is necessary to offer a brief description of some of the factors from what Sergei Bulgakov calls the "raging abyss of history"[1] that have given rise to the current crisis in evangelical identity in post-Soviet societies.

The historical experience of Ukraine, like many post-Soviet countries, has been riven by tragedy and trauma.[2] The twentieth century, in particular, has been described as "an era of terror and violence" in the troubled history of Ukraine.[3] Ukraine suffered disproportionately under both Soviet rule[4]

---

1. Bulgakov, *Unfading Light*, xli.

2. "The history of Russian culture," wrote Georges Florovsky, "is full off counter-currents, of clashes and contradictions of enthusiasm and disillusion." See Florovsky, *Ways*, 500.

3. Turij, "Das religiöse Leben," 258 (my translation).

4. Serhy Yekelchyk estimates that in the Holodomor (extermination by hunger) of 1932–33, between 3 and 3.5 million Ukrainians perished from starvation as a result of Stalin's policies. See Yekelchyk, *Ukraine*, 112.

and Nazi occupation.[5] The books of twentieth century Ukrainian history recount a tragic narrative of random killings, mass starvation and war. The burgeoning bureaucracy and the overbearing communist ideology, which distinguished the seventy-year period of Soviet rule, created a new type of human being, known as *homo sovieticus*,[6] characterized by a degraded sense of self-worth, a distorted code of ethics and a deformed social conscience. The Soviet mentality, epitomized by the *homo sovieticus*, has outlived the Soviet Union as a political entity. Patterns of socialization and the inculcation of Soviet values have survived and even flourished in post-Soviet society. Once the dust had settled after the political upheavals of the late 1980s and early 1990s, it became apparent how Soviet attitudes continued to govern the mentality and public life of the post-Soviet states.

The period between 1917 and 1991 has left an enduring critical legacy of crisis throughout the nations of the FSU. Although the manifestations of the crisis are primarily social, political and economic, there are also spiritual dimensions to the current predicament. The hideous buildings and unsightly slag heaps, which we can see from our windows as we write these words from our office in Donetsk, are part of the sad legacy of a defunct and malevolent ideology that controlled not only the outward architecture of the buildings but also the direction of people's innermost thoughts. The eyesores that blemish the scarred urban landscape in this region are a throwback to a materialist, functionalist worldview, which regarded architectural beauty and any sense of aesthetic appreciation as signs of "bourgeois decadence." A report was published in 2012, which analyzed the names of 20,000 streets in various parts of Ukraine. It was discovered that the main streets with old Soviet names (e.g., "Karl Marx Avenue," "Lenin Boulevard," "Komsomolskaya Street," etc.) outnumbered by twenty times similar streets with names connected with Ukrainian independence.

---

5. It has been estimated that 6.85 million Ukrainians perished in the Second World War. That constituted 16.3 percent of the whole population at the time. See Erlikman, *Poteri narodonaseleniia*, 23–35.

6. This term was invented by the prominent social critic Aleksandr Zinoviev in his book of the same title. See Zinoviev, *Homo Sovieticus*. The term is based on the notion of the "new Soviet man" (новый советский человек) developed by Soviet propagandists to promulgate the idea of a new generation of people who would be endowed with Soviet virtues of discipline, selflessness, hard work, and intelligence as a result of being nurtured in and by a Soviet culture.

Moreover, the main thoroughfares in 4,500 Ukrainian towns and cities are still named in honor of the discredited tyrant, Vladimir Ilych Lenin.[7]

The scars of the communist legacy are not merely nominal or aesthetic; they penetrate through to the collective consciousness of the people of the former USSR. According to one Ukrainian commentator:

> It is enough to visit any public institution to encounter the Soviet past thriving in the present. Examples include hospitals, post offices, libraries or preparing any form of official documents. Employees working at these institutions are often rude. People have to stand in long lines and each time it feels humiliating and uncomfortable. The Soviet mentality is also demonstrated in passiveness, unwillingness or an inability to change one's life for the better.[8]

The Soviet legacy has also left its mark on spirituality and mysticism, which were so embedded in the minds of Eastern Christians, particularly of Orthodox believers. Spiritual practices, such as prayer and worship, were repressed and set aside as useless and harmful preoccupations that diverted people away from the so-called real world of class struggle and control over the "means of production" that governed "real life."[9] Transcendence was suppressed under the iron weight of a godless, materialist, corrupt and immoral system.[10] Under communism, hope was directed not towards God, but towards an ideologically driven Marxist metanarrative of historical materialism, which anticipated the abolition of social stratifications and the triumph of the working classes. The ideological agenda of the communist regime posited a strict dichotomy between what Lenin called the "odious and vile superstitions of religion"[11] and the liberating force of modern science. Rejecting the "fog of religion"[12], Soviet thinkers argued in favor of

---

7. Kotaleichuk, "Yes, We Can," 61.

8. Ibid., 59.

9. Searle, "Learning from the Past," 10–21.

10. Christopher Marsh traces the origins of this suppression of transcendence to the philosophy of Hegel, whose grand narrative of the self-realization of the Absolute Idea throughout the course of history implicitly rejected transcendence and focused on immanence. This trend was elaborated and extended by the "New Hegelians," including Ludwig Feuerbach, whose critique of religion was formative in Marx's thinking on religion. See Marsh, *Religion and the State*, 42.

11. Lenin, *On Religion*, 71.

12. Ibid., 8.

what one leading scientist called the "creativity of the materialist world-view, without which it is impossible to build a communist society."[13]

Religion was regarded as the main social impediment to the establishment of a classless socialist utopia. As one article in the Soviet atheist journal *Nauka i Religia* (*Science and Religion*) put it, "If . . . the stage of advanced socialism will not be attained until religion has been defeated once and for all, then the measure of success of socialism is in direct proportion to the lessening of religious influence in society and to a decline in the number of believers."[14] A motto displayed at a high school in Trencin, Slovakia, made a similar point using more poetic and extreme language: "There will never be prosperity until the last remaining priest is struck down with the last remaining stone from the last remaining church."[15]

Such violent anti-religious discourse flourished in a context in which the sinister logic of dialectical materialism and historical progress subordinated human lives to the status of means to an end, resulting in what Berdyaev calls "a dead-levelling of human beings."[16] This end was regarded as the "greater good" of the world revolution and the dictatorship of the proletariat; if several people, even millions, had to be exterminated in order to realize this "greater good," this was regarded as an acceptable and even necessary precondition towards the realization of the communist vision. As the leading Ukrainian communist revolutionary, Lev Trotsky, famously remarked, "The end flows naturally from the historical movement. Organically the means are subordinated to the end."[17] Promising a materialist utopia of a classless society, Soviet ideology in fact delivered indescribable suffering and misery for millions of people. More than twenty years on, the scars have still not healed and the baleful legacy of the failed communist experiment continues to afflict not only Ukraine, but also many nations of the FSU.

13. Nesmeyanov, *Nauka i Religia*, 3.

14. Garadzha, "Pereosmyslenye," 2.

15. Cited in *Keston News Service*.

16. Berdyaev, *End of Our Time*, 177. On this point, it is important to note the clear discrepancy between Marx himself and many of the later radical Soviet leaders who claimed Marx's authority. Eric Fromm rightly notes that "the contrast between Marx's view and Communist totalitarianism could hardly be expressed more radically; humanity in man, says Marx, must not even become a means to his individual existence; how much less could it be considered a means for the state, the class, or the nation" (*Marx's Concept of Man*, 43).

17. Lukes, *Marxism and Morality*, 120.

One of the reasons why the communist legacy continues to exert such a strong influence—not only on post-Soviet society but also on post-Soviet religious identity—is the fact that the Soviet system represented not merely a political ideology, but a religious system.[18] Soviet Communism purported not only to offer the best of all possible modes of social and political organization, but also made grand totalizing claims about the meaning, purpose and destiny of human existence. The leading Marxist theorist, George Lukács, noted that communism taught that it was possible to "set forth a conscious teleological design for a future life and to use this design for the qualitative transformation of human existence."[19] Like a theocratic regime, Soviet communism, despite its profession of materialism, developed an *ersatz* religion that was equipped with its own moral system, which posited a clear and absolute demarcation between Good and Evil. Nikolai Berdyaev, noted, "It is difficult for a materialism to adopt a theory of knowledge which accepts absolute truth; Lenin was not troubled by this difficulty."[20] Moreover, as Nicholas Zernov remarks, Soviet communism, like the great world religions, also claimed to have "answered such questions as whether God exists, what the origin of the universe is, what happens to men after their death, where the source of their happiness lies, and how they can be liberated from misery and pain." The Soviet system, he adds, had "a distinctly religious flavor. It is presented as an alternative route to the perfect social order, as a substitute for Christ's teaching about man and his salvation."[21]

Lenin, like many followers of Karl Marx, believed that with the advance of science and the transfer of the means of production to the laboring classes, fewer and fewer people would turn to religion. It was assumed, in the words of V. I. Garadzha, Director of the Communist Party's Institute of Scientific Atheism, that "with the end of exploitation and the removal of conflict in society, a deepening crisis situation would follow in the area of

18. This claim was made as early as 1920 by Fritz Gerlich in his book *Der Kommunismus*, in which he described Communism as "ein Kind des neueren Chiliasmus"; see Walther, *Historische Zeitschrift*, 481. Nikolai Berdyaev likewise maintained that the Soviet communism of his time was "a transformation and deformation of the old Russian messianic idea" (*Origin of Communism*, 228). For a more recent account of the religious dimensions of Communism, see Crossman, *God That Failed*. Alistair Key focuses specifically on the messianic aspects of Marx's eschatological conception of history in his article, "Marx's Messianic Faith," 101–13.

19. Lukács, *Process of Democratization*, 103.

20. Berdyaev, *Ystoky y smysl*, 100.

21. Zernov, *Russian Religious Renaissance*, 310.

religion, leading to a weakening of its influence, which would culminate in the extinction of religion as a social phenomenon."[22] The determination of many believers to retain their religious freedoms after the communists had seized power persuaded the Soviet authorities that more active persecution was required in order to deliver people from the alleged soporific effects of religion, which Marx had denounced as the "opium of the people." Bolshevik leaders began a concerted press campaign against religion, publishing a weekly magazine, *Bezbozhnik* ("The Atheist"), which contained inflammatory articles against religion. For example, in one article published in 1923, the Bolshevik Commissar of Education, A. V. Lunacharsky, referred to "the hideous spectre of god, who has in truth inflicted diabolical evil on mankind throughout the whole course of history."[23] The destruction of the church thus became part of the official policy of the Bolshevik authorities.[24]

Throughout the period of the Soviet Union, churches were plundered and desecrated and millions of ordinary believers, together with thousands of church leaders, were persecuted, tortured or murdered as part of a systematic campaign against not only the Christian churches, but against the Christian faith itself. In the early years of the USSR, the dissemination of atheism and the war against Christianity became, in the words of Lenin, "the cause of our state."[25] Children, in particular, were to be re-educated according to the ideological requirements of the new regime.[26] In the school year 1927–28, scientific atheism became a compulsory subject in Soviet schools[27] and many people of older generations today can still vividly remember being taught "scientific atheism" as a subject at school alongside more traditional fields of study, such as mathematics, science, literature

---

22. Garadzha, "Pereosmyslenye," 2.

23. Lunacharsky, *Bezbozhnik*.

24. A detailed account of these early persecutions is given in McCullagh, *Bolshevik Persecution*.

25. Pospielovsky, *History of Marxist-Leninist Atheism*, 34.

26. A casual glance at the library shelves in the Keston Center for Religion, Politics, and Society at Baylor University reveals dozens of volumes published in the Soviet Union on "scientific atheism." For instance, one volume, titled *Ateicnicheskoye Vospitaniye v Semye* (*Atheistic Education in the Family*), published by the Ukrainian "politizdat" publishers in 1984, offers detailed instructions on how to initiate children into the worldview of scientific atheism. Notably, there are atheistic volumes clearly intended for teenagers or young adults, such as Komarov's, *Byt' Mudrym Bez Boga!* (*Be Wise without God!*).

27. Theodorovich, *Religion und Atheismus*, 220.

and history.[28] Contemporary sources demonstrate the extent to which the Soviet system promoted atheism as an official academic subject. According to the *Keston News Service*, in the academic year 1978–79, the organization, "Znanya," conducted a public examination for atheist lecturers in Ukraine in which 688,259 candidates sat the examination. It was further estimated that six out of every thousand Ukrainians worked as atheist lecturers, delivering a total of 290,000 lectures annually throughout Ukraine.[29]

The well-organized attempts by communist officials to actively promote atheism demonstrate that the communist regime aimed at nothing less than the systematic expulsion of religion from every sphere of life. Not only did they seek to drive religion from the public sphere; Soviet communism also demanded the eradication of every trace of Christianity from people's consciousness.[30] "For the first time in history," writes Paul Froese, "rulers of a modern state hoped to expunge not only the existence of religious institutions but also daily expressions of spirituality and, most dauntingly, belief in a supernatural realm."[31] The ideological justification for the suppression of Christianity was found in the "fact," established by Marxist theory, that religion was the opium of the people and the basic obstacle to human fulfillment and self-realization.[32] Taking his cue from Ludwig Feuerbach,[33] Marx asserted that religion was the psychological by-product of a basic human desire for immortality, which we project onto "God," thus creating a god in our own image.[34] This projection of immortality onto an imaginary god, claimed Feuerbach, was the root cause of human self-alienation.[35]

This belief was constantly reproduced in the popular literature published by communist authorities throughout the period of the USSR most notably in the atheist propaganda journal known as *Nauka i Religia* (*Science and Religion*). Although denunciations of "religious superstition" (as opposed

28. Bordeaux, *Gorbachev, Glasnost & the Gospel*, 24.

29. *Keston News Service*, 6.

30. Myklushchak, "Chelovek kak transendentnoe sushchestvo," 143.

31. Froese, *Plot to Kill God*, 1.

32. Marx, *Zur Kritik der Nationalökonomie*, 378.

33. Orthodox philosopher and theologian Sergei Bulgakov notes that "the atheist humanism of Feuerbach constitutes the spirit of Marxist socialism and is no less characteristic of it than the political and economic teachings of Marx, which may be compatible with a completely opposite world view" (*Karl Marx*, 17).

34. Marx, *Zur Kritik der Hegelschen Rechtsphilosophie*, 378.

35. Feuerbach, *Das Wesen des Christentums*, 70.

to "scientific knowledge") were to be found in almost every issue of *Nauka i Religia* between 1960 and 1989, a classic expression of the Marxist critique of evangelical-Baptist belief is found in an article by L. Mitrokhin, issued in 1964 under the title "Baptists on the Meaning of Life." The author juxtaposes the alleged escapist fantasies of Baptist unworldliness with the supposed noble and world-transformative qualities of Soviet atheist realism:

> Our [communist] understanding is diametrically opposed to the religious standpoint: in contrast to the "heavenly ideal," we emphasize the value of the "earthly ideal" . . . They [Baptists] dissipate their energies on the supernatural ideal of the notions of God and life after death. For a Marxist, the real interest lies in the actual social content of the supernatural ideal, to understand its influence on human beings and to appreciate its actual role in the social life.[36]

Likewise in 1972, the Soviet journal *Izvestia* (*News Bulletin*) published an article by the atheist philosopher V. Garadzha which echoed Feuerbach and Marx by claiming that religion was nothing but a "fantastically distorted reflection of reality in people's heads. It is a reflection in which the earthly powers assume the form of the unearthly."[37] Other popular regional journals also reproduced these kinds of Marxist critiques of religion. In April 1980, for instance, the Russian language newspaper of the youth wing of the Estonian SSR, *Molodyozh Estonii* contained an article asserting that, "the longer religion is maintained, the harder it will be to form a fully developed member of communist society. In the same way as hundreds of years ago, religion today provides an escape from life and the work of society."[38]

Despite the cruel, brutal and continuous oppression against the churches in the communism era, the Soviet authorities were unable to achieve the extermination of religious belief in the USSR, which their Marxist metanarrative had confidently prophesied and which their ideology demanded. Today the time in which atheism held unrivalled sway in the public sphere appears to be over. Religion seems not merely to have survived in Central and Eastern Europe, but, as several studies suggest, has steadily increased.[39] Recent sociological surveys continue to show

36. Mitrokhin, "Baptism o smisle zhizny," 24–29.

37. Garadzha, "Religion in an Age," 5.

38. Quoted in *Keston News Service*, 2. The Soviet magazine *Nauka i Religiia* (*Science and Religion*) likewise propagated the same dichotomy, arguing that whereas religion enslaves humanity, science liberates people.

39. Tomka and Zulehner, *Religion in den Reformländern*.

that the majority of Ukrainians believe in God. In 1993, 43–44 percent of Ukrainians affirmed belief in God,[40] whereas in 2009 this figure had increased to 60 percent and, furthermore, only 2.4 percent regarded themselves as convinced atheists.[41] Moreover, the results of a recent survey of the religiosity of the European nations demonstrate that Ukraine occupies fifth place in the league of "most religious countries in Europe," after Cyprus, Poland, Slovakia and Portugal.[42]

The growth of religiosity in the post-Soviet societies in the 1990s can to some extent be explained sociologically as the natural reaction to the collapse of a system of values, which had been imposed by Soviet ideology. The euphoric transition from the rigid Soviet system to an unrestrained pluralism of political ideas, social outlooks and cultural convictions entailed an unprecedented change in the lives of millions of Ukrainians.[43] When the USSR imploded, the moral vacuum created by this collapse needed somehow to be filled. For Ukraine, which had a rich legacy of Christianity stretching back one thousand years, the Christian Church was seen as the institution that could restore meaning, values and purpose to post-Soviet society. Given the historical association between Orthodoxy and the nations of the FSU, many looked to the Orthodox Church to fill the ideological abyss. As the Orthodox dissident, Vladimir Poresh, put it in 1990: "Never has so much been expected from it by so many people."[44] Only the Orthodox Church, it was thought, possessed the necessary intellectual, spiritual and creative resources for the resolution of the prevailing social and political crisis.

Unfortunately, from an evangelical perspective, although many people turned to religion, not everyone found a home in the church as a place in which they could express their spiritual longings. Rather, many found refuge in pagan or so-called New Age religious communities, which proliferated in the 1990s.[45] Thus, the rising levels of religiosity among the general population do not equate with a growth of the Christian churches in these

40. Dudar and Shanhina, *Vira y relihiya*, 267–70.

41. Turij, "Das religiöse Leben," 261.

42. Parashchevin, *Relihiya ta relihiynist'*, 13–16.

43. Turij, "Das religiöse Leben," 260.

44. Poresh, "Faith and Lack of Faith," 75. Quoted in Knox, *Russian Society*, 7. Poresh was a founding member of the dissident "Christian Seminar," which published the *Obschina* journal. See Bourdeaux, *Risen Indeed*, 34–35.

45. Ivakhiv, "In Search of Deeper Identities," 7–38.

countries. Moreover, many others continued to invest their hopes in the defunct Soviet regime.[46] Nostalgia became a powerful force in Ukrainian social and political life in the post-Soviet era.[47]

In a post-secular age, the search for a religious outlook that will inform contemporary political and social life has become an important feature of current intellectual activity. The contribution that post-Soviet evangelicals can make towards the formulation of a viable Christian social philosophy is enormous. The elucidation of this contribution will come into clear focus in the next chapter.

The Emergence of a New Threat: Consumerism

Now that the era of Marxist atheism has passed, the churches and the wider society now face a new threat: consumerism. The commercialization of the gospel message must be a serious concern to anyone who cares about the future of the Church in the FSU. Consumerism is ideologically at variance to Marxist ideology and also spiritually antithetical to the Orthodox tradition that has dominated the national consciousness of many countries of the FSU, particularly Russia, Ukraine and Belarus, for several centuries.

As in relatively affluent Western countries, consumerism is beginning to gain a foothold in parts of post-Soviet society. Large shopping malls are springing up in several cities throughout the FSU. Leaders of post-Soviet churches, like their counterparts in the West, now have to compete among themselves to gain new "customers" (i.e., church members and converts) to sustain their "businesses" (churches) and engage in aggressive "advertising campaigns" (i.e., evangelistic outreach initiatives) in order to promote their "brand" (i.e., denominational or congregational identity) and to sell their "product" (salvation from sin, spiritual joy and eternal life). Consumerism devours churches and regurgitates them into a form that is a pitiful hybrid of Christianity and consumerist ideology, which is a grotesque caricature of the true gospel message. Many churches have thus become like spiritual supermarkets where wor*shoppers* seek for new spiritual experiences.[48] The emergence of consumerism in post-Soviet society poses many challenges, but also some opportunities for the Church. According to some observ-

---

46. Wilson, "Communist Party of Ukraine," 221–25.

47. Bonnett, *Left in the Past*, 94–96.

48. These trends in Western churches are lucidly described in Drane, *McDonaldization of the Church*.

ers, the proliferation of consumer choice and the sudden emergence of individualism may even have caused people to turn to religion as a natural reaction to the lack of solidarity and fraternity to which they had been accustomed during the Soviet era.[49]

One of the consequences of consumerism for theological education is the fact that Christian universities can no longer take for granted the enrolment of the brightest and best young people from the churches, but must compete within a free market of various educational alternatives. This is not to say that consumerism and the idea of a free market economy are unequivocally malevolent or even wrong *per se*. Even the most vociferous critics of capitalism would admit that the open availability of consumer goods in modern, well-furnished retail centers is undoubtedly preferable to the long food queues and empty shelves that were a fact of everyday life for millions of people during the Soviet era. Furthermore, the new climate of competition generated by consumerism could have positive benefits for Christian educational institutions by providing a necessary stimulus to improve their courses, teaching and research outputs in order to compete with the best state-supported educational establishments. Nevertheless, sociologists have identified unbridled consumerism as both a cause and a symptom of cultural decadence and decline.[50]

By embracing Western models of consumerism to fill the ideological void left in the wake of the shattered Soviet system and a discredited institutional Orthodox Church, post-Soviet society may well be drinking unwittingly from a poisoned chalice. Even wealthy post-Soviet consumers, in common with their counterparts in Western Europe and North America, will sooner or later discover that "too much is not enough"[51] and that their spiritual discontents cannot be resolved by hoarding commodities. While the standard of living has increased for many, so too has the gap between rich and poor.[52] Although some are able to purchase goods of technology

---

49. Durkot, "Zwanzig Jahre danach," 219.

50. Jameson and Miyoshi, *Cultures of Globalization*; Tomlinson, *Globalization and Identity*; Stearns, *Consumerism in World History*.

51. This formulation (*zu viel ist nicht genug*) is taken from Marianne Gronemeyer's lucid diagnosis of the discontents of consumer society, titled *Die Macht der Bedürfnisse*.

52. A report on Ukraine (published in 2005) commissioned in connection with the Millennium Goals of the United Nations found that "the gap between the rich and poor is widening. A distinctly uneven income distribution is continuing to form in Ukraine, with majority of the population concentrated in the low-income category. The gross consumption ratio of the top 10 percent to the bottom 10 percent of population income

and fashion that would have been unthinkable for previous generations, many others have neither the economic means nor the education nor the family and business connections to participate in the emerging consumer society.

Moreover, in relation to the Church, the premise of consumerism (i.e., "minimum commitment and maximum return") is antithetical to the costly form of covenant relationships that characterize faith communities that claim to follow the example of Christ.[53] In a consumer climate, in which every sphere of human activity can be commoditized into a potential product that can be bought and sold on an open market, the Church must carefully guard the authenticity of the gospel message. There can be no place for the so-called prosperity gospel within any Slavic missiological paradigm. No church will be able to "sell" Jesus in the same way that the modern advertising industry sells shampoo and handbags. No false promises can be made to potential converts. We cannot say to people, "Come to God and you will experience happiness, inner joy and peace, emotional wellbeing. You might even become rich and be able to buy a bigger house, a flatscreen TV or a new BMW." The ideological void created in the wake of the demise of communism cannot be filled by the accumulation of consumer goods or by "McDonaldized"[54] consumerist caricatures of the gospel, but only by a genuine and robust hope and new vision of life in terms of costly discipleship and radical counter-cultural living for the sake of the Kingdom of God. The good news of the gospel is that this kind of "abundant life" (John 10:10) is freely available to all in Christ.

Economic Challenges

Despite the gradual emergence of a consumer society, a major factor underpinning the ailing economies of post-Soviet countries has been the political instability and corruption that have afflicted so many nations of the FSU since the demise of the Soviet system in the early 1990s. Although there is

---

groups over the 2004–2005 period was 6.9 times. The substantial increases in population income in 2005 driven by minimum wage and various social payments increases did raise the average monthly expenditures per capita, but unfortunately did not help to reduce the income gap." The full text of the report can be found online at http://www. undp.org.ua/files/en_24267mdgp.pdf (accessed 14 April 2013).

53. Merkle, *Being Faithful*, 128.

54. Drane, *McDonaldization of the Church*.

considerable variation in the economic fortunes of the various states of the FSU since the fall of communism, Ukraine is typical of the political chaos that was both a cause and consequence of major economic downturn, which affected most of these states following the disintegration of the USSR.[55] When Ukraine began its transition from an authoritarian, one-party ruled state to a pluralist democracy, the economic policies of neo-liberalism were touted as the "way of salvation" for Ukraine's future prosperity as a capitalist democratic state. This theological language to describe economic policies is consistent with the notion of "millennial capitalism," which assumed messianic connotations and which presented itself as "a gospel of salvation," which, "if rightly harvested, is invested with the capacity wholly to transform the universe of the marginalized and disempowered."[56]

The anarchic conditions that followed the collapse of the Soviet Union enabled some people to create immense industrial empires and amass enormous personal fortunes.[57] Meanwhile, the vast majority of Ukrainians became ever poorer than they had been under Soviet rule. The promises of "messianic capitalism" or "salvation" through the "gospel" of neo-liberal economics sounded hollow in light of their experience of abject poverty. It soon became apparent that the effective functioning of free markets depends on a basic system of morality buttressed by the twin pillars of honesty and trust[58]—qualities, which were in extremely short supply amid the widespread anarchy and corruption that characterized Ukrainian society in the early 1990s.[59] The economic deterioration continued for several years. Between 1991 and 1994, the Ukrainian economy was in a state of free fall.[60] By 1999, the per capita GDP of Ukraine was reduced to 40 percent of what

---

55. The Baltic states—Estonia, Latvia, and Lithuania—are exceptional in this regard. Not only have they developed relatively stable democratic systems of government, but these former Soviet states have undergone significant economic growth, especially since they joined the European Union.

56. Comaroff and Comaroff, "Millennial Capitalism," 1–56.

57. See Puglisi, "Rise of the Ukrainian Oligarchs," 99–123.

58. Fukuyama, *Trust*. Fukuyama's basic thesis is that low-trust societies do not prosper economically.

59. The same can also be said of the economic chaos that enveloped Russia following the dissolution of the Soviet Union. See Stoner-Weiss, "Whither the Central State?," 131. Stoner-Weiss uses the terms "stalled," "stunted," and "partial" to describe Russia's experience of economic reform in the 1990s.

60. Aslund, *How Ukraine Became a Market Economy*, 26.

it had been before independence.[61] Even though the economy underwent a period of growth, the global financial downturn of 2008 again led to recession, rising unemployment and declining living standards. Following the Maidan protests that led to the departure of Victor Yanukovych in February 2014 and the subsequent Russian invasion and occupation of Ukrainian territory on the Crimean peninsula, the Ukrainian economy has suffered another downturn. At the time of writing, the dangers of hyperinflation and total collapse of the Ukrainian economy seem ominously imminent.

A report published in relation to the United Nations' "Millennial Goals" identified three fundamental causes of economic stagnation in Ukraine, which can also be applied to other post-Soviet economies, such as Russia. These factors were identified as: "limited goods and services market (low demand)"; "widespread monopoly"; and "corruption." The report stressed that these problems are interrelated and interdependent.[62] The reference to the "widespread monopoly" is an allusion to the harmful imbalance in the Ukrainian economy, which in turn feeds the first problem of low demand and exacerbates the endemic corruption that debilitates the economy at every level. Since independence a small coterie of vastly wealthy business magnates has retained a stranglehold on almost all of the productive parts of the economy.[63] It was calculated that in 2012 Ukraine's fifty wealthiest oligarchs accounted for 85 percent of the country's GDP.[64] Moreover, despite the highly publicized philanthropic activities of these "benefactors," many Ukrainian industrial oligarchs have considerable political influence as well as alleged links to organized crime. Analysts from the World Economic Forum estimated that in 2008 the black market accounted for at least 40 percent of the Ukrainian economy.[65]

Moreover, a UN report confirms what every Ukrainian already knows: that corruption is endemic in Ukraine; for many Ukrainians, bribes are

---

61. Hanouz and Geiger, *Ukraine Competitiveness Report 2008*, 41. For further details about the state of the Ukrainian economy since 1991, see www.bank.gov.ua/control/uk/index (accessed February 2013).

62. The full report can be found online at http://www.undp.org.ua/files/en_24267mdgp.pdf (accessed 15 April 2013).

63. Pleines, "Political Role," 105.

64. Kuzio, "Oligarchs Wield Power." Moreover, of the 112 billion dollars held by these oligarchs, 34.5 billion dollars in 2013 were held by the inner circle of Ukraine's leading party, the Party of Regions. Kuzio further notes that in Russia, by comparison, the fifty wealthiest oligarchs account for "only" 35 percent of Russia's GDP.

65. Hanouz and Geiger, *Ukraine Competitiveness Report 2008*.

part of everyday life.[66] In a survey conducted in 2007, 67 percent of Ukrainian respondents who needed to use public services reported that they had to make corrupt payments in order to obtain the required assistance. It is widely acknowledged that Ukrainian businesses routinely pay bribes to government officials in order to undercut red tape.[67] Given the prevalence of bribery and other forms of corruption in Ukrainian culture, it is high time that the Christian community led the way in promoting serious theological reflection on how churches and individual Christians should deal with this very serious problem. In a context of rampant bribery and corruption, the gospel values of truth and integrity must be foundational to any Slavic missiological paradigm.

Problems of Identity and Politics

When the USSR collapsed in 1991, many people expected that Russia and all the newly independent states of the FSU would embrace Western values and become respectable members of the international community. In Russia, however, as in many countries of the FSU, capitalism did not give rise to democracy and neither did the emergence of a free market engender political liberty. In fact, as Zygmunt Bauman and Leonidas Donskis point out:

> liberalism planted in the soil of post-Soviet societies would become a caricature of itself, turning into an inversion of Marxism and celebrating and excessively associating itself with economics and financial power, instead of speaking up in favor of liberty and human rights . . . The caricature of liberal ideas in Eastern Europe, where liberalism has been confined to technocratic advocacy of the free market and the resulting vulgar economic interpretation of the human world, is a result of the Eastern European intellectual and moral vacuum after 1990.[68]

This vacuum was partly filled by old intellectual ideas and cultural practices associated with the Soviet regime. Despite the advance of

---

66. A detailed report on the extent of corruption in Ukrainian public institutions was published in 2011 by the European Research Association in cooperation with Kyiv International Institute of Sociology. The report (in English) is available online at http://uniter.org.ua/data/block/corruption_in_ukraine_2007–2009_2011_engl.pdf (accessed 17 April 2013).

67. Ibid., 52.

68. Bauman and Donskis, *Moral Blindness*, 74–76.

consumerism and the emergence of a free market economy, the symbolism and architecture of the communist era continue to form part of the everyday experience of many ordinary people in Ukraine today. In almost every southern and eastern Ukrainian town there remains a conspicuous statue of Lenin standing in prominent areas, such as in central city parks or outside government buildings.[69] In Donetsk, for instance, Lenin's statue stares ominously down onto a prominent McDonalds restaurant on the other end of the main central plaza of the city, which is still known as "Lenin Square."[70] Moreover, despite widespread revulsion at the odious and oppressive Soviet system, many Ukrainians, particularly those inculcated in the values of *homo sovieticus*, express a longing for order, stability and security that they associate with the former system, which is compared favorably against the endemic anarchy and corruption that have become part of everyday life for millions of people.[71] Recent events in Eastern Ukraine and Crimea have demonstrated that most Russians and some Russian-leaning Ukrainians are willing to agree to a Dostoevskian compact in which independence, freedom and truth are traded for stability, order and the consoling illusions of propaganda.[72] Yet it is not just the older generation that feels a sense of regret and disillusionment. Among many young Ukrainians there is a palpable sense a complete disillusionment with the political system, which they disdain as hopelessly corrupt, ineffective and overly bureaucratic. Although the trend towards cynicism seems to have been escalating since 1991,[73] there are hopeful signs after the Ukrainian Revolution of

69. In some instances, the condition of these statues may give rise to reasonable speculation about the locals' attitude towards Lenin and Communism in general. In some towns, for instance, Lenin's statue is freshly polished and clearly well kept. In other towns, by contrast, the tyrant's statue appears much more disheveled and in some cases his head is besmirched with bird droppings.

70. The university in Donetsk where we worked is located on "Ilych Avenue," which was named after Lenin. Ilych was Lenin's patronymic: Vladimir Ilych Lenin.

71. Following the collapse of the USSR, the countries that emerged from this breakup were hit by an unprecedented crime wave and a particularly high rise in organized crime, which, according to one account, "became a central element of the crime picture, bringing a violence and visibility previously unknown to Soviet crime." See Millar and Wolchik, *Social Legacy of Communism*, 135.

72. The reference to Dostoevsky alludes to the famous monologue of the Grand Inquisitor in the novel *The Brothers Karamazov*. In the parable told by Ivan Karamazov, the Inquisitor argues that people do not want freedom but instead want to be controlled and to be relieved by others of the intolerable burden of having to decide for themselves.

73. According to one survey, the share of Ukrainians who agreed with the statement "Democracy will never be established in Ukraine" was greater in 1996 than in 1991. For

Dignity and Freedom (2013/14) that the younger generation—particularly students, journalists and young church leaders—is beginning to re-engage with national politics and to campaign against corruption and for social justice.

Among many freedom-loving Ukrainians in the post-Maidan era there is a genuine fear of a resurgent Russia that represents a grave threat to the peace and stability of their country. There is particular apprehension concerning "Putinism," which represents a "vague and strange amalgam of nostalgia for the grandeur of the Soviet past, gangster and crony capitalism, endemic corruption, kleptocracy [and] self-censorship" and which implies "a total fusion of economic and political power combined with impunity and state terror, which overtly lends itself to gangs and criminal cliques of various shades."[74] "Putinism," according to Mykola Riabchuk, is "a system built upon the megalomaniac claim of a pan-Slavonic uniqueness and paranoid anti-westernism."[75] No one in the West should be in any doubt that the regime over which Vladimir Putin presides is one of the most corrupt political systems on earth. The Russian state parliament (the Duma) is occupied by Putin "yes-men," who are anxious to do the bidding of their master in the Kremlin. These kinds of democratic structures act as a kind of grotesque lipstick that is used to cover the very ugly face of the Stalinist despotism over which Putin presides. The sham "referendum," which took place in Crimea in March 2014 and the even more farcical "referendum" in Donetsk and Lughansk in May of the same year are further examples of the brazen attempt by Kremlin-backed criminals and stooges in Ukraine to create a supposedly democratic fig leaf to disguise the ugly scars of naked despotism, corruption, tyranny, and "gangster capitalism" that blemish the body politic of the contemporary Russian establishment. At the time of writing, Eastern Ukraine is under attack from a covert yet concerted invasion by Russian soldiers and armored units, who are assisting a minority of Russian-backed vigilantes attempting to impose their own vision of Putinism onto the occupied Crimean territory and other parts of southern and eastern Ukraine. As a result of the activities of these pro-Russian armed

---

further details of these and similar surveys, see Holovakah, "Popular Social and Political Attitudes," 203.

74. Bauman and Donskis, *Moral Blindness*, 78.

75. Riabchuk, "Blessing in Disguise," 67.

factions, the political future of Eastern Ukraine in 2014 remains precarious and uncertain.[76]

Ever since Ukraine gained independence, the Ukrainian political system has been blighted by the same kind of nepotism, corruption, inefficiency and incompetence that have tarnished the Russian government since the fall of the USSR. Even the hope and popular enthusiasm generated by the "Orange Revolution"[77] of 2004 were quickly smothered under the odious political machinery, which soon reasserted control under the corrupt governance of the Russian-sponsored reprobate, Victor Yanukovych. Since independence, the Russian "fifth column" in Ukraine has adroitly exploited differences of culture and language among ethnic Ukrainians in order to fabricate social division and foment political instability. The so-called "East-West" division in Ukraine was highlighted in the 1994 presidential elections, when the nationalist incumbent, Leonid Kravchuk, carried the provinces in Western Ukraine with huge majorities of up to 90 percent in some regions. His opponent, the Russian-leaning Leonid Kuchma, carried the eastern provinces with equally large majorities.[78] The election, which Kuchma won with 52 percent of the overall vote, reflected what a commentator in the *New York Times* referred to as the split between "Europeanized Slavs in western Ukraine and the Russo-Slav vision of what Ukraine should be."[79] However, this split should not be exaggerated. The Western media often give a false portrayal of Ukraine as a country sharply divided between "Ukrainians" in the West and "Russians" in the East. Recently, one British politician falsely asserted that Russians comprise 50 percent of the population of Ukraine. In fact, in 2014 Russians comprised only 17 percent of the Ukrainian population and even many of those eastern Ukrainians who speak mainly Russian still consider themselves Ukrainian in citizenship and national identity. Moreover, most Ukrainians are bilingual and in Ukraine, unlike in Russia, tens of millions of Russian speakers can read newspapers published by a free press, watch television broadcasted by independent media outlets and read and write blogs on an uncensored Internet—and they can do all of these things using the medium of the great Russian language.

---

76. The causes and consequences of political instability in Ukraine are explained in Shapovalova, "Ukraine," 65–66.

77. See Åslund and McFaul, *Revolution in Orange*.

78. Huntington, *Clash of Civilizations*, 166.

79. Ian J. Brzezinski, quoted in Erlanger, "Ukrainian Leader's Defeat Worries Kiev Bureaucrats."

In his well-known treatise on international relations, *The Clash of Civilizations* (1996), Samuel P. Huntington speculated that Ukraine might one day split into two countries with a fault line running between the Russian-leaning, Russian-speaking South and East, and the Europe-leaning, Ukrainian-speaking West.[80] Given the recent tensions in eastern Ukraine and the calls by a minority of small but well-armed bands of pro-Russian vigilantes for closer ties with Moscow, this prospect still seems to be an ominous possibility. Moreover, the threat of open conflict between Russia and the West will remain as long as Putin's Russia continues to dispatch tanks, BUK surface-to-air missiles, as well as truckloads of sophisticated military hardware into the hands of the Kremlin agents and Russian-sponsored mercenaries operating in Eastern Ukraine.[81]

Today the political future of not just of Ukraine, but of the whole region, hinges on the central issue of Ukraine's integration into the European Union.[82] As early as 1998, Ukraine made a formal declaration of its desire to become a full-fledged member of the EU. Despite deep-seated disagreements on other issues of foreign policy, all of the major parties in Ukraine now seem to be united in their desire for closer integration with Europe, including obtaining membership of the EU. This resolution has been galvanized since the tumultuous events that followed the Maidan protests in Kyiv. Successive Ukrainian governments have invested considerable political and diplomatic capital in their bid to obtain a clear pathway for full membership. However, the EU itself has been divided on the issue of whether or not to support Ukraine's membership aspirations and the prospect of a possible EU accession remains far from imminent, despite President Poroshenko's recent signing of the EU Association Agreement.[83]

In the heated debates concerning the national identity of the Ukrainian people and all peoples and nations of the FSU, there is an opportunity

80. Huntington, *Clash of Civilizations*, 37, 165–68. Huntington had earlier published his thesis in outline in an article for the journal *Foreign Affairs*, in 1993: Huntington, "Clash of Civilizations?," 22–49.

81. This threat of escalation is likely to increase if the United States votes for a more militant Republican president in 2016. Despite strong rhetoric and the application of limited sanctions, President Obama's policy toward Russia has been relatively conciliatory since Putin invaded and occupied part of Ukraine (Crimea) in March 2014.

82. Hoffmann and Möllers, *Ukraine on the Road*.

83. EU member states that have expressed support for Ukraine's long-term integration into the EU include the United Kingdom, Finland, and Sweden. France, Germany, the Netherlands, Belgium, and Spain have expressed their opposition. See Shapovalova, "Ukraine," 67.

for the Christian churches to make a positive contribution to framing the debate in ways that will facilitate peace and friendly relations among people of different political and national affiliations. However, the evangelical community will only be able to contribute to these debates on national identity and political allegiance, if it is clear about its own identity and allegiance.

Spiritual Challenges

It is against the backdrop of a Russian agitation and the Kremlin-sponsored terrorism and lawlessness in Eastern Ukraine that we should understand that Ukraine is undergoing not merely a political crisis, but a spiritual attack. As one anonymous author explains,

> Ukraine is experiencing not just a political and socio-economic crisis, but a diabolical onslaught that is intended to disrupt and control far more than just governmental, commercial, and social structures. Given the inevitable consequences of widescale societal breakdown, the enemy also seems intent on rendering Ukraine incapable of developing further as a center of moral and spiritual influence in the region.

This point is well made. Ukraine is a country of vast agricultural potential and rich repositories of raw materials. Despite widespread alcoholism and associated social problems, its more than 45 million population is generally highly educated, culturally aware and orientated towards civil society. Ukraine has the potential to become a major European power and a beacon of hope and a symbol of freedom and democracy not merely for the nations of Eastern Europe, but for the whole world. Ever since it gained independence in 1991, Ukraine has been the major hub for evangelistic and humanitarian activity throughout Eastern Europe, Russia and Central Asia. Despite strong resistance from entrenched Soviet mentalities and the passing of unfavorable legislation, Ukrainian Christians succeeded in establishing various NGOs, Christian missions and centers of theological education. For those with ears to hear and eyes to see, the activity of the Holy Spirit has been manifest in various ways in Ukrainian society in the past twenty five years. Given Ukraine's obvious potential as a spiritual center capable of bearing the torch of the gospel and dispelling the remaining dark corners of the enduring Soviet legacy, it should not be surprising that the powers and principalities should have descended on Ukraine with such vehemence and fury.

As well as the malicious destruction of life and property in Crimea and Eastern Ukraine, one of the most conspicuous signs of the diabolical powers at work has been the systemic campaign of falsification and fabrication undertaken by the news outlets controlled by the Russian State. This concerted campaign of misinformation and the blizzard of lies that it has unleashed will one day become a fascinating subject for many doctoral theses that will use it as a case study for how propaganda functions in the twenty first century. For now, however, the Russian misinformation campaign must be regarded as a diabolical menace. The aim of the Kremlin-sponsored propaganda is to arouse the fear and hatred of Russian-speaking Ukrainians toward the post-Maidan authorities in Kyiv by portraying the leaders of the Maidan as Nazis from the Right Sector. According to the Kremlin-controlled Russian news reports the Kyiv authorities aim to enforce "liberal" legislation (i.e., forced gay marriages) and to close down the mines of the Donbass before systematically butchering the Russian speakers who live in Eastern Ukraine.[84] Moreover, following the shooting down of flight MH17 over Eastern Ukraine—almost certainly by pro-Russian separatists with weapon systems supplied directly from Russia—Kremlin propagandists fabricated a theory that the airliner had in fact been loaded with rotten corpses, flown on autopilot out of Amsterdam's Schipol Airport before being blown out of the sky by Ukrainian forces using American missiles. This plot, which was supposedly hatched by the CIA and the Ukrainian intelligence services in order to discredit Russia's international reputation, was discussed as a serious explanation on leading Russian news channels.

There are countless other examples of fabrications, half-truths and flagrant lies propagated by the Kremlin-controlled news agencies that could be cited, but the underlying significance of this campaign is the way that it points to the influence of the dark forces that have been unleashed against Ukraine since the demonstrations on Maidan.

Social and Intellectual Challenges

Together with political instability and spiritual attack, Ukraine is afflicted with major social problems. Many of these issues, such as alcoholism, drug abuse, family breakdown, promiscuity and abortion, are interrelated.[85]

84. Lelich, "Victims of Russian Propaganda," 79.
85. Bromet et al., "The State of Mental Health."

Although these issues affect all societies, there are few European countries in which these problems are so endemic as they have become in Ukraine. The situation has now degenerated to such an extent that we were told by a Ukrainian social worker that an average Ukrainian woman, by the time she reaches the age of thirty-five, would have already undergone three or four abortions.[86] In conversations with social workers in Donetsk we were told that a shocking seven out of ten young men in Eastern Ukraine consume such copious quantities of alcohol that they would be considered by Western standards to be clinical alcoholics. Even if these claims are exaggerated, it is nevertheless the case that alcoholism affects the life of almost every family in Ukraine, particularly in the eastern regions, and these are staggering statistics of which all Christian missionaries who come to Ukraine—whether they be theological educators, medical workers, church planters, pastors or evangelists—should be aware. Behind these statistics lie hidden hundreds of thousands of stories and individual lives that have been marked, perhaps irreversibly, by despair, heartbreak and tragedy. Again, these contextual realities underline the imperative of compassion as the objective and point of departure of all our missionary efforts and evangelistic outreach.

One of the tragic consequences of these kinds of problems is the hopelessness of many young people whose lives are blighted by poor educational and employment prospects. This prevailing sense of despair among many young Ukrainians also presents a major challenge and opportunity for the Church and for theological education in particular. High incidences of substance abuse, alcohol dependency, family breakdown and other social problems are all symptoms of an underlying philosophy of nihilism.[87] Nihilism is a philosophical notion denoting the nothingness of a hopeless void and the radical absence of God and all traditional values and moral coordinates. In faith terms nihilism constitutes an abyss of unbelief and existential despair. One of the cultural manifestations of nihilism is hedonism or the pursuit of pleasure. Nihilism in culture creates an existential void, which people try to fill with experiences of pleasure. Pleasure and amusement become substitutes for meaning and purpose. If life has no purpose or meaning, then all that is left is for people to "have fun," to seek

---

86. The author of one article claims that she knew women under forty who had undergone "around 30 abortions." See Ushakova, "There Is No Sex," 1.

87. This term was popularized in Russian-speaking contexts by Turgenev's novel *Fathers and Sons*, in the unforgettable figure of Bazarov.

entertainment in all the superficial and prurient distractions that popular culture and the ubiquitous entertainment industry have to offer.

Nihilism is at once both a formidable challenge and great opportunity for the post-Soviet churches. Nihilism is not merely a social or cultural challenge; it is also has a spiritual dimension. Scripture teaches the sad truth that even when the light is clear to see, people often choose to remain in darkness: "And this is the condemnation, that light is come into the world, and men loved darkness rather than light, because their deeds were evil" (John 3:19).[88] Yet far from discouraging us, this fact should prompt us to redouble our efforts to shine the light of Christ into even the darkest and murkiest areas of our world, remembering that Christ died and rose again to redeem people from darkness and bring them into the light.

Nihilism posits a gloomy, somber world in which Nietzsche's prophecy concerning the "death of God" has been fulfilled. Christian faith once supplied the world with a narrative of sense and meaning. Nietzsche proclaimed that the exposure of the alleged "falsehoods" of Christianity now mean that the world has been emptied of meaning and purpose. The loss of God means the loss of hope for humanity.[89] Nihilism, as Nietzsche understood, can have a cathartic effect in its destruction, paving the way for a "transvaluation of values" (*Umwertung aller Werte*).[90] The way to counter the threat of nihilism is not through a naïve assertion of "absolute truth." Sometimes Christian preachers, particularly evangelicals, fall prey to the temptation to offer facile criticisms of the supposedly baneful aspects of "postmodernism," which they almost invariably misunderstand and caricature. Since the Christian faith is said to be based upon a foundation of absolute propositional truth claims, the postmodern disavowal of "absolute truth" is seen as a threatening development. Western evangelicals have thus spent decades tilting against the windmills of postmodernity and, like Don Quixote de La Mancha, have emerged from the fray looking ridiculous. Hopefully, their post-Soviet evangelical counterparts can avoid making similar mistakes and can be aware of the opportunities as well as the challenges presented by postmodern modes of thought.

88. Wright, *Theology of the Dark Side*, 38.

89. Referring to the demise of the Christian narrative, Nietzsche wrote that "the untenability of one interpretation of the world, upon which a tremendous amount of energy has been lavished, awakens the suspicion that *all* interpretations of the world are false" (*Will to Power*, bk. 1, §3).

90. Nietzsche, *Also sprach Zarathustra*.

The Christian faith addresses the challenge of nihilism not with simplistic or dogmatic professions of allegiance to abstract notions of "absolute truth," but with a vigorous affirmation of life in the face of death and despair.[91] Nietzsche's notion of the "transvaluation of values" corresponds to the Christian affirmation of life and hope, which is tested and purified in the fire of despair, suffering and death itself. One of the great truths of Christian faith, illustrated most strikingly by Jesus himself, is that the way to truth and vigorous affirmation of life leads down the road of radical doubt, despair and even death. The faith that finally emerges out of the fire of despair and devastation will be all the stronger for having dared to stare into the abyss. Faith is not a comfortable vague assurance that everything will turn out for the best; true faith, rather, is a touching of the void, a radical affirmation of life in the midst of overwhelming adversity and uncertainty; faith is at once paralyzing and invigorating. Christian education can help us to articulate this faith in our culture by finding a common language between Christian convictions and socio-cultural realities. Christian faith has a role to play in leading people out of the existential void by witnessing to a nihilistic culture that there is a more excellent Way that leads to enduring joy and lasting fulfillment (John 4:14; 6:35).

Religious Challenges

Christianity has dominated the rich and diverse culture of Ukraine for several centuries. The Ukrainian Catholic theologian, Oleh Turij, claims that, "One cannot possibly understand any aspect of the cultural, social, political, or even the economic life of the country in the last thousand years without taking into account the contribution of Christianity, its teachings, liturgical practices, ethical norms, social and personal spirituality, church art and popular piety."[92]

Notwithstanding the deep roots of Christianity in Ukrainian culture, which not even 70 years of communist atheism could eradicate, the period following the downfall of the Soviet Union has witnessed an upsurge in alternative religious groups that are challenging the traditional hegemony of Christianity. These alternative religions tend to be individualistic, private and unconnected to traditional religious organizations. Some are explicitly

91. Limited time and scope preclude the possibility of developing this point in detail here. For a classic statement of this thesis, see Tillich, *Courage to Be.*

92. Turij, "Das religiöse Leben," 257 (my translation).

pagan, identifying with the so-called New Age movement.[93] The revival of paganism in contemporary post-Soviet Ukraine has been attributed to the historical affinity between paganism and Ukrainian nationalist sentiment and to the infiltration of pagan beliefs and practices into mainstream Christianity.[94] These religious groups have a particular appeal among a new generation of spiritual seekers, who have become disaffected with materialistic lifestyles that prevail in post-Soviet Ukraine. These seekers are unable to find in our churches a sacred space in which their genuine spiritual longings can find proper expression and be directed towards the light of Christ. The phenomena of "churchless faith" and "believing without belonging" are apparent not merely in the cultural postmodernism of the affluent West, but in the mentality of an emerging generation of post-Soviet spiritual seekers. In Donetsk, for instance, a survey conducted in 1998 showed that 64 percent of respondents claimed to be "religious," but of these, over half defined themselves loosely as "believers in God," and only a tiny minority had any connection to a particular church.[95]

Another major religious challenge confronting evangelical theological education and mission in contemporary Ukraine, as alluded to above, is the dominance of Orthodoxy in Ukrainian culture. The Orthodox Church[96] and millions of Ukrainians consider Orthodoxy as an integral part of a pan-Slavic national identity. The Orthodox Church has played an important role in forming and guarding the identity of Slavic nations, including Ukraine, which derive their historical identity from the early medieval state known as Kyivan Rus.[97] Since the time of Kyivan Rus, Orthodoxy has

93. For an account of the varieties of pagan belief in contemporary Ukraine, see Ivakhiv, "Revival of Ukrainian Native Faith," 209–39.

94. See Proshak, "Paganism in Ukraine," 141–48.

95. Krindatch, "Ukraine: The Re-Awakening," 185.

96. It would be misleading to refer to *the* Orthodox Church in the singular because Ukrainian Orthodoxy is divided into three main churches: the Ukrainian Orthodox Church–Kyiv Patriarchate; the Ukrainian Autocephalous Orthodox Church; and the Ukrainian Orthodox Church–Moscow Patriarchate. The historical context and events leading to the emergence of the Ukrainian Autocephalous Orthodox Church are explained in Bociurkiw, "Rise of the Ukrainian Autocephalous Orthodox Church," 228–49.

97. The history of Kyivan Rus' dates back to 882 AD, when the Varangian people, known as Rus', moved their capital from Novgorod (situated in present-day Russia) to Kyiv (the current capital city of Ukraine). Vladimir the Great (980–1015) and his son Yaroslav I the Wise (1019–54) presided over the "Golden Age" of Kyivan Rus. The Christian Church of Kyivan Rus was heavily influenced by Byzantium and the Church fell under the jurisdiction of the Ecumenical Patriarchate of Constantinople after Kyivan Rus

provided a distinctive Slavic identity that contrasted to the Catholic West and the Muslim East, which at various stages in history, had threatened the independence and even the existence of the Slavic Orthodox states that originated from Kyivan Rus.'

The prevailing attitude of many, but by no means all, Orthodox clergy is that Ukraine does not require mission aimed at bringing people to faith because all Ukrainians already have a religious identity whether they choose to embrace it or not. Despite years of secularization and Church decline, some Orthodox maintain that to be Ukrainian is to be an Orthodox Christian. This is also true in other post-Soviet contexts where Orthodoxy confers both religious and national identity.[98] Despite the relatively high percentage of the population who claim to identify in some way with the Orthodox Church[99], in many cases this identity signifies nothing more than a nominal attachment to the history and culture of the Ukrainian nation. It does not justify the designation of Ukraine as a "Christian nation." Notwithstanding the deep-rooted Orthodox Christian heritage and the sustained efforts of missionaries, particularly after the collapse of the USSR, most Ukrainians, as in the West,[100] today live *etsi Deus non daretur* (as if God did not exist). Despite several shared theological convictions,[101] evangelicals and Orthodox believers have often viewed each other with suspicion.[102] As one ecumenical report puts it: "Orthodox frequently perceive Evangelicalism as Western and therefore unwelcome, particularly in countries which are going through a period of searching for new identities."[103] Moreover, many Orthodox Christians throughout the FSU have been wary of Western missionary activities, which are often thought to be directed

---

adopted Christianity as the official state religion in 988 AD. Kyivan Rus' disintegrated under the Mongol invasions in the 1230s, and Kyiv itself fell to the Mongol warlord Batu Khan in 1240.

98. Richters, *Post-Soviet Russian Orthodox Church*, 98–99. See also Thomas Bremer's fascinating survey of religious and national identity in Russia: Bremer, *Kreuz und Kreml*.

99. According to one survey, 72.2 percent of Ukrainians self-identify as "Orthodox." See the report of the EAAA titled "Effectiveness of Theological Education," 178–205.

100. Taylor identified the present era as a "secular age" in his acclaimed monograph, *A Secular Age*. Taylor hints, however, that "hegemony of the mainstream master narrative" may be waning.

101. These similarities are enumerated and analyzed in Cherenkov, "Evangelical Christians and the Orthodox Church."

102. Lewis, "Sobering Critique," 5–8.

103. Evangelical Alliance Commission on Unity and Truth among Evangelicals, *Evangelicalism*, 140.

towards the proselytizing of Orthodox churches into protestant Christianity.[104] The Baptist theologian, James McClendon, noted that one of the tests of the authenticity of a missional model is whether it can "be proposed in a spirit of love that will win friends, not enemies, for the good news it seeks to represent."[105] Any attempt to develop a generous, ecumenical missional vision in which evangelicals and Orthodox believers could participate as equal partners should take into account this astute maxim.

In a context in which Christianity and national identity are so closely connected, many Ukrainians look to the Christian churches not only to be active in social work and charitable activities, but also to develop the cultural heritage of Ukraine in order to form a collective national identity. Oleh Turij explains that, "In a society afflicted by moral and intellectual corruption, the citizens look to the churches in order to critically redefine the past." Many Ukrainians look to the Church for answers to the moral crisis in the hope that a revitalized Christianity may be able to offer genuine alternatives to the contrasting perils of neo-Soviet ideology and Western consumerism.[106]

Soviet and Western Approaches to Theological Education

Evangelical education in Ukraine after the demise of the USSR, as in many other post-Soviet countries, was heavily dependent from the outset on the West, particularly North America, to provide funding and resources. The history of Western involvement in theological education after 1991 has been extensively documented elsewhere and evangelical leaders and academics continue to debate its positive and negative impact. Given the influx of Western missionaries and teachers into Ukraine in the early 1990s, it was perhaps inevitable that friction would ensue between native and expat approaches to education and mission. This friction was particularly apparent in approaches to theological education as well as to teaching and learning more generally.[107]

---

104. Kenworthy, "To Save the World," 21–54.

105. McClendon, *Doctrine*, 44.

106. Turij, "Kirchen in der Ukraine," 216.

107. These differences are well illustrated and lucidly explained in Parushev, "East-West," 11–21. In this fascinating article, Parushev contrasts the difference between narrative convictions of Eastern students and logical thinking of Western students, and discusses how these different approaches produce different ways of thinking about the

Since at least the beginning of the nineteenth century, Western theology has generally been characterized by rational, historical investigation. The prevailing assumption has been that "real theology" is concerned with the ancient texts and the systems that theologians have built for interpreting them. All other types of theology are derived from this "pure" theology. So-called "real theological scholarship" involves the study of how ideas and texts interact. On this basis of this notion, Western theology—as Andrew Kirk rightly notes—has tended to separate theory from practice. "Applied theology" is regarded as a derivative pursuit that can be undertaken only after a long process of learning about biblical and historical issues and after gaining a sound grasp of systematic theology.[108] Moreover, Western theologians have displayed a particular propensity to compartmentalize their discipline into a vast range of disciplines and sub-disciplines and theologians are extremely hesitant about crossing the boundaries of other disciplines. A former colleague of ours who had spent twenty years teaching in a theology faculty of a distinguished Western university once said to us that he was "not a theologian." What he meant was that his doctoral thesis and main research interests were in biblical studies and Christian ethics, which apparently did not belong to "proper theology." Evangelical theologians and church leaders in the FSU do not have the luxury either of maintaining boundaries between "Applied Theology" and "Pure Theology"; neither do they have the resources to support narrow specialists to undertake highly particular studies of the minute details of an arcane area of theological scholarship. The demand in seminaries and colleges in the FSU, as Keith Jones maintains, is for experienced and qualified generalists who are able and willing to sacrifice their personal ambitions to become top-rank scholars in order to facilitate teamwork and to build relationships with colleagues for the greater good of the learning community as a whole.[109]

Another factor in theological education to bear in mind is the difference between the career options available for theology graduates from the West and those with degrees from institutions in the FSU. In contrast to Western theology graduates, whose degree will enable them to apply for paid placements within churches, such as pastors and missionaries, graduates from evangelical seminaries in post-Soviet contexts have no such

---

task of theology.

108. Kirk, "Re-envisioning the Theological Curriculum," 22–37.

109. Jones, "Leading a Theological Institution," 289–308.

opportunities to receive paid employment at the end of their studies. Alexei Melnichuk explains,

> In the West a demand exists for Christian workers—they go to seminary, and jobs are waiting in churches and missions that will pay them a salary, support them, and take care of them. The situation is different in the FSU. People here look with suspicion on a missionary without a job . . . now we see declining enrolments in seminaries and Bible colleges because many students are unable to find work afterwards. Mixed programs that provide students with a profession as well as good Christian ministry training practically do not exist.[110]

In the secular job market of post-Soviet economies, theological degrees— particularly those that are not state-accredited—are practically worthless. Very few churches can afford to pay the salary of a fulltime pastor, meaning that most pastors need to find at least one other job just in order to feed themselves and their families and to pay the bills and the rent. In light of these facts, evangelical institutions will need to think creatively about how to offer their students not just theological diplomas, but vocational, state-accredited degrees in non-theological subjects that will offer graduates the prospect and hope of finding meaningful employment once they have finished their studies. Instead of offering solely theological degrees, institutions that are sensitive to socio-economic realities and that want to survive and flourish in post-Soviet society will need to offer courses on a range of subjects, including philosophy, law, history, psychology, social work, business administration, economics and whatever else might be relevant to the particular setting of each institution. In other words, theological education in post-Soviet society will need to offer more than just an education in theology.

The main aim of theological education should not simply be to train people in the skills of practical church ministry, but to liberate people to become effective change agents of society and to bring their Christian faith to bear in every sphere of their professional lives. This paradigm shift in our approach to theological education will require a much greater integration with related disciplines that study human society. We will need to realize, as Andrew Kirk rightly points out, that "neither Biblical studies nor systematic theology on their own can be called theology proper. Only when they engage with every level of culture do they become part of a genuine

---

110. Melnichuk, "Keys to Re-energizing," 2.

theological undertaking."[111] This assertion echoes the classic arguments of John Henry Newman concerning the role of the university and the inter-dependence and mutuality that characterize the relation between theology and other branches of knowledge.[112] Newman's holistic conception of education is at variance to the compartmentalization and trends towards minute specialization that have come to characterize academic theology in much of the West.

Another point relevant to this section on the different perceptions of Western and national missionaries is that, contrary to the common assumption that Western Christians brought the gospel to Ukraine after the fall of Communism, Christianity had in fact been a central part of Ukrainian culture and identity ever since Vladimir the Great, who was said to have been impressed by the "beauty of the Byzantine liturgy" and the "intellectual superiority of Christian philosophy,"[113] established it as the state religion of Kyivan Rus' in 988. By far the most dominant form of Christianity in Ukraine has been Orthodoxy, which distinguishes itself from Western forms of evangelicalism on several points of doctrine and practice, although there are several points of commonality.[114] Western missionaries in the FSU should also realize that even the evangelical movement itself emerged in the Slavic territories not as an import from the West, but grew as a renewal movement within the Orthodox Church, as important historical studies have demonstrated.[115]

111. Kirk, "Re-envisioning the Theological Curriculum," 22–37 (27).

112. Newman, *Idea of a University*. Newman argued that "religious truth is not only a portion, but a condition of general knowledge. To blot it out is nothing short . . . of unraveling the web of university teaching."

113. Meyendorff, "From Byzantium to Russia," 86.

114. See Finger, "Anabaptism and Eastern Orthodoxy," 67–91. Likewise, Mykhailo Cherenkov lists some of the commonalities between evangelical and Orthodox Christians, as follows: communalism; mysticism; brotherhood; anthropology; submission and humility; eschatological consciousness; a "miraculous" understanding of grace; an emphasis on faithfulness; the idea of the local church; theocentrism; an accent on a conservative understanding of faith; polyphony of faith; and respect for history and traditions. See Cherenkov, "Evangelical Christians and the Orthodox Church."

115. Peter F. Penner notes that "For the evangelicals in the FSU, the translation of the Bible initiated a reform movement coming out of the Russian Orthodox Church." The reformers were known as "revivalists" and "separatists" and it was with these people that the Slavic evangelical movement arose. See Penner, "Scripture, Community, and Context," 25. Albert Wardin argues that although contemporary evangelicals in Russia and the FSU exhibit their indigenous character, they have incorporated foreign elements into their beliefs and practices, particularly from German Baptists. See Wardin, "How

Addressing the Theological "Brain Drain"

Given the general lack of educational opportunities, it is hardly surprising that, since independence, many intellectually gifted post-Soviet Christians have abandoned their native lands and have settled in other countries, particularly in the United States. According to one estimate, more than five hundred thousand evangelicals left the countries of the FSU to settle in the West in the period between 1989 and 2005.[116] From our experience of working in institutions of evangelical theological education, it became clear that the main aspiration for many bright young evangelicals was to find a scholarship that would enable them to study and emigrate, possibly permanently, to Western Europe or to the United States. This "brain drain" of some of the brightest and best evangelicals to the West presents a considerable challenge in itself.[117] Mark D. Elliott succinctly addresses the causes and consequences of the brain drain of Ukrainian evangelicals to the West:

> Seminarians' introduction to Western living standards and Western cultural values makes going home a difficult adjustment. The negative influences of narcissistic materialism and individualism are self-evident. But even defensible Western mores, such as the high premium placed on efficiency, productivity, and punctuality, pose problems for graduates attempting to re-enter societies that frequently value the building of relationships more highly than the completion of tasks by a set date.[118]

The loss of young evangelicals points to several broader challenges that confront theological education in Ukraine. There is currently a lack of opportunities for promising young evangelical students to receive a quality Christian education from universities in Ukraine or Russia. Given the shortage of suitably qualified teaching staff, the dearth of funding and resources, and corruption at local and national levels of the administration, it is extremely difficult for existing institutions to obtain meaningful state accreditation. The lack of accreditation creates a vicious circle of underachievement as capable students do not feel attracted to institutions that cannot offer degrees that will be recognized by employers outside the narrow confines of the evangelical subculture. Moreover, as Parushev notes,

---

Indigenous was the Baptist Movement?," 29–37.

116. Elliott, "Current Crisis in Protestant Theological Education," 215.

117. Graves, "Plugging the Theological Brain Drain."

118. Mark D. Elliott, quoted in Edgar, "Faculty Development."

distrust of secular accrediting agencies is particularly prevalent among Eastern Europeans, who can remember the strong atheistic ideology that drove state institutions. As a result, "Mistrust of the churches in formal education is widespread and not only in Eastern Europe."[119] This consideration leads us to address the issue of anti-intellectualism among evangelical communities.

Anti-intellectualism among Post-Soviet Evangelicals

Theology, once esteemed as the "queen of the sciences," is now regarded as a marginal or esoteric pursuit.[120] There is general distrust of theological education not merely by the state, but even among many post-Soviet evangelical churches. Certain churches exhibit an innate distrust of academic theology. One of the main challenges that evangelical academic leaders experience is strong opposition from denominational leaders, many of whom view theological education with considerable suspicion. For some church leaders, the concept of theological education itself is considered "liberal," even though, by Western standards, the education offered in most theological seminaries in the FSU would be considered very conservative. There is often the apprehension among the older generation, who never had the opportunity to benefit from a theological education that they will need to compete with younger leaders who will become better educated than they are. There is also the genuine fear among many regional pastors, who risk losing their most gifted leaders to a theological seminary. Pastors may therefore recommend mediocre students of limited ability who have no particular missional vocation in the hope that the experience of studying at the theological college will kindle a passion for mission. In the meantime, the most capable and mission-minded young leaders in the local church are withheld and retained by pastors and denominational leaders.

Distrust among evangelicals towards theological education is one of the legacies of the Soviet Union. Many evangelicals who lived under the Soviet system preferred to preach about the imminent end and preparing for the Second Coming of Christ. As one Baptist leader in the 1970s put it: "In a short time from now . . . neither Bibles, nor symphonies . . . will be needed, for we shall behold Him—Christ, as He is, will be all in all."[121]

119. Parushev, "Towards Convictional Theological Education," 191.

120. Jones, "Leading a Theological Institution," 300.

121. "Khristianam vsego mira!"

To the separatist Baptists, for example, the Bible correspondence courses established by the "official" Baptists in the 1960s and 1970s were seen as a means of educating pseudo-Christians who were obedient to the atheist authorities, rather than to Christ. The attitude of the "separatists" to education and theology followed from the tenets of "evangelical simplicity," the "imminent end of the world," and the primacy of practical love over dogmatic knowledge. These attitudes were expressed well in an article published in the journal *Vestnik spaseniya* (its ideas turned out to be so important that in another embodiment, it was subsequently republished in *Vestnik istiny*[122]):

> Christianity is the love of Christ; not the thought of love, not old memories of love, but that very first love . . . Let us remember not only our personal original, enthusiastic Christianity, but the nascent Christianity of the whole church . . . With the center, soul and passion of this sacred love there were not dogmas, no forms, no ideas, but Christ Himself. Love for Christ is burning, vanquishing, sacrificial—this is Christianity of the first and last days . . . We often live as if there is no living Christ; Once again, we fall under the burden of the past . . . and we live with such anxieties about the future, such plans and expectations, as if He will not come.[123]

> Even after the fall of the USSR, many pastors continued to express similar anti-intellectual sentiments. One pastor recalled that, "Western theologians wanted to help us to organize Bible courses. I specifically told some of them that we have no need of these . . . Indeed, we have no doctors of theology in the fellowship. But I say for those who are truly in awe before God, the Bible alone is enough to become a doctor of theology. So long as one is not lazy. Previously, we were persecuted from without, but now there is an onset of various false teachings and intrigues are being woven against the churches, against the narrow path.[124]

Rather than condemning the pastors who continue to express such sentiments, it is important that academic leaders in the FSU recognize that many church leaders have serious concerns about sending members of their communities to receive a theological education. A widespread prejudice exists among many evangelicals, who believe that they have nothing

---

122. Martsinkovskii, "Pervaiia lyubov.'"
123. Martsinkovskii, "Khristos gryadushchii," 12–16.
124. "Programma—nezavisimost.'"

to learn from the "liberal" and "ecumenical" theology of the West.[125] These attitudes reveal a deep disconnection between the evangelical churches and the universities and seminaries that must be addressed and overcome by anyone who cares about the future of evangelical theology and mission in the FSU.

Summary of the Challenges for Theological Education in Ukraine and the FSU

It is important to be aware both of the grave crisis confronting evangelical theological education and the enormity of the difficulties faced by those in positions of leadership whose task it is to envision new strategies and to pioneer new models. As recently as 2010, Mark R. Elliott made the bleak but accurate observation that "across the FSU many residential seminary buildings, built at great expense, are now nearly bereft of full-time students. From the Baltic to the Pacific one finds Protestant schools struggling with an enrolment shortfall that threatens their survival."[126] In his book *Baptism bez kavichek*, Mykhailo Cherenkov identifies several problems confronting the evangelical churches in the FSU, which he lists as "European secularism"; "Soviet atheism"; "aggressive Islamism"; "official Orthodoxy"; "folk paganism"; "global consumerism"; and "popular post-modernism."[127] Theological education cannot be unaffected by these broader social, political, economic and religious challenges. Post-Soviet society today is experiencing a period of profound transition; it is as yet uncertain how the evangelical churches can best respond to these various and multifaceted challenges.

One thing that does seem quite certain, however, is the need for a rigorous system of evangelical theological education, which is attuned to the contextual realities and challenges of real life and real people in the countries of the FSU. The evangelical churches will better be able to respond to the challenges if they can build up a generation of dedicated and well-educated Christian men and women. The evangelical churches in the FSU today need not only "professional Christians" (i.e., pastors, missionaries, evangelists, etc.) but also "Christian professionals" (i.e., Christian doctors, nurses, lawyers, entrepreneurs, architects, journalists, broadcasters,

125. Cherenkov, *Baptism bez kavichek*.
126. Elliott, "Current Crisis in Protestant Theological Education," 15–16.
127. Cherenkov, *Baptism bez kavichek*.

etc.), who are able to bring their Christian perspectives into these various spheres.

Following the sweeping changes of the late 1980s, many theological institutions were formed by national churches; others, such as Donetsk Christian University, were initiated by Western missionary organizations.[128] Walter Sawatsky has helpfully classified the recent history of missionary activity in the FSU according to three distinct phases. He describes the first phase from 1987 to 1993 as a period of "Frantic or even Frenetic Evangelism." The second period from 1994 to 1996 was more settled as missionaries tried to review their strategies. From 1997, Sawatsky argues, theological institutions that were founded in the first period of frenetic activity began a process of reorientation towards more realistic goals and priorities. One of the major priorities of evangelical theological institutions after 1997, maintained Sawatsky, was to develop a truly contextual theology. Several years on, the imperative of contextualization still presents a formidable challenge to academic leaders in universities and seminaries throughout the FSU whose task it is to develop courses of theological education, which are "both contextually relevant and biblically and theologically grounded."[129]

The diverse challenges enumerated in this chapter all illustrate the complexity of the crisis point at which theological evangelical education in the FSU has now arrived. Notwithstanding this pessimistic assessment, it is important to remember the central truth of Christian faith, which teaches that crises can be harbingers of hope. The manifestations of crisis in contemporary theological education imply not only dislocation and disarray, but also opportunity and hope. As Jürgen Moltmann put it, "Anyone who only talks about a 'crisis' without recognizing its implicit opportunity is talking because he is afraid and without hope. Anyone who only wants to have new opportunities without accepting the crisis of previous answers is living in an illusion."[130]

Philosophers have elucidated some of the main elements of "crisis" both as a category of existential dislocation and as a kind of social disruption. At the heart of a crisis, explains Alasdair McIntyre, is a breakdown

128. For more details on these initiatives and a critical analysis of the role of Western missionary activities, see Elliott, "Theological Education after Communism"; Brown, "Progress and Challenge in Theological Education," 1. A very critical account of Western missionaries can be found in Reimer's controversial and thought-provoking article "Mission in Post-Perestroika Russia," 16–39.

129. Kool and Penner, "Theological Education in Eastern and Central Europe," 102.

130. Moltmann, Church in the Power of the Spirit, xiii.

of epistemological norms through their exposure to new circumstances to which they no longer correspond.[131] Crises compel us to move out of our comfort zones and to move into thresholds where insecurity and uncertainty meet with new possibility and hope. Crises pulsate with the tension of unrealized possibility. The task of leadership is to actualize the latent possibilities in the crisis and to harness these synergies towards the positive transformation of the lives of those who fall under our sphere of effective influence. Such transformative leadership may prove decisive in enabling the evangelical communities in the FSU to stand at the vanguard of a new movement that will lead to a decisive break from the baleful legacy of Soviet communism and a thorough dismantling of the enduring processes of socialization that continue to produce *homo sovieticus*. The recent crises in the spheres of politics, society and education may herald the coming of a new epoch in the history of this region—an epoch that has passed through the post-Soviet transition and which will be determined not by the servile *homo sovieticus*, but by the freedom-loving *homo maidanus* prototype.

131. MacIntyre, "Epistemological Crises," 139.

3

Emerging from the Post-Soviet Transition

The Political Landscape and the Evangelical Church

The more persistently the Church stays silent about politics, the more numerous are the questions it faces: What is it protecting or justifying with its silence? What is its real position? Whose side is it on? Does it have anything to say about current concerns? Is the Church ready to move beyond the eternal, abstract and distant and weigh in on the tangible, burning issues of the present? The time for strict distinctions between "pure politics" and "pure religion" has passed; now politics is intertwined with economics, public morality, and religion. To assert that the Church prefers to stay out of politics is to admit that the Church shies away from public life and is afraid to get involved in the complex issues of our time. But our commitment to *missio Dei* will not allow us to remain silent on the pressing public issues of the present. Arcane reflection on esoteric ideas and principles will not suffice. Theology must engage with what is taking place now, in the current concerns of the public sphere.

In reflecting on the necessity of the Church to develop an appropriate socio-political theology, four helpful points of departure can be invoked: the witness of Martin Luther King Jr; the resistance of the Confessing Church in Nazi Germany; the ministry of the Church in Kyiv's Maidan Square; and the extreme nationalism of Russian Protestants. The first two of these were experienced through reading (and we rely not only on living history, but also on the texts of Martin Luther King Jr., Karl Barth, and Dietrich

Bonhoeffer); the second two were part of our lived experience. In this section we draw on personal experience and that of our contemporaries, as well as texts that were born from this experience. The first two serve as examples—we will always refer back to them. The second two define the context in which we live. Thus, we will look back on the first two stories, but speak from within the second two. We will voice only two thoughts—concerning the responsibility of the Church to the government and its responsibility to the public, and also how this responsibility is demonstrated.

We are used to professing the Church's responsibility to the government. This responsibility consists in obedience, that is, in maintaining order and staying within the law. The Church and individual Christians are obedient to the authorities if they carry out their activities in compliance with the laws of the land and in accordance with the higher, moral law of truth and justice. Obedience ends where evil begins. It is not the government that determines what is good and evil and, if a contradiction arises, "we must obey God rather than any human authority" (Acts 5:29). People can judge the good and the bad for themselves based on the critical discernment of their conscience. The Church, also, is called upon to distinguish between good and evil, and thus to legitimize the power that protects from evil, and to delegitimize the power that serves evil. When those in power violate their legal and moral boundaries, they should not only be denied obedience, but should be actively resisted, as Dietrich Bonhoeffer maintained.

Thus, in distinguishing between good and evil, the Church is responsible for submitting to legitimate authority (which acts in accordance with the constitution and moral law) and at the same time for resisting lawless authority (which rewrites laws for itself and violates moral prohibitions). Unfortunately among many post-Soviet evangelicals, we hear about obedience much more often than about resistance. Yet if we read the Bible carefully, we see many examples of resistance to oppressive power. Obedience to godless and lawless authorities is not only shameful and demeaning, but but also criminal and sinful. Such obedience constitutes a grievous violation of the natural order of good and evil and calls white that which is black (Isa 5:20). Proper obedience is manifested in the payment of taxes, in answering to the institutions of power, and in complying with existing legislation. Disobedience or resistance is manifested in criticizing transgressions, in denouncing injustice, in the withholding of bribes, in peaceful meetings and demonstrations, and in the refusal to take up arms against peaceful citizens.

It seems that the post-Soviet Church is enamored of loyalty and is forgetting about resistance. The times call for resistance, and if we do not want this resistance to acquire a destructive character, we must imbue it with a Christian content, well-defined limits, and appropriate forms of expression. Furthermore, the Church is responsible not only to the authorities, but also to the people. There appears to be a dangerous imbalance in the relationship between the Church and the State, on the one hand, and the Church and society on the other. Whereas the Church has built a separate relationship with the State, promising it its loyalty in exchange for benefits, patronage, and preferential treatment, society has lost respect both for the State and the Church. Society had been disregarded by the State, which has stood apart from it and become self-sufficient. Society has been disregarded by the Church, which has focused on the relationship with those who have something to give; it has colluded with those who are powerful and influential and who make the decisions.

The political system of a society includes both the State and civil society. The Church should be part of civil society, but still it prefers to be a supposedly separate entity. Nevertheless, the Church is, in effect, co-ruler with the State. The place of the Church is in society, but on the basis of extended autonomy, because it does not belong to society (and it is certainly not owned by the State), and it is directly subordinate to God. In terms of the responsibility of the Church to the State and society, a natural asymmetry is laid: first come one's neighbors, and then the State, and the State only insofar as it protects and looks out for the welfare of one's neighbors and the general well-being of the people. If we maintain that the responsibility of the Church is primarily to God, then the order of responsibility is as follows: firstly, to God, then to society (the people), and, lastly, to the State. Responsibility to society can be expressed in solidarity and disagreement.

In relation to society, it seems that the Church is enamored of disagreement and forgetful about solidarity. The Church's responsibility to the State therefore takes two forms: one positive (obedience and solidarity), and the other negative (resistance and disagreement). We need to restore the natural order of responsibility: first, before God; secondly, to society; and after these comes the State; and we also need to remember the forgotten forms of responsibility—the possibility and even the necessity of resistance to the State and the good that comes from solidarity with society.

Religious Freedom and the Difficulties of Dialogue

Even given the best intentions on the part of the Church, at this point interaction with society and the State is not possible. Why is it so difficult to achieve effective dialogue between the State, society and the Church? Why is the freedom to believe and to think differently under threat? Because in the post-Soviet transition, it remains the State that disseminates freedom. Because society is not ready for freedom. Because the State assigns to the Church a role that is not free. In this environment, churches fight for influence and survival, for proximity to power and concessions from the authorities, and they regard each other not as partners in dialogue, but rather as competitors. By focusing on the relationship with the State, and becoming dependent on it, churches have overlooked their dialogue with society and their communion with each other.

That is the short answer to how and why the Church, the State and society in the FSU have failed develop a dialogue and mutual respect for the freedom of the other. Yet not everything is clear, even concerning the concept of freedom. We can understand political freedom as proceeding from democratic values and principles or from the faith-based doctrine of human dignity, freedom and human rights. In Soviet times, freedom was a mirage, shimmering in the distance somewhere, almost like in Pushkin: "The heavy shackles will fall, the gloomy prisons will crumble—and freedom will joyfully greet you at the gates." In the post-Soviet era, freedom suddenly seemed within reach, but now it appears more and more distant, like an ever-receding horizon. Freedom was accepted as if it were a cheap offering, of limited value and fit to be disposed of. Dostoevsky's Grand Inquisitor seems to have been proved right by the history and experience of post-Soviet society when he said that, "I tell thee that man is tormented by no greater anxiety than to find someone quickly to whom he can hand over that gift of freedom with which the ill-fated creature is born." Now the freedom that was gained for such a high price is "going, going . . . gone," and we hypocritically lament its loss. This is because without freedom, even if we neither understand it nor value it, we can no longer live.

Christianity is a religion of radical emancipation. The Founder of Christianity came preaching a radical message of freedom: "The Spirit of the Lord is upon me, because he hath . . . sent me . . . to preach deliverance to the captives" (Luke 4:18); "And ye shall know the truth, and the truth shall make you free . . . If the Son therefore shall make you free, ye shall be free indeed" (John 8:32, 36). Christian theology teaches that truth is a precondition of true freedom: falsehood enslaves and truth liberates. In direct contradiction to the capitalist-consumerist notion of freedom as the absence of restraint or the superabundance of choice, Christian tradition and the teaching of Scripture posit a deeply counter-cultural conception of the essence of freedom. Christian teaching reminds us not to unthinkingly equate the condition of freedom with willfulness or arbitrariness. This kind of absolute freedom is a chimera. It amounts to what Dostoevsky called "living by one's own dumb will" and leads to spiritual self-enslavement and to the capricious will of one's own nature. This kind of "freedom" constitutes an existential abyss.

After the collapse of the USSR, this kind of "freedom" prevailed in the emerging post-Soviet society. Democratic freedoms were hailed along Western lines, so that everything seemed the way it should be, like in a civilized world governed by democratic values of liberty and equal rights. However, the abyss of negative freedom created an economic and moral vacuum in which anarchy thrived and nihilism flourished. The chimera of "absolute freedom" generated a void of chaos into which post-Soviet society ignominiously collapsed with disastrous consequences for hundreds of millions of people. As the year 2000 approached the situation was changing: stronger now, the State began to interfere in issues pertaining to freedom, regulating it, and metering it out. The results mirror what happened under Lenin's New Economic Policy: a weak state will give away freedom only in order to take it back once it has regained its strength.

As State structures have consolidated their hold on power, there has been a gradual curtailment of religious freedom throughout the FSU since the fall of the USSR.[1] In Belarus, under the despotic rule of Alexander Lukashenko, unregistered religious activity is a criminal offence. The Lukashenko dictatorship applies severe restrictions on so-called non-traditional religions, which include evangelical communities. The Russian Federation likewise places severe restrictions on religious freedoms and officially distinguishes between what it calls "religious organizations" and "religious groups." Zoe Knox makes the telling point that "the great paradox of Russia's post-Soviet religious renaissance was the transition of the Moscow Patriarchate from a suppressed organization, directed and regulated by an

---

1. Lauren B. Homer painstakingly enumerates the various ways in which the Putin regime has passed legislation specifically aimed at curtailing the freedom of non-Orthodox Christian groups. Homer's analysis reveals that the passing of this kind of legislation has been accelerated at an alarming pace since mid-2012. See Homer, "Growing Russian Restrictions," 16–21.

atheist regime, to an institution which directs considerable effort to suppressing other religious bodies by discouraging religious pluralism and enjoying state-sanctioned privileges in a secular country."[2] Ukraine, by contrast, is relatively pluralistic and, at the official level, much more tolerant of minority faith groups than many other countries of the FSU.[3] Nevertheless, discrimination against evangelicals remains widespread throughout the FSU, particularly in Russia, where the official church institution has aligned itself so closely with the State.

But the responsibility is not only on the State. A weak civil society, even if it does not surrender freedom to the State, in any event will not mount resistance when deprived of it. Today a maturing civil society is both a major threat to post-Soviet states and the basic condition of democratic freedom. This is why, to the State, nongovernmental organizations, which promote the consolidation of the infrastructure of civil society, are branded as "dangerous foreign agents" (Russia is now trying to impose this fiction it created onto Ukraine). This is also how the State authorities regard any church or Christian organization that dares to adopt a free and independent position.

Given these conditions, the Church remains the sole authority, the main agent of influence capable of representing the interests of their people to the State. But here, too, not all is in order. Christianity as an influential voice in public life has not yet emerged. Frequently, a denomination will look out for itself rather than for the common good and the people as a whole. When the Ukrainian Ministry of Culture threatened to punish the UGCC [Ukrainian Greek Catholic Church] for their participation in the Maidan protests, most denominations opted to remain silent. The State authorities are trying to employ the Church for State needs, to impose upon it peripheral duties, or even forcing it to perform functions that are altogether alien to its mission and ethos. The Church is regarded as the nation's backbone, the spiritual bond connecting the "Russian world." But it should also retain its own prophetic voice and the right to criticize and speak out.

We were reminded of this by the events in Kyiv in the winter of 2013. The peaceful Euromaidan protests, which expressed the spontaneous outpouring of discontent and disgust of millions of ordinary Ukrainians, were met with bulldozers, batons and police brutality. What happened in Ukraine in February was a popular revolution against a murderous and

2. Knox, *Russian Society*, 1.

3. Wanner, "Evangelicalism and the Resurgence of Religion," 1–21.

corrupt regime, which had long ago lost legitimacy and the confidence of the people it was supposed to serve and represent. This was a regime which had even resorted to murdering dozens of its own citizens. The general will of the people was expressed in an overwhelming expression of popular disaffection with the inveterately corrupt regime of the criminal-turned-politician Victor Yanukovych, one of the most miscreant and reprobate figures ever to have occupied high office. Christians were at the forefront of the peaceful protests on Maidan. Among the "heavenly hundred" who were murdered on Maidan by Yanukovych's snipers were dozens of Christians. These Christians took a stand against the oppression, injustice, criminality, and exploitation of the pro-Russian kleptocracy headed by Putin's man in Kyiv, Victor Yanukovych. The Ukrainian people had suffered long enough, and history will record to their credit that the majority of Ukrainian Christians stood in solidarity with the protestors.

The response of the Church to the Maidan protests signals a seismic shift in the Church's public engagement in post-Soviet society. The implications and significance of Maidan extend beyond the national boundaries of Ukraine. Maidan may become a symbol of hope for Church and society throughout the nations of the FSU. Maidan has signaled a new era in which the post-Soviet Church is awakened to its social responsibilities and is able to demonstrate solidarity with the people. While the protests were taking place in Kyiv, the bells of Mikhailovsky Monastery awakened the Christian community of Ukraine to their responsibility as citizens, to their solidarity as Christians with society. The Head of the Ukrainian Orthodox Church, Patriarch Filaret, made the following statement:

> Our church has supported Maidan because it stands on the ground of morality. The people stepped forward against the lies and deception of the government which had not signed the Association Agreement despite spending a year preparing people for its signing. When snipers shot at people at Maidan, the church stopped praying for the government and then the government fled. Now we are facing an even bigger trouble—Russia's aggression against Ukraine and the occupation of Crimea. This is an act of immoral behavior by the Kremlin officials because Ukraine gave up its nuclear weapons while Russia, USA and Great Britain were to guarantee Ukraine's territorial integrity.[4]

4. Filaret, "We Think." Filaret was referring to the 1994 Budapest Memorandum, according to the terms of which Ukraine relinquished its Soviet-era nuclear arsenal in exchange for assurances by Russia, the United States, and the United Kingdom to respect

What have the recent events in Kyiv taught us? They have served as a powerful social impetus for the Church's participation in public affairs. What is needed are words of love and peace, of hope and the future. What is needed is the intermediation of the Church, a participation that is critical and prophetic, but at the same time, promotes peace and reconciliation. As the Church rediscovers its prophetic voice, it will recognize that a serious commitment to evangelism means not only entreating individuals to repent, but also, as Lesslie Newbigin put it, "a radical questioning of the reigning assumptions of public life."[5]

On the political plane, dialogue has hit a dead end. We need to return it to Christian foundations. It is only on such a foundation that national accord is still possible. Vibrant political and social life cannot flourish in the ideological void left over from the moribund Soviet era. We need to reveal the social potential of the Church and the universal, reconciling nature of Christianity. Only Christianity can explain how peace is attained through sacrifice, through forgiveness and love toward one's enemies, through the unity of those at enmity with each other through the reconciling power of Christ. What must be done today in defense of freedom? We must invest in that which the churches and the politicians have almost completely shunned: an analysis and unmasking of the social potential of the Church to transform society, not only just for the sake of responding and rendering aid, but for the sake of effecting authentic transformation. We must help activate the work of experts, in social-theological studies, in monitoring relations between the Church and society, and in this the role of the international community is vital in connecting us with global experience, diplomacy, wisdom and a dialogue between traditions. The Christian community should help unleash the potential of the Church—well-informed and unpartisan Christian assessments, analysis, recommendations should serve as guidelines and voices in a civil society. All of this is needed for the Church itself as it fashions a responsible and transformative social theology.

The Russia Factor

Post-Soviet space remains heavily, almost one-sidedly, dependent on what is happening in Russia. The year 2013 was a successful one for Putin's

---

the territorial integrity of Ukraine. Russia's invasion and occupation of Crimea in March 2014 constitutes a flagrant violation of this treaty.

5. Newbigin, *Truth to Tell*, 2.

diplomacy. Russia was able to regain influence in Ukraine, Armenia, and Kyrgyzstan, which are actively being pressed into a tight form of economic and military cooperation. In Belarus and Kazakhstan, already members of the Customs Union, tightening political and religious repression has been surfacing in the wake of Putin's own clampdowns on religious freedom. The dependence on hydrocarbons and loans from Russia is unquestionably evident in their imitation of his religious policy. What the naïve American fundamentalist Pat Buchanan has rashly called Putin's "conservatism" and his defense of "traditional values" is just a way of legitimizing Russia's imperial policy toward its neighboring territories and its repressive policies against non-conformist religious groups.

In Russia itself, manifestations of civil and religious liberty are severely limited for purported reasons of national security. Demonstrations in memory of the Bolotnaya Square prisoners, gatherings by the people against crime and government inaction, and even a meeting of sympathizers after the attacks in Volgograd—all have been violently dispersed by the State authorities. The Sochi Olympics were preceded by extraordinary security precautions and restrictions in freedoms. At the same time, there have been symbolic concessions made to the international community, including in December 2013 the release of victims of political repression: Mikhail Khodorkovsky and members of the band Pussy Riot, Nadezhda Tolokonnikova and Maria Alyokhina, who had all previously been recognized by Amnesty International as prisoners of conscience.

Characteristically, the Kremlin's tough stance against prisoners of conscience is fully endorsed by the Russian Orthodox Church. This can be explained by its typically "harmonious" relations with the State. What is harder to explain is the sympathy in Russian society and the Christian community to the Kremlin's rigid policy, the demand for a "strong hand," anti-Western sentiments, legal nihilism, and the widespread nationalism and anti-democratic ferment. In part, this can be explained by fear, in part by the lack of available information, and in part by religious traditions.

Fear causes people to avoid dangerous topics, to bury their heads in the sand and to focus on the most prosaic personal interests. In a society of fear, believers do not talk about social responsibility, justice, truth, freedom, solidarity or the transformation of society. They turn, instead, to discussions about distant and abstract categories, such as the soul and eternity. The information deficit justifies their passivity and conformity. Aggressive propaganda and restrictions on the independent media have resulted in a government monopolization of the information sector. This has also impacted religious organizations in terms of their official position and information policy. As the Russian proverb puts it, "The less you know, the sounder you sleep." In an environment where knowledge is dangerous, people prefer not to know, and if they do know, then they would rather not talk about it, and if they do talk, then it is only in the most general terms.

Yet the post-Soviet religious traditions restrict civil and even religious activism, in particular when it acquires a social dimension and touches on pressing issues. In local traditions, the custom is to suffer in silence, to make any compromises that are necessary to safeguard the Church. This is why even the evangelical churches, which suffered the most from Stalinist repressions, sent congratulatory telegrams to Stalin as the "great friend of all believers," and their leaders assured the West that "within the Soviet Union there is not a single prisoner of conscience." This is why the Russian Orthodox Church, which was almost completely destroyed by Stalin in the 1920s and 1930s, put out an obsequious 2014 "Stalin calendar" (issued by Dostoinstvo, publishers of the Holy Trinity St. Sergius Monastery). This is why the leaders of the Protestant unions of Russia in the same Stalinist spirit talk about the machinations of the West concerning Maidan in Ukraine. This is why we hear constant repetitions of the myths about the fraternal Slavic nations and the elder Russian brother, who is in fact suffocating its neighboring republics with its rough brotherly embraces.[6]

Signs of Change and Hope

What lessons can we take from the events of the past year so that our attitude to what is underway in the post-Soviet world is more objective and sympathetically active? The primary problem for civil and religious liberties is not the overly active intervention of the State, but the passive indifference of society and religious organizations. As the Ukrainian proverb says: "my hut is on the edge of the village," meaning, "That's not my headache. It doesn't concern me."

Only a strong society can stand up to the State by defending its legitimate rights and freedoms, and, in so far as society stands up for these, the Church should demonstrate its solidarity with society. How can we awaken

---

6. As a recent popular song has put it, if Russia and Ukraine are brothers, then Russia is Cain and Ukraine is Abel. "Eto, detka, rashizm! Pesni vremen ATO na Vostoke." See http://nbnews.com.ua/ru/news/126663.

and strengthen society in the absence of civil institutions? Who can do this, who is capable of coming forward with an inspiring and transformative initiative? In the context of a weak civil society, the most effective of its members may just be the Church. This is why the keys to the transformation of society are in the hands of the Church. In its turn, the transformation of the Church, critical self-examination, reassessment and renewal of its traditions are possible only in a dialogue between traditions, in the close cooperation of national churches with the global Christian community, through international partnerships and networking experts, through educational, and social projects aimed at creating a new generation of leaders for the Church and society.

Thus it is that in a post-Soviet society, the way to the transformation of that society is through the reformation of the Church. What is it that can transform the Church? Training new leaders, inter-denominational partnerships, a mass media that is also accountable to society, the commitment of independent experts, constructive analyses of trends in relations between Church, State and society, international support for progressive initiatives, and a broad movement by lay Christians spreading beyond the walls of the church into professional spheres. At the same time, we are observing the most disturbing current trends in the social and theological positions of the post-Soviet Churches. This includes Church nostalgia for Soviet stability, the demonization of "unspiritual" Europe and anti-Americanism, and disappointment in the Christian ability to effect social transformation, the disengagement of the younger generation from the life of the Church. These negative trends are not likely to be reversed in the short term. Hope lies with the new Christian generations growing up after the collapse of the USSR. As Thomas Kuhn put it in relation to scientific paradigms, more often than not the advocates of a new paradigm win out not because the representatives of the old order are persuaded to accept the new paradigm, but because the latter simply die out.

The most positive sign of the new times, of the new (post-) post-Soviet era, is, we believe, the Ukrainian Maidan. Maidan is a manifestation of civil society as a peaceful form of protest against a corrupt government. Maidan has become a symbol of liberty. The students—the generation of the future—were fundamental to the protest movement. They bore the brunt of the violence inflicted by the police on 30 November 2013, the night of the brutal dispersal of the protesters. The second force was the journalists, who were the only independent authority in the country. The third force was the

Church. It is the Church which opened its doors and protected the students being persecuted by the special police units. On the night of 11 December, the troops began their second attack on the Maidan and the Church sounded the bells, summoning people to help. This echoes the events of 800 years ago, when the armies of Batu Khan's Golden Horde stormed Kyiv. At that time, the last defenders took shelter in Desyatina Monastery. And today, the Church has become the last refuge for freedom and a stronghold of civil society. It is regrettable that after more than twenty years of "freedom," other institutions of civil society have failed to take shape. But we can take encouragement from what happened. The Church, the students and the journalists—together this is a worthy triad and the future of post-Soviet nations belongs to them.

The Ukraine Factor

Despite the missionary enthusiasm and euphoria that led to a "religious renaissance"[7] and "a rebirth of faith"[8] that ostensibly occurred in Ukraine following the demise the USSR, many churches in the nations of the FSU are now in decline. Even Ukraine, which has been called the "Bible belt" of the FSU[9], is no exception. However, despite the decline of Christian institutions and dwindling church congregations, Christianity in Ukraine remains the focus of attention of many foreign scholars and researchers—missiology sociologists, theologians and journalists. Unlike other former Soviet republics, with Ukraine not everything is clear. Ukrainian Christianity has preserved momentum, and diversity is thriving. Interest is growing within society toward Christianity, along with calls for renewal and a more active role for the Church.

Along with this is the need for a calm, steadfast and responsible analysis of data. Moreover, it is not objective data or numbers that are fundamental to this assessment. Statistics themselves cannot serve as a reliable basis because they, in turn, are based on methodological assumptions and specific procedures. While statistics from missiological centers continue to make

7. Wanner, *Communities of the Converted*, 2. Wanner's optimistic predictions, unfortunately, are not grounded in the socio-religious realities of post-Soviet Ukraine and do not take sufficient account of the diversity of theological and social convictions within Ukrainian evangelical subcultures.

8. Durkot, "Zwanzig Jahre danach," 219.

9. Wanner, *Communities of the Converted*, 1.

claims about the ongoing Christian boom in Ukraine,[10] more fundamental and extensive research suggests the existence of a traditionalist consensus and slowdown in the growth of new denominations.[11] According to Ukrainian analysts, a slowdown in the pace of growth has changed to a reduction in the numbers of both communities and parishioners, a blurring of affiliations, and an increase in the numbers of the "simply Christian."[12] Regulatory bodies and national expertise centers analyze the number of religious organizations, but do not say anything about the number of parishioners affiliated with churches. At best, they use public opinion polls. Denominations also prefer to speak only of how many organizations they comprise, offering only ballpark figures of membership. This may be an indication of the weak communication between church leadership and its members and an inefficient accounting system. It could be because the speakers are hesitant to talk when in the company of sociologists, but are confident about inflating the numbers to audiences that are less "in the know." For example, the Orthodox Churches put out the numbers of their parishioners not in absolute terms, rather as a percentage of the total population of the country. This makes it easy—according to this method, you simply subtract the ones you know are "not yours" and then count everyone else as "yours."

Among Ukrainian Protestants, the situation is just as opaque. Often, data verification is hindered by denominations with a propensity for mistaking what they want with what really is, in fact, wishful thinking. Each neo-Protestant denomination aspires to be the most dynamic. Each traditional church tries to display at least moderate growth. Overall, the data confirm the steady growth of charismatic churches and the slowdown in growth of evangelical Christians. But we must note that the constituency of the neo-charismatic churches is notoriously unstable. Even though there is evidence that these churches are experiencing moderate growth, this church is characterized by the fluidity of its flock, the frequent change in denominational affiliations, and the inflation of membership statistics.

The numbers for Baptist and Pentecostals are more stable. According to data from the All-Ukrainian Union of Churches of Evangelical Christians-Baptists (UUCECB), over the course of 2012, almost half of all parishes in

10. See *East-West Church and Ministry Report* 21.2 (2013) 10.

11. Center for the Study of Global Christianity, "Christianity in Its Global Context, 1970–2020."

12. "Relihiya i vlada v Ukrayini."

the union had not baptized even a single person that year.[13] Meanwhile, the strategic plan for the development of the union whereby membership is to be doubled by 2020 remains unchanged. It is surprising that the statistics of foreign researchers often rely on unproven data from the denominations. Thus, the membership of the All-Ukrainian Union of Churches of Evangelical Christians-Baptists for 2010 was assessed at 151,000 members.[14] These data cannot be verified because there has not been a single parallel count. There are, however, reliable data from the Razumkov Centre establishing a decrease in Protestants as a proportion of the Ukrainian population from 2 percent (in 2000) to 0.8 percent (in 2013).[15]

Outside the scope of international agreements, other new trends linger that have caught the attention of national experts—increases in the numbers of the "simply Christian," "simply Orthodox," and "simply Protestant," the complexity of the religious identity of Ukrainians, which includes not only those who are Orthodox, but also Greek Catholics and Protestants, the disappearance as a social group of atheists and the ambiguity of the "nonbeliever" label. To be Ukrainian today is to be primarily Orthodox, but also Greek-Catholic. With the weakening of the Ukrainian Orthodox umbilical cord, the opportunity to become part of the Ukrainian identity is extended to Protestants as well. At the same time Catholics are part of the "Latin" or "Polish" Christian culture. Against the backdrop of the Orthodox consensus in Ukraine, the number of atheists and nonbelievers continues to decrease. Apparently, some freethinkers and agnostics are housed in the too broad category of "Orthodox." If being counted among the Orthodox is enough to be called such without clarification of your credo, it is quite possible to be an Orthodox atheist or at least an Orthodox occultist.

Thus, Ukraine impresses not so much with the number of new religious organizations and their parishes as it does with the new structure of religious life. Social demand for traditional and new forms of Christianity is growing steadily, but the existing denominations are less and less capable of satisfying it. Herein lies a key difference between sociology and missiology: sociologists merely record demand, while Churches should respond to it.

13. "Skorochuyetsya chyselnist baptystiv v Ukrayini."

14. *East-West Church and Ministry Report* 21.2 (2013) 10.

15. "Relihiya i vlada v Ukrayini," 27.

Ukraine between Eurasia and Europe

The future of the post-Soviet space depends on the civilized choice between Europe and Eurasia. For all its apparent "decay," it is Europe that remains the center for post-Soviet countries, in terms of both its power to attract and its power to repel. For many Ukrainians Europe signifies, firstly, economic development, political liberty and democratic choice; secondly, Europe exemplifies higher living standards and, thirdly, it denotes a cultural identity that has deep roots in the Christian tradition. The politicians debate about the first. Nobody debates about the second, because everybody wants it. Regarding the final point, everybody debates about it, especially the religious leaders. The problem is that discussions about tolerance, minority rights, freedom and human dignity can easily progress into disputes about the fate of traditional values and the Christian heritage, which is only one step away from the demonization of modern Europe. It is strange that the "face of the anti-Christ in Europe" is so poorly covered and easily discerned. It is also peculiar that "Holy Russia" remains completely untouched by the same kind of bad influences that allegedly afflict Europe, although according to the Scriptures, the Beast "was given power to wage war against God's holy people and to conquer them. And it was given authority over *every* tribe, people, language and nation" (Revelation 13:7).

In this simplistic division of territories into "holy" and "profane" we see a somewhat naive and biased attitude. The fanatical belligerents railing against the "corrupting influence of the West" forget that "the Earth is the Lord's and the fullness thereof, the world and those who dwell therein" (Psalm 23:1). The Antichrist acts throughout the earth, seducing its inhabitants, and the Holy Spirit works everywhere, maintaining a beneficent influence. This is a more complex picture of the world in which there is not an inch of pure Christian territory, but anywhere and everywhere there is the presence of God. This picture is much more Christian than the simplistic division into East versus West, Europe versus Russia, and the lands of the Antichrist versus the holy land.

Recall that Paul, the "apostle of the Gentiles," walked from East to West, from Jerusalem to the center of culture—Athens, and then to the imperial capital—Rome. "I appeal to Caesar's court," he said after the Jews accused him of blasphemy and the violation of laws. The "profane" city of Rome, and not "holy" Jerusalem became his venue for judgment and debate. By employing his civil right, the apostle appeals to the authority of the Emperor for a fair trial. In response to the question of Festus, "Will you go up to Jerusalem?" Paul says: "I am now standing before Caesar's court, where I ought to be tried. I have not done any wrong to the Jews, as you yourself know very well. If, however, I am guilty of doing anything deserving death, I do not refuse to die. But if the charges brought against me by these Jews are not true, no one has the right to hand me over to them. I appeal to Caesar!" (Acts 25:10–11). Christ was crucified in Jerusalem. The righteous were sacrificed to defend traditional values. In Rome, justice was prized over religion. But there, too, Christians were dying, whether at the amphitheater or on crosses.

A democratic Europe and traditionally religious East are equally dangerous for Christians who dare to follow their Teacher, and not for the sake of traditional values or changeable imperial fashion. Not so long ago, the Ukrainian publishing house Colloquium released a translation of the Christian philosopher James K. A. Smith's *Who's Afraid of Postmodernism?*[16] The author is not afraid of postmodernism, and recommends that others cease being afraid of it. Indeed, he presents a good example of a positive Christian reading of postmodern theses. The first chapter of the book is "Is the Devil from Paris?" and urges Christians to receive the ideas of the "unholy trinity" (Derrida, Foucault and Lyotard) without prejudice. You cannot make Christians out of Derrida, Lyotard and Foucault, but neither should you demonize them. The questions put forth by Smith can be extended not only to postmodernism as a dominating mindset, but to the entire modern world, as long as it is Eurocentric: "Who's afraid of Europe?" and "Is the Devil from Europe?"

In connection with this, there is an obvious need for theological reflection not so much on the political, but rather on the cultural, spiritual, and religious aspects of the current debate about a possible European integration of Ukraine. Which of the calls for a revival of Ukrainian cultural and spiritual traditions have come from a pro-European (or anti-European) perspective? How are the manifestations of the Christian presence in society changing in a post-secular environment? How flimsy is the thesis about the supposed vitality of Russian spirituality and the apparent spiritual decadence of Europe? What might be the actual image of faith in the conditions prevailing in an infinitely pluralistic society?

The topic of relations in a post-Soviet world and a European world are multifaceted. For a long time now and with varying degrees of success a debate has been waging about the political vector of development and its

16. Smith, *Church and Postmodernism.*

nebulous consequences. Only recently have economists joined the debate, and today they are more closely weighing the pros and cons of the alternatives. But the fiercest fighting today centers around values and traditions. In this, all the values are tangled up with a single issue—the clamor for the protection of "the Orthodox faith" and repeated calls to defend the Soviet legacy, caught up with corruption, shady schemes, base populism, criminality, servility, collectivism and so on.

In these arguments, the communists (or, more accurately, the "Orthodox communists") are held up as the most ardent defenders of "our" "spiritual" traditions. But the people will not desist in their defense of "tradition." "What do we need Europe for?," they ask. "Why let ourselves be deceived by those crooks? Never will we reach agreement, and we don't know how to live under the law anyway." Thanks to the work of the communists and those Christian "traditionalists" of the pro-Russian party, the Ukrainians were presented with a contrasting picture of the spiritual life "with them" and "with us." The argument went something like this: "Europe is in decay, it is soulless and non-Christian; with us, at least for now, faith is still alive, so we had better stay away from those depraved Europeans"

Is it really so good for us and is it really so bad in Europe? And if we really are so spiritual, what is wrong with our faith if we cannot convert it to the public good, apply it to an economic development, or at least to the creation of an independent judiciary and the overcoming of rampant corruption that continues to afflict every sphere of post-Soviet society? Why, if we are so "spiritual," are we incapable of converting this spiritual prowess into at least a basic respect and common courtesy for one another and why have we failed so lamentably in creating the bonds of unity among our people?

Even if we agree with the special nature of our spirituality, then how can we, and how should we protect it? Here we can compare two high-profile cases: the Italian Lautsi case (the Lautsi family opposed the display of Christian symbols in schools) and the Russian Pussy Riot case (where the State and the Orthodox community joined forces against the participants in a punk prayer). In both cases, a battle was waged over the fate of Christian values, but the "spirit" of the two battles differed. In "secular" Europe the Italian courts and then the European Court of Human Rights spoke in the language of justice and culture. In "Orthodox" Russia, they spoke in the language of censorship. Here is how the Italians put it: Yes, the crucifix is a Christian symbol, but it has long been a part of secular culture now, so it does not offend anyone and cannot reasonably be construed as provocative. It is merely a manifestation of our cultural heritage. By contrast, this is how "Orthodox" Russia defended its persecution of the Pussy Riot: "We should have dragged them out of the church . . . by the hair and locked up these slags so that they think twice before they mock the Russian Orthodox faith . . . Don't be surprised if next time we break your legs. We Christians are tired of being weak. If I had been there instead of the church officials, I would have stripped them down to their underwear, covered them in honey and feathers, shaved them bald, and driven them out into the frost under the crowd of cameras that would have gathered around by then. For their desecration of the church, I would have had them burnt in public! These girls are sluts. They should hang for such a thing. I wonder, would it be better for them to drop dead tomorrow or should they be tortured a bit first?"[17]

A difference in belief, in values, in traditions is most pronounced in the methods employed to defend them. On this topic, the Vice Rector of the Ukrainian Catholic University, Miroslav Marinovich, spoke eloquently: "We believe that in the West, faith is in decline, and it is with horror we say that churches are being closed, because for us the most important are the external attributes. However, unlike us, in Western Europe we see 'inculturated Christianity' embedded in human relations."[18]

Of course, the European perspective opens up a series of challenges for our "spirituality," for Ukrainian Christian traditions. Here are just some of them:

- The challenge of pluralism: We are not alone with our tradition, our authority is not obvious, and our claims to exclusivity are dubious;

- The challenge of tolerance: No one should take their faith so seriously that others feel excluded;

- The challenge of total control against the background of unprecedented freedom: Nobody is going to die for his principles, no one is going to kill anyone; but those who are willing and able to do this need to be isolated;

- The challenge of memory: Recall and renew one's tradition so as not to get lost in the "big world";

- The challenge of personal faith, personal intellectual courage: Learn to live without the Iron Curtain, to orient yourself on your own, to

17. Uzlaner, "Pussy Riot Case," 106.

18 Marinovich, "Authenticity of Eastern Christianity."

demonstrate the benefits of your faith and to defend your position in the language of debate, and not from a position of power and authority.

The question arises, why is all this important? Knowing about these challenges, why should we move forward? The answer is simple: because we need to modernize our society. The period of the post-Soviet transition is over. All that has remained of the Soviet legacy has already been used and squandered. Ukraine is not a whole or self-sufficient entity, but part of the European cultural space, and especially of its core: the central tradition of Christianity. If it remains outside of Europe, Ukraine will remain in a cultural limbo, where powerful forces and vested interests will seek to harness Ukraine's economic, political and cultural resources to serve their own agendas, and the Ukrainian people will remain as pawns in an ill-fated civilizational battle between East and West. Outside Europe, all that awaits Ukraine is a new era of Russian-led serfdom—no courts, no free elections, no education, no medicine, and no freedom of movement. For only in an open dialogue, in a free world of permeating cultural ties, can Ukraine overcome its cultural and scientific isolation and emerge from the cul-de-sac of economic stagnation and endemic corruption.

Openness and accountability—this is what our Orthodoxy needs. This is what our public officials need. This is what our universities need. The "principle of Europe" is the principle of coexistence, plurality and unity in diversity. The great Ukrainian national poet, Taras Shevchenko, also spoke about this: "Learn from the alien, but do not be ashamed by the familiar." This principle of the "alien" and the "familiar" is European, corresponding to the values of pluralism, while preserving for each their special place and unique role. There are certain risks inherent in this, but there are even greater possibilities. There are crises, but there is also the experience needed to overcome them. The future has its uncertainty, but it also has its hope, and the past will no longer hold us back.

One question still remains: What will happen to our Christian traditions in a European future? They will compete freely, without invoking authority, but growing in credibility. The Church and faith will become open movements on the side of change, rather than closed institutions that promote the status quo. People will know that Christianity is more than what we know about it or our experience of it: that it is diverse, and that this diversity should be valued and protected, rather than simplified inside a self-contained unity and locked within its own tradition. Faith will not fear the most challenging questions. There will be doubts and disputes, but thanks to this there will also be conscious choices. Individuality will not be suppressed, the Church will be comprised of free people who consciously chose the Christian tradition, deepening their knowledge of it and continuing it in a spirit of enterprise, freedom and creativity. Our values will no longer be only spiritual, but will be either incarnated in or in conflict with the social, cultural, political and economic reality. We will live in an increasingly complex world, where few will immediately agree with us, but this competition will make us stronger and allow us to hone our skills in "giving an answer to everyone who asks you to give the reason for the hope that you have" (1 Pet 3:15). The Christian tradition will receive the opportunity to undergo a renewal and become more relevant, and our values will demonstrate their competitiveness. We move from reservations to the real, big world, where the dangers are many, but the prospects are even greater. Knowledge of one's local culture alone will not save one from assimilation. A deep knowledge of Christianity from its primary sources is needed. Effective mission requires conviction, passion, and deep and authentic personal faith. These are worth fighting for; perhaps they are even worth dying for. This is why, for example, Ukrainian Christians need to not only mark the 450th anniversary of the Peresopnytsia Gospels, but also to read them, study them, and know their tradition from the primary source.

As Ukraine takes its place among the nations of Europe, the path towards this goal will be difficult but will also present manifold opportunities. On this point, one representative of the Ukrainian Churches spoke eloquently in the address to the Ukrainian people on European integration:

> It is clear that a contemporary united Europe offers not only a litany of cultural achievements. It also presents challenges and problems which indicate the need for reform—and this also pertains to Ukraine. Traditional religious, cultural, family and moral values, which for centuries served as the foundation for the life of the peoples of Europe—these are precious treasures that we need to appreciate. Together we must protect, defend and augment them. We know concerning the situation in Europe there are a lot of like-minded people here with whom we are ready to join forces.[19]

Despite our support for Ukraine's European prospects and the tangible benefits that would accrue from Ukraine's full integration into the European family of nations, we nevertheless maintain that the Kingdom of God, rather than any worldly political entity must claim our ultimate

19. "Zvernenniya Tserkov."

allegiance. Archpriest Georgy Kovalenko, a spokesman for the late Metropolitan Vladimir, spoke well concerning the ultimate loyalty of the Church: "It seems to me that our politicians exaggerate the importance of the issue of geopolitical integration. For the Church, the issue of the possible signing of an Association Agreement with the EU is neither Good Friday with its suffering, nor Easter with its joyousness."[20] For the Church, the main thing is to remain true to itself, true to its own foundations, to its mission, and to not change its values in response to the vagaries of government policy.

Transformation of Society or Rejection of the World?

Post-Soviet evangelicalism stands at a historical crossroads. The choice presents itself as two alternatives: either to continue rejecting the world or to take responsibility for transforming society. Obviously, any prospects for development and influence are connected with the second option. But, for historical reasons, the first option has generally prevailed. Rejection prevailed in the Tsarist era, and also throughout the Soviet period. The vision of the Church influencing society was characteristic only for Ivan Prokhanov and turned out to be utopian in the conditions of the time. His projects for an Orthodox-Protestant alliance, for Christian education, political parties, civil initiatives, cities and communities were adopted with great popular enthusiasm, but then were stopped and wiped out by a government crackdown. Since then, a focus on withdrawing from the world, on avoiding confrontations with a hostile society, on preserving one's faith in light of the imminent Second Coming have once again come to prevail.

Even after the collapse of the Soviet empire, during the peak activity of evangelical churches, experts were openly skeptical about the social potential of post-Soviet evangelicals. In particular in 2001 Victoria Lyubaschenko used Weberian "ideal types" to designate Ukrainian evangelicalism as a popular, radical version of the Reformation:

> Limited access to the classical heritage, isolation from the world's centers of theological thought, prolonged civil underdevelopment have created in Ukraine a rather peculiar form of evangelicalism. It is enervated by the low educational level of its adherents, but this is offset by their missionary zeal and communal egalitarianism. It lacks developed religious and philosophical doctrines, but is replete in straightforward, pragmatic ideas that facilitate their

20. Kovalenko, "Politiki pryeoovyelichivayoot znachyeniye."

79

reading of the Bible. The average Ukrainian evangelical is far removed from doctrinal modernism and political slogans, but is very committed to maintaining his Christian family, and demonstrating piety and civil obedience."[21]

In fact, both the "transformation of society" and "rejection of the world" are no more than idealizations. In practice, it turns out that often "the transformation of society" is reduced to altering individual elements to one's advantage, rather than transforming the entire structure; in like fashion the "rejection of the world" is a convenient way to mobilize internal forces when there is a deficit of vision, to maintain control in the right hands during difficult times and to prolong the old way of life. Upon closer inspection, it becomes apparent that both the one and the other approach can be easily manipulated. Thus, in Soviet times legal congregations were drawn into the struggle for peace and the education of the "new Soviet man," and thus suffered from internal problems, such as weak leadership, lack of spiritual content and theological illiteracy. All of these factors, compounded by State repression, incapacitated the public witness of the churches and prevented evangelicals from exerting a transformative impact on society.

Today it is becoming clear that, in reasonable proportion, we need not to choose between two polarized alternatives, but to maintain the creative tension between transformation and rejection. We need to protect both values: solidarity with others and loyalty to one's own principles. This combination is possible only with a solid theological basis, which, in turn, can be obtained only by a renewed vision for theological education and mission in post-Soviet society, which can be expressed in the metaphor of "Church without Walls."

21. Lyubaschenko, "Protestantizm v Ukraïni."

4

Building a Church without Walls

Fulfilling the Great Commission in the FSU

After the flurry of "frantic and even frenetic"[1] missionary activity that followed in the wake of the collapse of the Soviet Union, evangelicals in recent years have begun to take stock. Although some continue to hope and pray for imminent revival, many seem to be coming to terms with the decline and what it means to live as a missional people on the margins who ask the painful question of lament and hope that was asked by an ancient people that found itself in a parallel condition of exile: "how shall we sing the Lord's song in a strange land?" (Ps 137:4).

The realization that the evangelical community is declining has provoked considerable soul-searching among Ukrainian evangelical leaders. In 2008, the vice president of Kyiv Theological Seminary explained that "Ukraine is like a hub of Christianity in a sense because we have the largest number of churches and percentage of Christians of all Soviet countries. But if you look at how we are doing as evangelicals after all these years—almost 15 years of freedom—the statistics show a decline. It started to disturb us. Weak churches can't fulfill the Great Commission."[2] Similarly in 2009, a veteran Ukrainian evangelical wrote that, "We now see that the number of converts has stopped growing or has slowed down significantly. We

1. Sawatsky, "Return of Mission," 95.
2. Konstantin Goncharov, quoted in Wunderink, "Faith and Hope in Ukraine."

must ask ourselves: did we do something wrong? Did we use our time and resources unwisely?"[3]

Instead of building church empires through short-term, Western-funded evangelization initiatives, the aim of our mission in the FSU must be to build the Kingdom of God by loving and serving people in costly discipleship that persists long after the sound and fury of the revival event or mass evangelistic rally have subsided. The veteran missionary Walter Sawatsky sets out the challenge lucidly:

> The task . . . of mission in the CIS [Commonwealth of Independent States] remains profoundly massive. It involves introducing persons to Jesus Christ for the first time and it involves the long drawn out process of deepening the faith for those who claim to be believers but who know and practice their faith poorly. Indeed, throughout history mission that mattered has usually had more to do with the slow formation of a people into the likeness of Christ than with the initial introductions. How do the workers sustain their vision after the initial euphoria—how do they manage that necessary relentless persistence?[4]

A proper, contextualized missiology that is in tune with the realities of life in the FSU has an important role to play in answering Sawatsky's question about how missionaries can cultivate the kind of "relentless persistence" required to renew and transform the Church in these changing times.

The recognition of the integrated relationship between mission and theological education builds on a long tradition of scholarship, which has broadened our notion of mission. We are following a well-established approach that refuses to consider mission and theological education as two separate tasks. Once considered practically synonymous with "evangelization," the word *mission*[5] now has a much wider currency, encompassing not only proclamation or *kerygma* (κήρυγμα) but also community or *koinonia*

---

3. Melnichuk, "Keys to Re-energizing," 2.

4. Sawatsky, "Return of Mission," 115.

5. We use this term with an awareness of its complexities and problems. Many Christians dislike the term *mission* because historically it has been linked to imperialist aggression and forced "conversion" of indigenous people to Western Christianity during the colonial period. Some argue that the term should not be used at all; see Cottrell, *From the Abundance*, xi. We use the term in the conviction that it can be redeemed both from the abuse to which it was subjected during the colonial era and from the often bland and meaningless connotations that it carries in relation to certain "mission statements."

(κοινωνία) and service or *diakonia* (διακονία).[6] Theological education *as mission*[7], which encompasses three aspects of *kerygma, koinonia* and *diakonia*, does not occur within a cultural vacuum, but is necessarily connected to local economic, social and political conditions. The challenge is to train people to respond in relevant, authentic and creative ways to the diverse challenges that culture presents to our Christian witness, without thereby compromising either our personal integrity or the ultimate claims of the gospel on our lives as individuals and as communities. Education is the seed from which, if it is carefully tendered and nourished, the evangelical communities in Ukraine and throughout the FSU will reap a rich harvest of Christian leaders who will become salt and light in every sphere of society.

In a context such as Ukraine, where evangelical beliefs and practices are regarded as unconventional or alien to the mainstream culture, the kind of "relentless persistence" referred to by Walter Sawatsky is even more necessary. Western missionaries must understand that when a Ukrainian converts to evangelicalism, the response of his or her family and friends will most likely range from mild derision or ridicule to outright hostility and even violence, in extreme cases.[8] Moreover, given the strict moral standards of most Ukrainian evangelical communities, the new convert would be expected to give up common practices, such as drinking, smoking and lewd language, which were once part of everyday life and which previously guaranteed acceptance among friends and family. There would be persistent social, cultural, and peer pressure on new believers (particularly young believers) to abandon their evangelical faith. Whereas the ecstatic frenzy whipped up by an evangelical preacher at a revival event may be enough to stir people to "make a decision for Christ," it will not be enough to sustain new believers on a lifelong journey of faithfulness in costly discipleship. Above all, the new convert needs to find a church where he or she will be welcomed into a covenant community, a spiritual home where he or she can be encouraged and nurtured and receive acceptance and recognition of the contribution that he or she can make to the collective life of the community.

Only when our evangelistic campaigns are buttressed by long term commitments to building covenant communities, can we truly claim to be

---

6. Fedorov, "Orthodox View," 69–101.

7. Penner, *Theological Education*, 7.

8. This is also the case for evangelical converts in other FSU contexts, especially in the Muslim-dominated states of Central Asia, where persecution is a fact of daily life for many Christians.

fulfilling the Great Commission as commanded by Jesus in Matt 28:18–20: "Therefore *go* and make disciples of all nations, baptizing them in the name of the Father and of the Son and of the Holy Spirit, and *teaching them to obey everything I have commanded you.*" The fact that the crucial final part of this commission ("teaching them to obey . . .") is often overlooked prompted Dallas Willard to coin the pun "The Great Omission,"[9] to critique certain models of contemporary evangelism that focus exclusively on conversion and require that people make a "decision for Christ," while neglecting the imperative of discipleship and costly obedience. When Jesus sent his disciples out into the world to "make disciples of all nations," he was not commanding them to persuade people to "make a decision for Christ," but was exhorting them to persuade people (as much by their lives and by their verbal proclamations) to open up their lives to receive the abundant life of God and to be continually sustained and challenged by the call of Jesus on their lives. Furthermore, as John Drane rightly maintains, "In terms of practical evangelization, the most striking conclusion is that the New Testament, the experience of the majority of Christian people, and contemporary developmental thinking all converge in suggesting that conversion to Christ is not a single event, it is a process."[10]

Evangelism aims at conversion, but the notion of conversion, according to the biblical concept of *metanoia*, is far greater than the thin evangelistic conceptions of individual repentance or saving individual souls so that people can "go to heaven when they die" that prevail in many evangelical churches. David Bosch makes a strong case for a more integrated understanding of mission that reflects the depth and all-encompassing implications of the notion of *metanoia*—a word which is often mistranslated into English as "repentance." Evangelism, for Bosch, is

> that dimension and activity of the church's mission which, by word and deed and in the light of particular conditions and a particular context, offers every person and community, everywhere, a valid opportunity to be directly challenged to a radical reorientation of their lives, a reorientation which involves such things as deliverance from slavery to the world and its powers; embracing Christ as Savior and Lord; becoming a living member of his community, the church; being enlisted into his service of reconciliation, peace, and

9. Willard, *Great Omission.*

10. Drane, *Faith in a Changing Culture*, 107.

justice on earth; and being committed to God's purpose of placing all things under the rule of Christ.[11]

The evangelical churches thus need a broader and more biblical conception of evangelism that is as concerned with sanctification and "growing in grace" as it is with the "event" of salvation in the lives of individual believers.

The Relevance of Contextual Missiology

The good news is that foreign missionaries can learn from the mistakes of the past. Rather than trying to impose Western models onto FSU contexts, missionaries from North America and Western Europe can use their creative gifts to encourage, empower and equip native Christian leaders to develop a contextual theology that is in tune with the social, cultural, economic and spiritual realities of the region. This is not a new thesis, but has been at the heart of the understanding of many protestant missionary communities since the early years of Western involvement in Ukrainian evangelicalism and theological education. When a group of theological education institutions met in the Romanian town of Oradea in 1994 with the aim of developing a concerted strategy for equipping the evangelical churches in the nations of the former Soviet bloc, the participants were able to agree on the essential point that: "the mission of the church is multidimensional and operating within a pluralistic and multi-ethnic situation, with spiritual, relational, social and physical consequences."[12]

In recent years, more and better resources have become available as indigenous historians and theologians have published scholarly works that are rooted in local contexts. This development signals a useful departure from previous practice, which used to involve translation of English-language textbooks that did not address the context of Eastern Europe and its Catholic and Orthodox heritage. As recently as 2009, Scott D. Edgar notes that, "While the investment of Western resources and faculty has been valuable to theological education in the FSU, a common weakness has been the lack of contextualization as educational models, methods, and goals have been imported from the West."[13]

---

11. Bosch, *Transforming Mission*, 420.

12. Paragraph 7 of the Oradea Declaration, 4–7 October 1994; cited in Penner, "Case Study," 254.

13. Edgar, "Faculty Development."

Although these kinds of critiques are accurate and important, it is necessary, in raising the issue of contextualization, to bear in mind that there are several ways of understanding this term. In terms of theological education, contextualization is much more than the translation of Western course materials into native languages or finding local examples to illustrate materials and ideas that have been imported from the West. Contextualization is not even simply a matter of replacing Western teaching staff with local teachers, although this is undoubtedly a desirable and necessary condition for the emergence of a contextual theology.

There are very few people today who would still advocate the uncritical adoption of Western models of theology and mission to FSU contexts. The debate has moved on and the main focus has shifted away from the contextualization of theological education and towards the contextual integration of theological studies with both ministerial practice and other non-theological academic disciplines. The reports of several student attitude surveys and the findings of numerous research projects have all demonstrated conclusively that many students enrolled on theology courses at FSU institutions have been unable to integrate their studies with their ministerial practices or Christian vocations. Reporting on these findings, Insur Shamgunov makes the following insightful observations:

> Graduates who believed they received the most benefit from their training for their later professional practice were the ones who were either actively involved in a local church ministry or who actively participated in student mission activities during their training. The theory-practice gap was minimal for them, as they were able to quickly transfer the learning that they needed and to rapidly contextualize information for immediate use. At the same time, the majority of the criticisms from graduates were directed not at culturally un-contextualized theological training, but at the larger issue of the theory-practice divide, which is relevant not only to Central Asia, but to theological education everywhere.[14]

Shamgunov criticizes "the traditional framework of ministerial training with its fourfold divisions of biblical studies, systemic theology, church history, and practical theology." He argues that what is needed instead is "a more holistic model, centered on the actual ministry of the church."[15] The

14. Shamgunov, "Protestant Theological Education," 12. See also Shamgunov, "Listening to the Voice."

15. Shamgunov, "Protestant Theological Education," 13. This call for a more integrated approach has long been promoted by notable leaders in theological education in

point is well made, but what is missing from this critique is a recognition of the fact that the gap between theory and practice, which has undermined theological education in many institutions, is itself a product of the importation of Western theological presuppositions.

Perhaps some evangelical readers may entertain doubts about the theological credibility of contextualized missiology, preferring instead just to "preach the gospel." It may be necessary, therefore, to dispel from the outset certain misunderstandings concerning what is meant by "contextual theology." Lesslie Newbigin rightly critiques the false dichotomy that is sometimes posited between a "contextual" and a "pure" gospel message: "We must start with the basic fact that there is no such thing as a pure gospel if by that is meant something which is not embodied in a culture. The simplest verbal statement of the gospel, "Jesus is Lord," depends for it meaning on the content which that culture gives to the word, Lord."[16]

Contrary to the misguided assumptions of some evangelical critics, developing contextual models of mission does not mean being conformed to or imitative of culture; rather, a truly contextual theology is a flexible paradigm that is rooted in Scripture and which is able to provide a critical lens through which to refract contextual realities in the light of the gospel. Recognizing that "cultures differ significantly in their reception of the word of God,"[17] contextual theology attempts to grapple with the question of what a meaningful and empowering gospel would look like for people in a particular culture or community.[18] As one Orthodox theologian helpfully remarks: "In the same manner in which it was necessary for the Second Person of the Trinity to assume human flesh to communicate the message of salvation, the truth of God must assume a form in which the message of salvation can be communicated. The Living Word became incarnate; thus the written word must also become incarnate."[19] Moreover, the notion that contextual theology, paradoxically, can and should be applied universally is predicated on the understanding that the gospel of hope and new life in Christ has universal and cross-cultural meaning. Compassion, the universal and timeless principle of the gospel message, must be applied and prac-

---

Russia, as is clear from Holovaty's useful article "Ideal Theological Education."

16. Newbigin, *Gospel in a Pluralist Society*, 144.

17. McClendon, *Witness*, 61.

18. See Bevans, *Models of Contextual Theology*; Schreiter, *Constructing Local Theologies*.

19. Stamoolis, *Eastern Orthodox Mission*, 62.

ticed in specific contexts in order to address particular needs. Contextual theology proceeds from the conviction that it is possible for the gospel to be relevant to the culture without being captive to it. From the perspective of *missio Dei* the task of contextual theology is not to follow prevailing social trends, but to discern the activity and purposes of God in the midst of cultural change and to participate intelligently and reflectively in these purposes.[20] As John Drane rightly maintains:

> The Bible unhesitatingly affirms that God is constantly at work in the world in many ways, times and places. Evangelism is not about Christians working on God's behalf because God is powerless without them. Effective evangelism must start with recognizing where God is already at work, and getting alongside God in what is going on there.[21]

Thus the Church should demonstrate solidarity with those in society, whether Christian or not (e.g., social workers, doctors, nurses, community leaders, orphanage directors, teachers, street cleaners, etc.), who, whether they are aware of it or not, are participating in the *missio Dei*.

The Role of "Expat" Missionaries

Western missionaries should be conscious of the inevitable fact that when they come to work in Ukraine or any nation of the FSU, they become apostles not merely of the gospel, but also of their culture. Westerners bring with them a set of cultural convictions and moral values, many of which are at variance to norms that govern Ukrainian and other post-Soviet societies.[22] Failure to recognize and respect these differences will have various consequences, ranging from giving minor offence by committing a certain *faux pas* to more serious issues of misunderstanding, leading to acrimonious relationship breakdowns.

The pace of change in the Soviet bloc in the late 1980s and early 1990s was so rapid that many Western mission agencies were caught by surprise as new opportunities opened up for reaching the people of the so-called evil empire with the message of the gospel. When the reforms of *glasnost*

20. Bosch, *Transforming Mission*; Kirk, *What Is Mission?*

21. Drane, *Faith in a Changing Culture*, 63.

22. Chapman, "Collectivism in the Russian World View"; Parushev, "East and West," 31–44.

and perestroika were underway, one Western missionary, Gary Cox, wisely noted that, "The temptation for us in the West, especially mission organizations committed to these lands, is to move in and do the job for them, often imposing unfamiliar and even culturally unacceptable programmes, methods and materials."[23] Thankfully, there were missionaries in this period who did not seek to use or control the local missionaries for their own agendas, but instead saw their task as one of encouraging and equipping local churches to engage in missional activities that were sensitive and appropriate to the local context.

A few well-researched studies have critically analyzed Western involvement in mission in the post-Soviet societies and which have offered helpful suggestions about how Western educators and missionaries can make a positive contribution to the work of local churches and seminaries. Miriam Charter, for example, wrote a PhD thesis on models of theological education in the FSU and came to the conclusion that "the most redemptive role for Westerners in the inevitable partnership of East and West in the development of theological education . . . must be one of encouragement, intentionally encouraging . . . educators not to allow the West, unchallenged, to replicate the educational models and styles that they have implemented in countries around the world."[24] In similar vain, Andrew Christian van Gorder maintains that missionaries are "learners and beneficiaries and not simply . . . those who are coming to give and direct."[25] Mary Raber, an American Mennonite missionary with several years experience as a theological educator in Ukraine, offers a helpful perspective on how native evangelicals respond to their expat counterparts:[26]

> on the one hand, foreign professors are seen as desirable friends whose very presence confers prestige and who possess the vital stores of information that will strengthen and sustain the evangelical community in the future. But on the other hand they are unknown and potentially dangerous entities who can disseminate false doctrine, weaken morals, and arrogantly usurp authority from recognized church leaders. Naturally the visitor's own attitude largely determines how he or she will be received.[26]

23. Cox, "Making Mission," 7–8.
24. Charter, quoted in Elliott, "Post-Soviet Theological Education," 9–10.
25. Gorder, "Post-Soviet Protestant Missions."
26. Raber, "Expectation and Reality," 33–37.

The last twenty years have witnessed a change in native evangelicals' attitudes towards Westerners. Greg Nichols, an American missionary who worked in Odessa for several years, notes that, "Western missionaries are still viewed as useful partners, but are no longer seen as the key ingredient in a successful ministry."[27] This changed attitude is a positive development because it militates against a culture of Eastern dependency on the West that characterized the early years of theological educational initiatives in the FSU. As Nichols remarks, whereas Westerners were once seen as essential donors, they can now be regarded as genuine partners.

Western missionaries who work in the FSU therefore need to demonstrate humility and even vulnerability. Their task is not to set the agenda, but to equip local Christian leaders with the tools, training and resources that they need to minister faithfully to people in their localities. On this point, Johannes Reimer offers simple, yet useful, guidance for Western missionaries working in Russia, which can be applied by missionaries working throughout this region:

> Let the natives determine what type of congregation needs to be established. Plant a church for the people, and while planting, stay with the people . . . Try your best not to copy your home congregation. This will always be your biggest challenge. Even if you believe your home church has developed the best model ever, don't think this can ever be universal as it may not apply to your Russian community at all . . . Establish a community- and need-oriented church. Mission must aim at the transformation of society as a whole. Russians will almost automatically measure your missionary work holistically. Pure evangelism which neglects social responsibility will sooner or later fail in this country.[28]

Expat missionaries should also jettison any pretension to be intellectually or spiritually superior to those people they are serving and enabling. Pete Rollins's understanding of the role of missionaries is instructive in this regard:

> In Christian mission the goal is not that some people "out there" are brought closer to God by our work, but rather that we are all brought closer to God. Such an insight may actually help expand the numbers of people who want to be involved with mission organizations rather than diminishing them, for there are many

27. Nichols, "Reflections on Twenty Years," 4.
28. Reimer, "Mission in Post-Perestroika Russia," 8–9.

who have been put off by the apparent superiority they are often required to assume in such environments.[29]

In keeping with these shifting trends in mission, John Papavassiliou predicted that,

> sooner or later the missionaries will not be able to work in underdeveloped countries as carriers of a higher civilization, of a civilization foreign to the local conditions of life . . . I foresee a radical change of the structure of missionary work. Missionaries, as carriers of the great message, will not behave also as carriers of a message from a higher civilization, but as brothers and teachers, as well as disciples and students of local cultures.[30]

Missionaries who abandon the perceived need to demonstrate their superiority and who adopt this more vulnerable posture may be surprised to discover that, "Many believers in the Soviet Union have long . . . shown the ability to retain spiritual values in seemingly hopeless conditions" and that we have "as much to learn from them as they from us."[31] Moreover, the success of our mission cannot be determined by crude numerical calculations (i.e., counting numbers of "converts" or copies of Bibles distributed); rather, success becomes apparent when our lives become transformed into Christ-likeness and when the hope of the Gospel reveals itself through the incarnational witness of our lives to the watching world.

Church Without Walls

Our reflections on the future of mission and theological education in the FSU have led us to a basic question: What is the Church? The formal academic answer to this question can be stated thus: The Greek word, ἐκκλησία, translated in English Bibles as "church" or in Russian Bibles as "tserkov," contains two primary significations. The first part, "ek," indicates "out from" or "out to," and the second part, "kaleo," signifies "to call." In a strictly linguistic sense, therefore, the church is that which is "called out from or to" something. As well as this notion of being "called out," the term ἐκκλησία in the Bible signifies two meanings: firstly, the "Church" is the local community of believers gathered for the sake of worship and witness in

---

29. Rollins, *How (Not) to Speak*, 54.

30. Papavassiliou, quoted in Stamoolis, *Orthodox Mission*, 73.

31. Bourdeaux, *Gorbachev, Glasnost and the Gospel*, 212.

a particular place; secondly, as the mystical body of Christ that constitutes the fulfillment of God's eternal plan of creation, redemption and glorification. It is significant that in the whole Bible there is no single reference to the Church as an organization or as a building.[32]

The Church, in the sense of a community that is "called out," is thus both an empirical and an eschatological reality. The fullest expression of the meaning and nature of the Church is to be found in the last book of the Bible, Revelation. The New Jerusalem of Revelation 21 represents a transfigured world and the fusion of the entire human community into a spiritual fellowship without barriers or distinctions of any kind.[33] The Church is a radical eschatological community: the Church, as the people of God, constitutes "a spiritual house, a holy priesthood . . . a chosen generation, a royal priesthood, a holy nation, a peculiar people" (2 Pet 2:5–9). A universal priesthood requires a Church without walls. If the Bible depicts the Church in the guise of a "new heavens and a new earth" in which all barriers and separations have been abolished, why, then, is the reality of our contemporary church life (not just in the FSU, but throughout the world) at such variance to this biblical paradigm? Why, particularly in our evangelical churches, instead of dismantling these barriers and separations, have we actually fortified them through our use of trite categories: "saved" and "unsaved" people; "Protestant" and "Catholic"; "Baptists" and "Pentecostal"; "Calvinist" and "Arminian"; "historical post-millennialism" and "premillennial dispensationalism," etc.? A radical vision of "Church without walls" can help us see these ridiculous categorizations for what they really are.

The great scandal of World Christianity today (and the post-Soviet Church is no exception) is the proliferation of denominations. In today's world, denominations have become impregnable walls, which unchurched people need to climb over before they hear the good news about Jesus. The churches of the FSU need a generous ecumenical vision that is focused only on Christ and the teaching of Scripture, rather than on denominations and the philosophies and traditions that are based on devotion to sinful organizations or individuals. The focus should be on the biblical teaching of the redeemed humanity, particularly as it is depicted in the gospels—including the "fifth gospel" of Isaiah's prophecy and its elaboration and culmination in Revelation 21 and 22. A renewed focus on the eschatological vision of

---

32. Bulgakov, *Bride of the Lamb*, 255.

33. Ibid., xvii.

hope can serve as the true theological foundation for a Church without walls in post-Soviet society.

One of the promises of the eschatological vision of the Church without walls is that we will one day be able to perceive things as they really are (1 John 3:2). Walls are those barriers that prevent us from seeing things as they truly are. There are physical walls that block our view as well as walls of prejudice that close our minds and obstruct our worldviews. In response to perturbing cultural trends, many churches have gone on the defensive. Panicky churches have sought to preserve the purity of their doctrine, forgetting that fundamentalism and dogmatism are possibly the most dangerous heresies that have ever threatened the Church. Other churches have tried to become relevant by mimicking cultural trends. There have been moments while attending evangelical churches in Ukraine when we were unsure whether we were in the House of God or whether we were watching a rehearsal for *Ukraine's Got Talent*. A. W. Tozer made the same point much more eloquently:

> A few churches accept fossilization as the will of God and settle down to the work of preserving their past—as if it needed preserving. Others seek to appear modern, and imitate the current activities of the world with the mistaken idea that they are being creative . . . but the creatures of their creative skill are sure to be toys and trifles, mere imitations of the world and altogether lacking in the qualities of eternity—holiness and spiritual dignity. The hallmark of the Holy Spirit is not there.

The central hallmarks of the Holy Spirit are not signs, wonders, miracles or other spectacular manifestations of God's activity. They are important, but they are manifestations, rather than the presence or essence of the Holy Spirit. The crucial hallmark of the Holy Spirit is God's people living together peaceably in a community (κοινωνία) of mutual love (ἀγάπη).

In the accounts of Jesus's life in the gospels, nowhere do we read of Jesus establishing a religious institution. In fact, quite the opposite is the case: far from founding a religious institution based on order and hierarchy, he built a community in which the values of love (agape), acceptance, hospitality were lived out in the context of a new order of existence made possible by the Kingdom of God. In fact, Jesus even explicitly discouraged this kind of hierarchical order and power relations that governed the "kings of the Gentiles" (i.e., the secular powers that govern the systems of the world—see Luke 22:24–26). The problem in many post-Soviet churches (as in the West) is that missionaries and church planters have tried to build the Kingdom of God through programmes and evangelization outreach strategies, which have had little relationship value. God—as Father, Son and Holy Spirit—has ordained community as his chosen means to build his Kingdom on earth. The early churches were not "churches" in the modern sense at all; the earliest Christians had no designated buildings of worship, but would congregate in each others' houses, offer hospitality, share each others' stories and read and reflect together on the meaning of Scripture.

Another lesson that we can learn from the early church is that in the first few centuries of its existence, the Christian Church had a terrible reputation; it was hated, despised and even brutally persecuted by the rich and powerful in society. Nowadays respectability is one of the walls that prevents the churches from fulfilling their vocations to be the Church. A respectable church is a compromised church. It is time that churches once again had a bad reputation, and for churches to become counter-references to (rather than imitators of) the State and dominant cultural trends. Radical witness for the sake of the Kingdom of God will inevitably incur the wrath of the ruling social powers, as Jesus himself warned (John 16:1–4). As James Mc-Clendon avers, "The Christian church must break out of its socially fixed roles in society in order to become the bearer, catalyst, and servant of a new and liberated society being created worldwide."[34] In witnessing faithfully to its radical calling, the Church without walls would follow the radical example of Jesus, who always valued relationships more than reputation to the point of being stigmatized by his religious and political enemies with the sneering sobriquet, "friends of sinners." Jesus was not concerned about his reputation and neither should his Church without walls today.

Crucially, the Church without walls is a church which invites people into fellowship without first insisting that they immediately conform to accepted patterns of "Christian behavior" or that they subscribe to certain creeds that uphold "sound doctrine." In the same way that the disciples journeyed with Jesus and gradually came to a realization of their faith, so should the Church without walls, the people of God, welcome people into fellowship and allow them to journey with us as they (and we) become more integrated into the Way of Jesus. Jesus's "method" of evangelism is expressed perfectly in the simple invitation, as recorded in John's gospel, to "come and see" (John 1:45–51). If this is the case, why do so many evangelicals make it a precondition of Christian fellowship that one must be "born again"?

34. McClendon, *Doctrine,* chapter 5.

On this point, Timothy Radcliffe offers this helpful comment: "We should travel with people as they search for the good, the true and the beautiful . . . Our contribution is to remind people of these deepest desires, which are rooted in our nature like the migratory urges of salmon or terns, making us restless until we arrive. We should be with people as they search for the good, the beautiful and the true." This search is rooted in the knowledge that the source of the good the beautiful and true are to be found in Christ as the one in whom, according to a passage from the New Testament, "are hidden all the treasures of wisdom and knowledge" (Col 2:3).

The task of the Church is to witness to the compassion of Christ for the benefit of the watching world. The Church thus serves as "the beach-head of the kingdom, the place in which the reign of God begins to be made manifest here and now."[35] Churches that thrive in the FSU will be those communities of believers covenanted together in the love of Christ and exhibiting a radical witness guided by faithfulness to Christ, obedience to Scripture and an openness to listen to the leading of the Holy Spirit. Above all, the Church without walls is a church that builds community and thus becomes the answer to its own prayer that, "thy Kingdom come, thy will be done, on earth as it is in heaven." Such a notion of community is built not by programmes and strategies, but by *compassion*, which is the central value of all Christian education and mission.[36] Compassion is expressed primarily not through programmes and initiatives, but through relationships. Compassion is the defining character of the Kingdom of God. This Kingdom is concerned with relationships. Lesslie Newbigin rightly remarks that, "From its first page to its last, the Bible is informed by a vision of human nature for which neither freedom nor equality is fundamental: what is fundamental is relatedness."[37] Compassion rooted in a vision of covenant relationships, generous hospitality and inclusive community must be both the object and point of departure of all of our educational and evangelistic endeavors. Compassion (agape) stands to mission in the same relation as fire to flame; compassion is the heart and soul of mission, its most basic essence and condition of its being. This integration of mission and compassion is consistent with Newbigin's notion of "mission as love in action."[38]

---

35. Stassen and Gushee, *Kingdom Ethics*, 230.

36. Penner, "Scripture, Community, and Context," 22.

37. Newbigin, *Foolishness to the Greeks*, 116.

38. Newbigin, *Open Secret*, 40–55.

Compassion thus remains a constant gospel principle to be practiced regardless of the cultural context, even though the ways in which compassion is demonstrated will vary according to the setting. In a context of social breakdown and deprivation, such as parts of urban areas in Eastern Ukraine, the element of compassion becomes particularly paramount. In a context where broken families, substance abuse, alcoholism, destitution and poverty are facts of everyday life for the majority of people, any "gospel" message of salvation, hope and new life in Christ that does not reach out to people with the compassion of Christ, however well intentioned or doctrinally sound, will not be heard and may even do more harm than good. There may even be some truth in Berdyaev's remark that Soviet communism was a judgment on Christians for their denial of Christ's teachings concerning human equality and social justice.[39]

On a related point, cross-cultural missionaries and theological educators should always be aware that certain scriptures will appeal more to one group of people than to another. For instance, when one of us asked a young Ukrainian student in our class what her favorite book of the Bible was, she replied without hesitation, "the Book of Revelation." When she was asked why, she replied that she was particularly struck by the poignant depiction of the heavenly city, the New Jerusalem, with its golden streets that radiated with the light and shekinah glory of God. She said that it offered her a heart-rending contrast to the filthy, murky, grey, litter-strewn streets that she had become accustomed to from spending most of her life in the industrial city of Donetsk. This was a striking example of the relevance of ancient prophecies to the contemporary context. The student had integrated the biblical horizon of future hope with the cultural horizon of contemporary reality. This kind of "fusion of horizons" (*Horizontverschmelzung*)[40] is a primary task not just of biblical hermeneutics, as Anthony Thistleton persuasively argues;[41] it is also a vital task of contemporary missiology. The biblical narrative provides a horizon at which Christian visions and aspirations for the coming of the Kingdom fuse with the reality of living in a fallen world that does not (yet) reflect the heart of God. The task of reaching out to people with compassion is connected to the challenges and opportunities of theological education in the FSU. The aim of theological education should be to teach a holistic knowledge of God's work of salva-

39. Berdyaev, *Ystoky y smysl*.
40. Gadamer, *Wahrheit und Methode*.
41. Thistleton, *Two Horizons*.

tion so as to imbue in students such a sense of missional vocation that they will be inspired to participate in God's plan to save the world through the redemption wrought in Christ and realized by the Holy Spirit.[42]

The notion of "Church without walls" has a particularly transformative application to the communal context of post-Soviet society. At the heart of the "Church without walls" paradigm is a trinitarian understanding of God as an inclusive community of three persons: Father, Son and Holy Spirit. Stanley Grenz writes that

> At the heart of the Christian understanding of God is the declaration that God is Triune—Father, Son and Spirit. This means that in his eternal essence the one God is a social reality, the social Trinity. Because God is the social Trinity, a plurality in unity, the ideal for humankind does not focus on solitary persons, but on persons-in-community.[43]

Jürgen Moltmann likewise contends that the conception of God as "Absolute Subject," developed by philosophers such as Fichte and Hegel, has undermined what he calls the "social doctrine of the Trinity,"[44] which, in turn, has contributed to a culture of excessive individualism in Western culture. The nature of God is community and as people made in God's image, we are made for community. This perhaps self-evident theological axiom, expounded at great length by several leading theologians,[45] is vital to a proper understanding of mission and theological education. The major task of foreign missionaries who come to serve in post-Soviet mission field is to create communities by facilitating relationships that are based on gospel values. Rooted in Scripture and grounded in its trinitarian identity, the Church can truly be the people of God,[46] a community infused with missional vocation,

---

42. The Orthodox theologian Anastasios Yannoulatos writes that "since the Christian mission is incorporated into God's mission, the final goal of our mission surely cannot be different from His. And this purpose, as the Bible . . . makes clear, is the 'recapitulation' (*anakephalaiosis*) of the universe in Christ and our participation in the divine glory, the eternal, final glory of God" ("Purpose and Motive," 4).

43. Grenz, *Theology*, 76.

44. Moltmann, *Trinität und Reich Gottes*, 5. Moltmann offers a convincing critique of Karl Barth on account the monotheistic horizon of understanding within which Barth frames his "doctrine of the Trinity."

45. Hilberath, *Der dreieinige Gott*; Volf, *After Our Likeness*.

46. This notion is addressed from a Baptist perspective in Haymes et al., *On Being the Church*.

which can be empowered by the Holy Spirit to reach out to a new generation of disaffected spiritual seekers in post-Soviet society.

Tomorrow's Churches:
Open Christianity in an Open Society

The tendencies of our time are converging toward an immediate future that will demand a radically open image of Christianity and the Church. What is all the more visible in the yearning for openness is a fatigue with clerical bureaucracy and a desire for a proper clarification of the relationship between the Church and society. Such a demand is not the opium of the people, but a sip of clean water from a wellspring of authentic "simple Christianity." The public demands a transparent, candid, honest relationship with the Church. While talking about salvation and eternity, all too often the Church has engaged in underhand business deals and political machinations. It sometimes happened that its interests in its own institutional survival were placed above the true gospel message of salvation and compassion for those in need.

The Church can respond to external criticism and internal weakness by either embarking on a path of renewal, and experimentation with new forms of "open Christianity" or by immersing itself in a search for answers in the depths of history. The relationship of the Church to history should be critical, but also grateful for what has already been given and discovered. The openness of the Church presupposes an openness toward both the future, and the past.

The open Church inhabits a different type of space than that which is occupied by social institutions. Dietrich Bonhoeffer spoke about this very topic, urging a rejection of "spatial thinking": "If we are talking about the space of the Church, we must be sure that this space at every moment is already penetrated, taken, overcome by the testimony of the church of Jesus Christ. Thus all false spatial thinking is ruled detrimental to understanding the Church."[47] Why? Because "the world is not divided into parts between Christ and the devil, it is the holistic world of Christ, whether or not the world itself knows this."[48] The trouble is that not only does the world not know and not accept the integrity of the world under the rule of Christ.

---

47. Bonhoeffer, *Ethics*, 38.
48. Ibid., 39.

Theology should aim to make creative connections between faith and the whole of life. A robust Christology of the kind developed by Bonhoeffer exposes the fallacy of dividing the world into "sacred" and "secular" dimensions. Faith should be joined to every sphere of life, including politics, business and the media, as well as religion and education. Faith must not be confined to private morality or to church life, but the rule of Christ should be extended to all of life in recognition that "the world is the Lord's and all that is therein" (Psalm 24:1).

The mission of the "open Church" is to proclaim the gospel of the Kingdom, to discern, to bless, to participate in its highly diversified forms, directing people both within and outside of the Church in their spiritual search towards an encounter with Christ, wherever this meeting might occur. The Church loses its special place so that it might be present everywhere. In what new manifestations might this omnipresence be expressed? What internal church *perestroika* would it require? These are the questions that belong on the theological agenda at this time, so that the "Church without a place" does not end up becoming the "Church out of place." These questions have become all the more pressing in light of recent events precipitated by the Maidan protests. Such is the magnitude of these events for the spirituality and history, not just of Ukraine, but of the entire region, that they call for serious theological reflection on their meaning and significance.

5

The Church after Maidan

The Church on Maidan

As the debates continue about the Church *and* Maidan, we propose a discussion on the Church *on* Maidan. The Church on Maidan presents itself as a fortuitous phrase in many respects. Maidan has demonstrated the extent to which the Church belongs in the city center, near the central square; Maidan and the Church are always nearby as special places—the center of public life and center of spiritual life are almost completely congruent. So it was long ago, and even in Soviet times the link between Maidan and the Church could not be completely severed. Once again the cry is raised: "On the square near the church there's a revolution taking place."

The Church should be at the epicenter of what is happening and in the midst of social processes; that is, it should follow in the path of Maidan. Where Maidan is, that is where the Church should be. Where the people congregate, where they go in quest of truth, where they call out for freedom, where they raise the voice of truth against the abuse of power, that is where the Church should also be, as represented by its clergy or laity, in the words of sermons and in the compassionate service of the Christian community. It should be recognized that the Church as an institution is inherently conservative and even inert, so it may well see in Maidan a threat to its own stability. At the same time, the Church, wishing to remain true to its Founder, cannot fail to follow him. And he, as we know from the

Gospels, certainly found himself in the thick of things, among the people and their needs.

And so Maidan, as the geographical center of the city and the social center of its life, is a natural place for the Church. This thesis seems so self-evident as to hardly be worth theological justification; it follows directly from the Gospels and resonates with their spirit. The Church's calling on Maidan is another thing. What should be said? What should be done? How should it dispense with its potential "to be in the center," "to be on Maidan"? These questions relate to a number of socio-theological and socio-philosophical topics that are actively under discussion in a post-secular landscape. What kind of landscape is this? This is not a retrospective return to the Church's dominating role over society and the State; nor is it nostalgia for the theocracy of the Middle Ages. This is a forward-looking vision of a more complex relationship between the Church, society and the State, where the entire triad plays an active role, but none lays claim to a monopoly with respect to the specifics of the other and their openness to the partnership for the common good.

If we concur with the understanding of the Church as a beachhead of the Kingdom of God, we have to agree with Cardinal Kurt Koch's thesis concerning the necessary "self-relativization of the Church" as the penultimate, not the last, resource to be called upon "in the events, needs and desires, which it shares with the other members, to recognize the real signs of the presence or plan of God."[1] Thus, the Church is called upon to recognize what is happening in society ("on Maidan") as part of what has already come to pass, in the fullness of the impending and increasingly evident manifestation of the Kingdom of God. If the Church has its own special place—even if it is near the Maidan, in the city center, but still confined within boundaries, the Kingdom cannot be limited (and therefore it is difficult to define, i.e., to assign semantic and territorial limits to it). New vistas of the Kingdom are emerging everywhere, including in politics, economic relations, and even in social conflicts.

The post-secular perspective reveals the absence—and, even more than this, the fundamental impossibility—of a clear break between the social and the religious, between society and the Church. And this complex connection has its analogies in theology—in Christology ("indivisibility" and "disembodiment") and teachings about the Kingdom of God, which is everywhere, but for the time being is not visible. Thus, in the words of

---

1. Koch, *Khrisiyani v Evropi*, 81.

the Apostle Luke, "And when he was demanded of the Pharisees, when the kingdom of God should come, he answered them and said, The kingdom of God cometh not with observation: Neither shall they say, Lo here! or, lo there! for, behold, the Kingdom of God is within you" (Luke 17:20–21). "Within you" (or better translated, "among you") means that the Kingdom is already present among the people. The Kingdom is among us and we feel its presence, but it cannot be reduced to our spatio-temporal awareness. The Kingdom is not a human construct, but is growing and manifesting itself in the human environment by transforming it and infusing the social space with spiritual values of love, humanity, compassion, forgiveness and solidarity.

Within the Kingdom of God boundary lines will be drawn differently. We can no longer posit clear distinctions between the holy space of the Church and the secular world outside. As is rightly asserted by Reformed theologians, "The boundary is laid not between the two spheres, but between the two regimes of power. The dividing line runs through all areas of created reality . . . This is a broken line, not straight; it resembles the front line, the boundary between two rival systems."[2] In other words, in the future Kingdom of God, we can see the full scale, so that the Church is part of society, but also the Church and society are part of the Kingdom. Thus the Church, aware of itself as a symbol and a herald of the Kingdom, cannot find neutral territory for itself; rather, she lives together as one with society and together they share a common history, her realm and her network are the same world in which wheat and tares, and the sheep and the goats live side by side and in which God causes the "sun to rise on the evil and the good, and sends rain on the righteous and the unrighteous" (Matthew 5:45).

The Church represents the interests of the Kingdom of God throughout society and in all its spheres. As James McClendon contends, "Christ's salvation is for the whole human reality, in all its social, economic, political, and religious dimensions, overcoming all divisions and ending all injustice and oppression."[3] The maps of the sacred and profane, religious and social all overlap. The task of the Church is to discern between good and evil, between God and gods, to illuminate the front line in what Chuck Colson calls the "kingdoms in conflict," and to manifest the presence of God in a variety of social situations. And then it turns out that on any social issue,

2. Walters, *Renewed Creation*, 110.
3. McClendon, *Doctrine*, 427.

the Church cannot be neutral. It is fated, or rather, it is called on to engage with society. It has no option other than that of being a participant. By not protecting the victims, the Church is complicit in the crime; by not calling evil that which is evil, the Church supports the criminals.

The public participation of the Church as a religious organization is restricted by law and its own social doctrine. But it may bless all its sons and daughters as representatives of the Kingdom of God, in their struggle for civil rights and in the confirmation of their gifts and professional callings. This aspect of the Church's activity will not be overwhelming or domineering, but will bring us together and enrich us. This presence implies that it is not everywhere that the Church, as a religious organization, will make its presence known. This may require some sort of restructuring of the Church: Christians are not to be found where the Church purports to be, rather the Church is found where the Christians are. This means that the Church can be implicitly present on Maidan—in the embodiment of its faithful representatives. In this case, the Church must acknowledge its participation through its voluntary representatives by blessing and supporting them. Without dissembling, we must clearly state: The Church is present both on Maidan, and on the Anti-Maidan, both in the opposition and in the government, insofar as its members have always acted according to their understanding of Christian responsibility. Then the task of the Church becomes not so much positioning itself as yet one more player in social processes, but to provide a public context in which Christians can speak out on behalf of Kingdom values of hope, reconciliation and compassion. In its social role, the Church is thus called to encourage the faithful and to expose the "wolves in sheep's clothing." Then the vocation of the Church becomes a concern for all societal parties: some will be rebuked, some will be encouraged, some will receive aid, and others will be reprimanded.

Through her people, the Church can exert influence on society, reminding others of the fundamental values of human dignity and freedom, of the primacy of the spiritual and the common good, of charity and self-sacrificing love, and of solidarity and grace. In this, the Church does not dictate to people their right choice as citizens, but rather defends what this choice has to offer and what it requires. The Church cannot agitate for either the European Union or the Customs Union; the Church can only emphasize the importance of a free and responsible choice. But the Church cannot fail to condemn the use of force against the defenseless, and to speak out against corruption, selective justice and political repression.

Thus it is that the Church finds itself on Maidan. It is there that, by its very nature, it is endowed with the amazing ability to be "in the world." Once on the Maidan, the Church must maintain its otherness, the ability to live and say it is "not of the world." The Church does not put itself alongside other organizations and parties that act on behalf of some and against others, and thus limit themselves. Aware of itself as the focus and messenger of the Kingdom, the Church represents its interests through its children, the citizens of the earthly city and the citizens of the future city of God. Its task is to distinguish between good and evil and to instruct people in the fear of God, in how to nurture virtues and life skills. Only in this way, giving up its place in the background of society and its conflicts, through the sacrifice and risks inherent in participation, the Church may be the leaven that causes the dough to rise; the seed that grows into a tree whose branches will spread to shelter all.

What provides an understanding of the Church in the future Kingdom for an understanding of the State, society and religion in a post-secular perspective? The fact that Christians are citizens of the Kingdom of God, but are simultaneously citizens of society. The Church cannot rule over society, but it can influence it through her people. An active Christian presence in society can transform social ties in their entirety, making society more just, cohesive and humane. By disavowing a special role for itself as a separate organization, the Church can activate its presence in culture through the participation of Christians in civil society. The relationship between the Church and society is crucial to optimal relations between Church and State, and society and State.

The Lessons of Maidan: The Interests of the Church

Post-secularism creates opportunities for the Church's return to the public sphere. Public space is no longer considered necessarily secular. For the Church, the door is open. The Church's main interest in an open society should be society and not the State. Until now, the Church has sought harmony with the State, but the time has come for her to demonstrate solidarity with society. The Church can return to society, and the current revolutionary situation may be a particularly auspicious time for the Church to engage with society. The Church may agree with the State about the division of power, but then it all may be taken away by society. Instead of playing political games and engaging in struggles for influence on high, the Church should educate its people, because the future of post-Soviet society belongs to them—and *not* the foreign, Kremlin-backed unholy alliance of bandits, mercenaries, gangsters, and oligarchs who rule over society and use the State for their own selfish interests.

The post-secular world offers opportunities to renew Christian unity. If only the priests of the Ukrainian Orthodox Church of the Moscow Patriarchate prayed more often for the pacification and blessing of the inhabitants of Lviv, and the priests of the Ukrainian Greek Catholic Church (UGCC) prayed more fervently for the unfortunate inhabitants of Donetsk. If only the Ukrainian Baptists named as their brothers not only the Russians, but the British, Germans, Italians, Lithuanians, and other European evangelicals as well. If only the Kyiv City State Administration was graced with not only a portrait of the Ukrainian nationalist, Stepan Bandera, but an icon of Rublev's Trinity.

In addition to the fidelity of tradition and concern for the contemporary, the Church must foresee tomorrow. The prophetic vocation of the Church is expressed in its capacity to sense the future, to warn of danger, and to serve as a harbinger of hope. The Church must serve the future, because with it comes the Kingdom of God. It should anticipate and embody renewal, awakening and rebirth. It should prepare and educate its people to live out their prophetic calling as agents of the Kingdom of God. We must focus on preparatory work for the future, rather than on responding to and struggling with what we have already outlived and agonized over. The best help right now for the living is to struggle to make the future a better place for them. It is obvious to everyone that the current order has lost legitimacy: "the emperor has no clothes." The Church is called not only to engage in politics, but should itself become a *polis*, which embodies an alternative vision for political engagement and mediation between society and the State.

Maidan forced Christians to address a question that they long avoided: In what ways is the gospel not only the source of personal salvation, but also the source of social transformation? Post-Soviet evangelical churches are known for these two features: their focus on the personal relationship with God and on evangelistic activity. Both features are distinguished against the backdrop of the historical Churches. The latter underscore the importance of tradition and history. Tradition alone includes the newcomer into the community of faith and limits the role of the individual, while the historical-cultural and political significance of the Church in society attracts and inspires people far more than the isolated calls of the evangelist to personal repentance.

Today, both the evangelical and the historic Churches have been faced with the challenge of Maidan. Personal faith and evangelism alone, or tradition and complacent authority are no long sufficient. The events of Maidan illustrate that both approaches of the Church toward society have been exhausted and are in need of revision. What the historical Church longs for is what the evangelical movement has been strong in: namely, greater focus on the individual, a personal relationship with God, the living gospel, and simple sermons that can be understood and applied by ordinary Christians. As for the evangelical churches, what they want is what has been the exclusive purview of the historic Church: namely, greater attention to the social dimension of faith, integration with the broader Church tradition, connection to local cultural features, and the history of the people. Far from being confined to proselytism and individual conversions, the task of mission must be "concerned with the course of world history, with the gospel encounter with culture, with the shape of life on this planet."[4]

As we noted in chapter 1, the emphasis on personal salvation and gaining individual converts has been misguided: these emphases have been carried away with narrowly defined personal issues at the expense of social responsibility. Moreover, any kind of "mission," which is aimed solely at eliciting individual repentance through dire warnings about hell and eternal damnation, raises serious concerns about the motivations of the "convert." Pete Rollins explains,

> If someone is convinced that there is a place where they will be tormented after death, and that the only way to avoid this terror is by affirming that Jesus Christ is Lord, then they will no doubt make that affirmation, regardless of whether they are genuinely moved by Christ or not. This type of discourse endeavors to compel individuals to bow their knee regardless of their motives or the nature of their desire. Like a lover of nuts who is offered thousands of shells with no center, so we offer God thousands of "converts" with no hearts.[5]

These words call to mind the disturbing words of Jesus, who said: "Woe to you, teachers of the law and Pharisees, you hypocrites! You travel over land and sea to win a single convert, and when you have succeeded, you

---

4. McClendon, *Doctrine*, 430.
5. Rollins, *How (Not) to Speak*, 36.

make them twice as much a child of hell as you are" (Matthew 23:15). One leading Baptist theologian has even argued that this focus on making converts constitutes a demonic perversion of the true task of mission. "The perversion associated with evangelism," notes McClendon, "is potentially the more demonic . . . just to the degree that in a crass way it succeeds. Members are added; the institution grows; but in this phony evangelism, the gospel is choked out by that growth." This is what happens when the highest goal of mission becomes the making of converts, which results in "an infinite regress of mere recruitment" that takes the place of any "real (or realistic) understanding of the point of evangelism."[6]

A further critique of traditional evangelistic methods in post-Soviet churches is that the active preaching of the gospel and the coming of the Kingdom has often degenerated into tedious moralizing and an unhealthy preoccupation with the spiritual dimension to the detriment of solving evident and concrete problems. As a result, evangelical Protestants know all too well what the "I" is, but do not know the "we." Despite our theoretical commitment to the doctrine of the Trinity and the communal context of individual salvation, we continue to sing hymns about "*My* Jesus, *My* Savior."[7] Our prayer and worship often reflect the "me and Jesus" spirituality that replicates much more the imported ideology of Western individualism than it expresses the true values of the gospel. Moreover, we claim to know what the "Word of God" is, but we seem incapable of expressing it in the material reality of our lives and working in solidarity with society and the wider Church. Accordingly, the reaction of most evangelical Christians to Maidan was "neutral." They thought it was not their business to mix in politics. If they did participate in society, it was only to preach the gospel in the narrow sense of "preaching."[8]

Abdicating their social responsibility, the churches have reduced the task of mission to exhorting people to join *their* church. Pastor Sergey Golovin remarks that, instead of fulfilling Christ's Great Commission to

6. McClendon, *Doctrine*, 439.

7. This song, produced by Hillsong (a Pentecostal megachurch that originated in Australia), has been translated into Russian and is regularly sung at evangelical Christian gatherings throughout the former USSR.

8. Thankfully, not all evangelicals were passive during the Maidan protests. For the first time in the history of the post-Soviet nations, an evangelical Christian, Oleksandr Turchinov, became the interim president. The polls demonstrated that despite the hugely difficult challenges he faced and the unpopular decisions he was forced to make, his approval ratings were consistently high among the Ukrainian population as a whole.

"go and make disciples of all nations," evangelical Christians say, "go and lure them into church buildings." As a result, the mission serves only the Church institution. Society remains without a transformative influence as churches relinquish their vocation to be salt and light. The light shines only upon the faithful and the salt is distributed only to members of the Church. But this is not what Christ meant when he said,

> You are the salt of the earth. But if the salt loses its saltiness, how can it be made salty again? It is no longer good for anything, except to be thrown out and trampled underfoot. You are the light of the world. A town built on a hill cannot be hidden. Neither do people light a lamp and put it under a bowl. Instead they put it on its stand, and it gives light to everyone in the house. In the same way, let your light shine before others, that they may see your good deeds and glorify your Father in heaven. (Matt 5:13–16)

We need to reject exclusivity, and return to the holistic mission, when both the person and society, the sermon and co-partnership, the spiritual and the social, the moral and the political become complementary parts of the overall Christian vision of biblically informed action on behalf of the overriding biblical imperative of social justice.

In the last century, the theologians of the Lausanne Movement proposed speaking about the mission as transformation. For evangelical churches this was a radical rethinking of mission. The call of the people in the Christian community was supplemented with calls upon the Church to go forth into society and transform it. This launched within the global evangelical movement a renewal of missiology that should be extended to the national level, as well. Unfortunately, the influence of the Lausanne Movement remains rather weak among evangelical churches in Ukraine and the FSU. There are several reasons why the gospel should not only save individuals, but also transform society: exclusivity is dangerous; Christ's teaching about the Church and its mission in the world was part of his teachings about the Kingdom; the global evangelical movement can offer us a wealth of experience on holistic missiology and inspiring stories of how the gospel changes the destinies of nations. The hope that underlies all the pages of this book is that the history of Ukraine and other nations in the former USSR may become one of those stories. The responsibility for this possibility lies with the Christians of these nations.

Out of the ferment of Maidan new questions have arisen for evangelical Christians, the answers to which might give birth to new missiologies.

More than twenty-two years after the collapse of the USSR, the Church has, in fact, remained shackled by the Soviet legacy. The Church has remained in the past and is now struggling with a future where she is afraid of losing her place in the status quo and forfeiting all the privileges acquired through her servility. So we see that the same post-Soviet evangelicals who so vehemently criticize the non-Christian West did not utter a word of protest against the flagrant iniquity of the President of Ukraine (Yanukovych) or the corruption of the local traffic cop. We also see how many post-Soviet evangelicals gladly participate in parents' committees and family forums, where "Christians" join forces with the local communists to uphold "traditional values" and to decry the sins and "spiritual decay" of Europe. These evangelicals tilt vainly against the windmills of "Western decadence," "postmodern culture" and "liberal propaganda," apparently oblivious of the extent to which their churches have colluded with degenerate forces, such as consumerism, corruption and authoritarianism, which are rife in contemporary post-Soviet society.

In light of this, we need to ask ourselves some searching questions: Why is it that we as evangelical Christians seem to take an unseemly relish in exposing the sins of ordinary people in our churches, but maintain a cowardly silence concerning the sins of those in power? Do we not see that our silence is a sign of consent, and that with our acquiescence we untie the hands of the wrongdoers? Do we lack the moral imagination to envision the possibility of living in a country without bribes and without lies? Is it even possible to live the Christian life if the entire structure of society requires people to compromise their Christian principles of honesty, openness, integrity and compassion? If the State and society are corrupt, should we simply endure it and take no steps to address this social evil? Why do we call those standing on Maidan "rebels" and "lawbreakers" if, under the Constitution, it is the people who are the source of power? If we lack the moral courage to take upon ourselves the legal responsibility for the government and the situation in our country, then why do we wonder at the immorality of society and the nihilism of ordinary people? If we as the Church are not in solidarity with the people, then why should the people be in solidarity with the Church? Who needs us if we nothing to offer? Who will look out for us if we are not willing to be our brother's keeper? Just imagine that you had been standing there in place of those on the Maidan, in the sniper's line of fire—if that were you, would you want to enter a church that stayed silent during the national disaster or that approved of the regime that was opposing its people? Do we not think that instead of calling the people to repent and make peace, the Church itself must repent for betraying the people, and for failing for so many years to speak truthfully to those in power and to stand on the side of the oppressed?

The Post-Maidan Era and the Birth of *Homo Maidanus*

The "post-Maidan era"—that is how historians one hundred years hence will talk about the new era in the history of Ukraine and the post-Soviet world. Maidan was an expression not only of social and political changes, but of a deep, tectonic shift in thinking, culture and relationships. The Maidan demonstrations signaled a "transvaluation of values" marked by a paradigm shift from *homo sovieticus* to *homo maidanus*, which echoes Nietzsche's understanding of the *Übermensch*, who supplants the "last man" (*der letzte Mensch*). *Homo sovieticus*, as one young Ukrainian commentator, Anna Kotaleichuk, notes, "does not accept any nonconformity, nor tolerates freedom of thought. Nor does it show any respect to himself or herself, or others." *Homo sovieticus*, she continues, is "characterized by an adherence to a bureaucratic culture, routine rudeness, a fear of everything new and a fear to show individuality." *Homo sovieticus* is a Dostoevskian caricature of a degraded humanity which is paralyzed by the existential tension arising from the tragicomic situation of being, on the one hand created for freedom, but, on the other, being too feeble and afraid to embrace the risk responsibility and vulnerability that freedom brings. For *homo sovieticus* freedom is not a blessing, but a curse, or (as Berdyaev put it) a "fatal gift" that condemns him to perdition.[9] The revolutionary events in Ukraine in 2013–14 can now be understood as the painful birth pangs that presaged the birth of *homo maidanus*, which will eventually "overcome" (in the Nietzschen sense) *homo sovieticus*. *Homo maidanus* is a very different kind of species from her *sovieticus* counterpart. She is more civil-minded, open to change and is endowed with an innate love of freedom.[10]

Maidan has thus opened the door to evident and irreversible social and anthropological metamorphoses that have long been in the making. After Maidan the takeover of Crimea was launched, and it was immediately apparent who was supporting President Victor Yanukovych's kleptocratic

9. Berdyaev, *Destiny of Man*, 23.

10. Kotaleichuk, "Yes We Can," 58; Parusinski, "Poroshenko's Historic Opportunity," 81–86.

regime and its criminal activities. Russia removed its mask. The "brother at the gates" appeared, armed with weapons and outright hatred. The launch of Russian aggression marked the final end of the "Russian world," about which President Putin and Patriarch Kirill had spoken in such grandiose terms, using pseudo-Christian language. Ukraine can be a good, reliable neighbor to Russia, but a clear and unambiguous majority of Ukrainians have rejected the rhetoric about the organic, spiritual brotherhood and unity between the Russian and Ukrainian peoples. The vast majority of Ukrainians, particularly the young and the educated, supports the unity of Ukraine against Russian incursions into its eastern and southern provinces. As Riabchuk notes, "The Kremlin is well aware that any normal electoral process in Ukraine will result in the defeat of the radical pro-Russian forces and therefore will do its best to sabotage and derail any normalization."[11] As well as trying to bully Ukraine into submission by charging exorbitant gas prices, the Russian government has also supported the extreme nationalists of the so-called "People's Republics" of Donetsk and Lughansk, which have been involved in vote rigging, extortion, corruption, hooliganism, and even torture and murder. Putin and his fellow mobsters in the Kremlin are trying to turn Ukraine in its own image: an authoritarian failed state controlled by the mafia, in which the organs of state power become instruments for racketeering, repression and corruption. In Russia itself an uncontrolled chain reaction of decay has been set off. Russia as a unifying territorial power of the post-Soviet space is receding into the past.

After Maidan Ukraine, too, is left isolated, but for now this may be to her benefit. She breaks away from the rough, bear hug of her bigger brother, but her place in Europe is not yet ready, and she herself is not yet ready for Europe. This is an auspicious time to prepare for reintegration into the European family. At the same time, Ukraine should be aware of her special status as a transit region, on the edge of Europe and in close proximity to Russia.

After Maidan, the entire post-Soviet world can no longer ignore the real force of civil society. Maidan revealed the remarkable ability of ordinary citizens to organize and mobilize in battle against a criminal state. Ukrainians themselves were dubious about their abilities. The Russians and Belarusians were even more doubtful. Now there is already a precedent, so the post-Soviet State sees in civil society an entity with which it must contend, and therefore it does everything to forestall its development and

11. Riabchuk, "Blessing in Disguise," 66.

crush its slightest signs of awakening. As it turned out, it is not the opposition, not pressure from the West, but rather it is the solidarity of ordinary people that is the critical factor in the transformation of post-Soviet State and society.

After Maidan, two forces step onto the stage of history, the real significance of which to this day is underrated: the students and the journalists. Maidan started as an uprising in November 2013 organized by students from the Kyiv-Mohyla Academy and the Taras Shevchenko University. These students, and the hundreds of thousands of others who supported the revolution, are the vanguard of the future. Their focus on the future can transform them into an organized social force. They grew up in independent Ukraine, have almost no connection with the Soviet past and are less susceptible to traditional forms of propaganda. Students are natural advocates of change. The same can be said of journalists. Any journalist who seeks and disseminates accurate and pertinent information thereby becomes an enemy of the totalitarian State, which is propped up on a crutch of lies, intimidation, fear and violence. Students and journalists were the main forces supporting Maidan and the main targets of the propagandists. But now it is with them that the hopes lie for transformation, transparency and government accountability, the shake-up of elites, a reboot of the system, and a root and branch modernization of post-Soviet society.

After Maidan, the role of the Church and society's attitude towards it are changing. In an environment of corrupt institutions, the Church had the highest confidence rating, but took little advantage of its influence. Instead of serving society, the Church served the interests of the State. Maidan, having become the judge presiding over the State, also became a judge presiding over the Church. The Church that was part of Maidan has a future. The Church that let Maidan pass by is left behind. Church leaders who preached "neutrality" or reassured the authorities of their unswerving devotion revealed themselves to be spiritually bankrupt.

"Post-Maidan" is the label and method of defining a new era: that which has a future should pass through the experience of Maidan, through the questions it raised and the values of honesty, integrity, freedom, sacrifice, activism, and solidarity on which the revolution was based. It is precisely these values that challenge and undermine the Soviet and post-Soviet ethos around us and within us. Maidan thus hammered a wooden stake into the heart of what was called the USSR, and pushed out the shoots of a new life, which is not a (post) Soviet life, but one that is truly new. In the near future our generation will be witnesses to the changes "after Maidan," although it would be even better to become active participants in the process of transformation.

The past is behind us. The future is before us. Maidan has liberated us from our customs and routines, from our familiar life and our complacent satisfaction in the idols of wealth and status. There can be no return to "business as usual." The old ways have gone and the new has come. Everything has changed—themes, issues, values, the tone, objectives, meanings, questions and answers. In the words of W. B. Yeats (albeit writing about a very different context): "All changed, changed utterly: / A terrible beauty is born."

Maidan was a vital first step away from the post-Soviet vices of corruption, cynicism, and irresponsibility, and marks a return to the values of freedom, compassion and solidarity. Christianity, too, is liberated and uncoupled from the façade of fake, hypocritical, State-sponsored religiosity. When President Yanukovych, the Prosecutor General, and their entourage of ministers fled the country, many icons, holy relics, and stolen biblical manuscripts were found in the palaces that they had abandoned, but absent were any traces of Christ. In light of this, our Christianity, too, is reset to zero. We have an historic opportunity to return to the simplicity of the gospel, to reflect on what really matters in our faith and to distinguish between what is genuinely important and what is insignificant, extraneous or transitory. Although this is a time of new hope, there is also apprehension generated by uncertainty of not knowing how these events will culminate. Nevertheless, the note of hope prevails as we witness the demise of the old and the birth of the new.

In times such as this, the following words of Christ, which so fascinated Dostoevsky,[12] are especially pertinent: "Truly, truly, I say to you, unless a grain of wheat falls into the earth and dies, it remains alone; but if it dies, it bears much fruit. He that loveth his life shall lose it; and he that hateth his life in this world will keep it for eternal life" (John 12:23–25). It is in this hope that the conditions for our rebirth lie. Jesus died and was resurrected. We also are passing through death to a new life—a life that is "life indeed" (John 10:10). So the future is in Christ's hands. He frees us from the past for the sake of the future and forms us into part of his "new creation" (2 Cor 5:17). Everything that is happening is under the banner of his coming Kingdom. The history of all hitherto existing society is the his-

---

12. John 12:24 is inscribed on Dostoevsky's gravestone in St Petersburg.

tory of liberation and the establishment of the Kingdom of God "on earth, as it is in heaven."

In this history of the world, Maidan is an episode in a linear chronology. But in the history of the Church, it may be the *kairos* moment ushering in a new series of opportunities and challenges. We may now bid farewell to the ideological remnants of a moribund and defunct (post-) Soviet system and to a society whose attitude towards Christianity wavered between grudging acceptance and outright hostility.

Images of post-Soviet Missiology in Light of the Post-Maidan Era

Post-Soviet missiology is seeking out and constructing its new, up-to-date images. Two tendencies can be identified in this search—the biblical-theological and socio-cultural. Future missions to FSU countries are connected with the formation of a number of suitable, local, authentic, effective, holistic missiological approaches within the paradigm of global Christianity. These missions must be based on biblical principles and be embedded in a complete theoretical system, which is in tune with the historical experience of the various churches and theological approaches, and takes into account local contexts by focusing on the needs and issues of local communities.[13] The gap between the biblical and theological bases and local contexts discredits missiology as "inappropriate" ("out of place," not suitable for the location), divorced from reality, irrelevant, or as too limited by their place, too trapped in its context, and divorced from biblical universal truths. Post-Soviet missiology errs in its excessive reliance on ecclesiocentrism[14] and almost complete disregard for the social dimension. Neglect and ignorance of the sociocultural context suddenly give way to its absolution, canonization, and sacralization. We witness this phenomenon in modern Russia, where "official Christianity," instead of being the transforming factor of "salt" and "light," serves as a rubber stamp or a divine legitimation of Putin's policies.

Relevance, holism, depth and openness—these characteristics enable post-Soviet missiology to keep different aspects, directions and dimensions together. A relevant missiology creatively applies the biblical principles and

13. Cherenkov, "Toward a Relevant Missiology," 49–58.

14. As Johannes Reimer rightly observes, the ecclesiocentric mission is aimed at the church itself, "the consecration and the preservation of the status given to her by God"; "The purpose of such a church is to survive" (*Transformation*, 35).

objectives of the mission to the local situation, directed from the world of Scripture to the world of present material reality. What is primary here is the focus on the context, adapting to it and zeroing in on it with the greatest precision. A holistic missiology evokes multidimensionality and complementarity, inseparability and non-convergence, the need to see the big picture and not just the immediate situation, no matter how urgent. Deep missiology emphasizes the historical dimension, which understands mission as an ongoing process that has its own logic and development. History teaches us about the continuity of memory and experience and the role of tradition. If valid missiology is concerned with the "here and now," then deep missiology looks at the roots, because the current situation is predetermined by the past. Accordingly, for most people in the post-Soviet space, the best approach is not likely to be a verbal presentation of propositional truths about Christianity, about which they likely know nothing or very little. Rather, a more appropriate approach would be to work towards a renewal of long-known truths that are deeply embedded in the collective national memory of a people who were once Christian.

Recent missions in the post-Soviet space have mainly been concerned with making occasional forays into society for testimony and to "catch" a few converts and bring them into the church. But open mission signifies movement in two directions. The Church not only teaches society that which God reveals inside the Church, but also learns from what God reveals to the Church through social events and processes. With openness, the Church ceases to be a "holy place" that is rigidly separated from the "secular world." Social reality is seen as part of God's creation. Society is the sphere of God's effective action. Society is the public space which is sustained, redeemed, and sanctified by God's presence. God works inside and outside those spaces which we designate as "sacred." All around the world God is active, beckoning us to participate with Him in the great work of redemption.

The requirements for missiology to be relevant, holistic, deep and open lead to a series of unexpected adjustments to traditional views of the mission as an invitation to people to join a church. First, a distinction is introduced and tension arises between the missiology of the Church and missiology of the Kingdom. Missiology of the Church expresses the responsibility of "our church" for carrying out the Great Commission of Christ and implementing this responsibility in a religiously acceptable manner. Missiology of the Kingdom points to the unity of *Missio Dei* and the Church's mission, to a wider scope of God's saving work, with or without the Church. The scope of God's redemptive activity in the world cannot be confined to the Church and the evangelistic activities of Christians. As Drane notes, "To imagine that God is somehow helpless, locked away in heaven with no capacity to do anything unless Christians set up church programmes, is to have a very impoverished—and maybe heretical—notion of who God truly is. The Bible emphasizes that this is God's world, and God is at work in it."[15] Second, the holistic ethos of missiology in practice is revealed in its diversity, multiplicity, and the sum of local missiologies, both in succession and complementary to each other. We can talk not only about changing paradigms of mission in history, but also about the co-presence of "missiologies in the genitive case" (i.e., "missiology of . . ."), each of which occurs in response to a specific missiological challenge. Third, post-Soviet missiology requires a new biblical hermeneutics "for every day," which follows from radical and fresh readings of the Bible in the light of the challenges of each new day. Fourth, the success of missiology is expressed not in the triumph of Christianity over society, but in compassion for and involvement in society. It makes sense to talk about the missiology of the Cross (by analogy with *theologia crucis*) and the missiology of solidarity. What is preserved here is the social responsibility, the desire to influence and change, but without the naive optimism about Christianization and Christendom. Fifth, missiology justifies not so much the movement from the Church into the world, but also a constant presence in the world, not only through evangelistic activity, but also through the sacrament of living. This is not so much a course of action as it is a way of thinking and being. The Church's mission in the world is realized in imperatives to proclaim and encourage, to send and convert, to go and teach, but also in non-binding forms: being, living, sympathizing, loving, salting, and shining the light of Christ in places of darkness. Sixth, the renewal of missiology will require a reconnection between mission and discipleship, teaching and preaching, sanctification and conversion. The Great Commission of Christ speaks not only about a hasty transfer of the truth, but the long and difficult work of missionary teachers with students, about the Christian enlightenment of nations, about educating entire peoples.

In this regard, the words of the Russian writer Nikolai Leskov that "Russia was baptized, but not enlightened" underscore the most important task of the mission in the post-Soviet space after Maidan. Indeed, we can

---

15. Drane, *Faith in a Changing Culture*, 61.

speak similarly about the evangelical awakening: Rus' was awakened, but not enlightened. People began to read the Bible. They learned to believe and to live according to the Scriptures. But until now, Orthodox and Evangelical Christians have been deprived of clear theological landmarks and the nurturing influence of Christian culture. The mission of the Russian Christian Student Movement in the early twentieth century offers a good example in the history of the evangelical mission. Its founder, Paul Nikolai, believed that the new Christian thinking could be developed through the students, who would be the future elite of the country; what was needed was to educate those who would contribute to the establishment of God's Kingdom. He wrote about the problems of the student mission as follows: "Think about how the men and women devoted to faith will occupy all the positions of leadership in society: that's a goal worth working toward. Just think about what they can accomplish: they will face no obstacles."[16] This precedent can serve as a starting point for the creation of new forms of mission that combine preaching the gospel with rigorous Christian academic engagement.

A Vision of the Kingdom and Local Idols: The Challenge of Fundamentalism

A vision of the mission of the Church that takes the Kingdom of God as its object and point of departure surpasses the parochial interests of particular churches or denominations. Within the post-Soviet evangelical churches various idols and stereotypes have built walls of prejudice around narrow interests that have impoverished and circumscribed the vision of the Kingdom. These idols include fundamentalism, national exclusivism, historical myopia and anti-intellectualism. Taken together, they limit the potential of evangelical churches, lock them in cultural and theological isolation and make them captive to the past under the unwritten and non-reflexive tradition of "fellowship." The light of knowledge, the advance of science and the use of the critical faculties are viewed as a threat rather than an opportunity for growth.

The chief impediment on the path to the vision of the Kingdom is fundamentalism, which can rightly be called the most odious heresy in the history of the Church. Post-Soviet evangelicals often proudly assert that their commitment to the unshakable authority of the Word of God

16. Gundersen, *Pavel Nikolai*, 47.

distinguishes them from their secularized Western counterparts. However, the appeal to the authority of the Scripture easily morphs into the canonization of one's own reading, in opposition to all others and condemnation of those who disagree as "liberals" and "heretics." Fundamentalism naively, yet aggressively, lays claim to exclusive and direct knowledge of the truth of Scripture, bypassing theological reflection, the witness of tradition and the necessity of hermeneutics. Fundamentalists are thus particularly fond of claiming biblical warrants for their convictions. A fundamentalist is generally unperturbed by allegations that his (fundamentalism in the post-Soviet context is usually, though not always, a male phenomenon) convictions are "unpopular," "old-fashioned," or even "bigoted," so long as he can establish to his own satisfaction that these beliefs are "biblical." The trouble is that these "biblical" convictions often turn out, upon mature reflection, to be little more than cultural or ideological prejudices that the fundamentalist has brought to his readings of the Bible. The reading strategies of fundamentalists thus become tainted by presuppositions of which the fundamentalist might be completely unaware. Fundamentalists will mine Scripture in search of a verse, a phrase or a even a single word that will substantiate the preconceived prejudices which they bring to their reading of the text. The Bible is plundered for proof-texts, which are then used to validate certain preconceptions which, owing to their supposed warrant in Scripture, are posited as "biblical." Furthermore, out of these interpretive conditions there can arise states of sectarian enmity in which anyone who challenges the fundamentalist "biblical" interpretation is ostracized and their interpretations are branded as "unbiblical," "liberal" or "heretical." This occurs even though those who have a different opinion can usually cite a contradictory proof-text from other Bible verses, which support a point of view that dissents from that of the fundamentalists. Under these interpretive conditions the Bible can become a savage text of divine sanction for cultural chauvinism and religious bigotry. A recent "official statement" of Russian Baptists on the situation in Ukraine, which cloaks implicit support for the Putin regime in the language of Scripture, affords a classic example of how Christian fundamentalism functions as an ideology in post-Soviet society. The text is peppered with numerous biblical proof texts quoted out of context, thus giving the aura of being "biblically based," whereas in fact the document is devoid of theological or biblical integrity and the thin biblical veneer constitutes little more than expression of Putinism translated into the language of "biblicism."

The trouble is that fundamentalism does not exist in isolation; it blooms in the vicinity of the other idols, such as national pride, cultural myopia and anti-intellectualism. Under a consistently fundamentalist approach, neither theology nor theological education is necessary, unless such an education is directed towards inculcating mindless adherence to stale doctrinal formulas. Moreover, in a climate of fundamentalism, theology becomes entangled in networks of control in which power is held in the hands of a few unaccountable individuals, around whom a personality cult emerges. Under such conditions, the only function of theology is to perpetuate these networks of power, illusion and deception—often under the guise of defending "sound doctrine." In combination with primitive Calvinism, which supporters of John MacArthur have actively promoted in post-Soviet churches, fundamentalism also renders missiology superfluous. Such churches can confine themselves to the interests of the select "little flock." This kind of austere Calvinism promoted by some North American fundamentalists has caused untold damage to the spread of the gospel in Ukraine and the FSU. Not only is Calvinism alien to the history and tradition of Christian theology and spirituality in this region, but it also posits a false and servile doctrine of divine sovereignty,[17] which, as the case of the Russian Baptists' recent support for Vladimir Putin demonstrates, can easily morph into a pseudo-theological justification of unjust and tyrannical secular ideologies, such as Putinism.

This kind of fundamentalist Calvinism exported from North America has indoctrinated some post-Soviet evangelicals with a monarchical image of God as an autocratic head of state who commands Christians to denounce "liberals," "heretics," and "charismatics." These denunciations are remarkably analogous to the Soviet regime's purges against dissidents, nonconformists and "heretics," who deviated from the prevailing orthodoxy of State-imposed Marx-Leninism. According to the severe Calvinism preached by fundamentalist Christians, demonstrating animosity towards adherents of other religions, particularly Muslims,[18] becomes a gospel

17. On this point see Berdyaev, *Divine and the Human*, 8.

18. See, for example, MacArthur, *Terrorism, Jihad, and the Bible*. This book is typical of the kind of weak scholarship that one has come to expect from an ill-informed pastor, whose knowledge of the nuances of Islamic belief and practice can be charitably described as "limited." MacArthur has preached through translators to Ukrainian evangelicals in which the same kinds of distortions and straw man arguments against Islam are found to prevail. It is difficult to see what these sermons are trying to achieve, apart from eliciting animosity and mistrust on the part of Ukrainian evangelicals toward Muslims.

imperative. The graceless, stern, disciplinarian god that is worshipped by these fundamentalists is a blasphemous caricature of the gracious God of gratuitous mercy whose heart overflows with compassion and whose likeness we see revealed perfectly in Jesus Christ. Berdyaev thus concluded that "nothing but a dreadful state of fear could make men become reconciled to Calvin's doctrine of predestination."[19]

For the fundamentalist things are either black or white; the rigid lines that define the contours of their worldview allow for no grey areas or shades of truth. There is neither acceptance nor generosity of other viewpoints that diverge from their personal understanding of truth. The emphasis on dogmatic systems of thought and propositional statements about God which aspire to truth also betrays a dangerous foundationalism that restricts God to the realm of thoughts and ideas. Trusting in the allegedly unimpeachable credentials of a system that posits "sound doctrine" can thus lead to a neglect of the vital truth of Christianity that "God is testified to in the transformed lives of believers rather than in some abstract doctrinal system."[20]

It is therefore no coincidence that young post-Soviet theologians call fundamentalism an "inhibiting factor"[21] in the theological development of the Church. By denying to the sciences, including theology, the right to credibility and relevance, fundamentalists immensely simplify reality and its *veritas*, depriving themselves of perspective. After all, if "the Bible does not contain anything that is not comprehensible, and is no more complicated than a child's primer"[22] then everyone has the right to interpret the truth in their own way and to consider themself as the infallible interpreter. Another peculiarity of post-Soviet fundamentalism is that it reads in the Bible not a guiding idea that can be creatively implemented, thus meaning the preservation of freedom in the process; rather, what is read is a concrete regimentation of thought and behavior. Thus the portrait of the Soviet and post-Soviet Baptist that emerges is not drawn along theological lines, but along contours of external behavior, and not in positive, but in negative colors: "Baptists are those who do not drink, do not smoke, do not watch

---

We hope that the next generation of post-Soviet evangelicals will be able to eschew these kinds of islamophobic distortions by working toward a more constructive and respectful engagement with their Muslim neighbors.

19. Berdyaev, *Divine and the Human*, 10.

20. Rollins, *How (Not) to Speak*, 40.

21. Dubrovskij, "Fundamentalizm kak tormozjashhij faktor," 27–45.

22. Manzhul, "Verit, chtoby znat," 23.

TV, do not go to the movies, do not have icons, are not baptized, do not vote and do not pledge allegiance to the flag."

Today fundamentalism is manifested primarily in the form of a distrust of academic theology and theological education, of dialogue between traditions; in opposition to "ecumenism," "secular science," and the "secularism" of modernity; in the worship of the letter of the Bible (bibliolatry) and fear of hermeneutics and semantics; in the cult of "correct" interpreters and the constant attempt to ferret out "liberals." Many Baptist theologians today preserve a commitment to the Bible as an inerrant text, but in so doing they adhere to a fundamentally biased relationship to the Bible known as "Bibleism."[23] Rather than reading the Bible as a book of life that invites readers to discover and experience the depth, beauty, mystery and sacrament of life, the fundamentalist is fixated with approaching the text as an academic document that details "facts" about God. In this approach, the fundamentalist thus unwittingly capitulates to the agenda of secular humanists, who insist that all claims to truth must adhere to positivistic criteria of empirical verification by corresponding to a proper understanding of "the facts."

The flaws and deficiencies of this kind of positivistic foundationalism have been exposed by many notable philosophers, scientists and theologians since the 1950s. Ironically, therefore, in its commitment to the notion of the Bible as an infallible repository of unimpugnable facts about God, modern biblicist fundamentalism has become one of the last remaining citadels of positivism in contemporary postmodern culture. As Pete Rollins notes, "both biblical criticism and apologists for the idea of inerrancy are primarily concerned with the rational legitimacy of the text when viewed as a description of factual claims." The fundamentalist claims that the truth of the Bible is bound up with propositional statements, which correspond to "the facts" about God, sin and salvation. Instead of reducing the Bible to an "inerrant" compendium of descriptive statements, the reader who seeks to honor the God revealed in the pages of Scripture should instead approach the text as "a means of approaching its life-transforming truth, a truth that dwells within and yet beyond words."[24] Unfortunately, such critical approaches are not very popular in the post-Soviet cultural space. Much more popular are the ill-informed rants of John MacArthur on how the Bible is not merely the only inerrant text, but also the only guide you need

23. See the excellent book by Smith, *Bible Made Impossible*.
24. Rollins, *Fidelity of Betrayal*, 47–62.

for whatever you encounter in life.[25] For many, it seems that rigid, literal interpretations of Scripture offer a kind of indolent certainty and cheap grace that avoid the necessity of having to grapple with the problems of semantics and hermeneutics that are raised by the biblical texts and by the inevitable tension involved in trying to render the Word of God into terms understandable to the limited and subjective human intellect and imagination. By objectifying the text as an authority in its own right (apart from the witness of the Spirit), the exponents of inerrancy thereby render the Bible susceptible to human reasoning and empirical criteria of verification.

Fundamentalism violates the harmony between the authority of Scripture and the freedom of conscience, which can rightly be understood as the two foundational principles of evangelical conviction. It is noteworthy that attempts to restore the harmony of authority and freedom come precisely from the educational environment. Thus, Fyodor Raychinets, Dean of the Ukrainian Evangelical Theological Seminary, calls for the hermeneutics of freedom and the contra-fundamentalist revision of the individualization of evangelical churches, citing Walter Shurden, a representative of moderate Baptists: "Baptist identity is freedom, not control, the principle of voluntariness, not coercion; individualism, not the herd instinct; personal religion, not public, diversity, not conformity."[26]

Fundamentalist belief in the unassailability of one's own understanding of truth is linked to another certainty: namely, in one's own national superiority. A notion prevalent in post-Soviet churches is that Russian-Ukrainian churches have a special spirituality and are called to a universal mission. These messianic feelings are rooted in the concept of "Moscow as the Third Rome," which was prevalent in the thought of Dostoevsky and Soloviev, and also Prokhanov and Martsinkovsky. Western rationalism is contrasted with a mystical sensibility, dogmatism with doxology, cognitive theology with awe and mystery, and the quest for knowledge with contemplation on divine love. Thus, if in the West theologians have been engaged in a quest for truth, understanding and reason, then in the East the evangelical movement has inherited from Orthodoxy the conviction that the truth is already known, and that it need only be preserved. Hence the well-known arrogance exhibited by uneducated, but "spiritual" Christians, who demonstrate their suspicion and even contempt towards "theologians." This partly explains why, after the fall of the "Iron Curtain,"

---

25. Smith, *Bible Made Impossible*, 7.

26. Raychinets, *Svoeobrazie baptizma*, 71; Shurden, *Baptist Identity*, 59.

interest in theological education first experienced a peak and then waned. Systematic knowledge, methodical study, intellectual work and deep theological reflection were not considered to be Christian virtues.

This problem is compounded by the fact that claims of exclusivity are combined with historical myopia. If the tradition is deeply rooted and rich enough, it can, given time, lead to spiritual conceit and an indulgence in isolation. But evangelical churches in the FSU live within the confines of a "minor history," the most "ancient" of which dates back a mere 150 years. Acute myopia revolves around canonizing a tradition that is neither ancient nor proven. The experience of Soviet years is canonized, not because it is worthy, but because post-Soviet evangelicals know no other history. Soviet history is the history of a marginal existence, or, rather, a constant struggle for survival in which intellectualism seemed liked an unaffordable luxury. The projection of this experience to current times engenders the idealization of marginality and withdrawal from the world as the most faithful mode of Christian existence. In conditions such as this, neither an active mission, nor theology, nor education is possible. Moreover, nor is education seen as necessary, because living in constant marginality, without prospects, without hope for the transformation of society is to be essentially in a perpetual waiting mode for the "end times."

It would seem that the opening of theological schools after the collapse of the Soviet Union was the advent of a new era—an era of long-term plans for training leaders for churches and missions. But here too, everyone expected instant results, and no one had an eye on the future and was prepared for it. When no one saw results from "theology," then it was quickly replaced by missionary training programs, and then by more practical courses in "leadership." Not until today has it dawned on all concerned that without a theological basis, leadership programs and missionary projects hang in the air. Without a clear theological identity, without a coherent strategy for theology-education-mission-church, outside activity will bring only short-term gains.

Given the range of regional differences, post-Soviet evangelical Christians, that developed in Soviet times under the decisive influence of the Baptist tradition, find themselves following the same trends as their foreign counterparts, for whom "to be a Baptist is a calling," which requires overcoming a "scandalous past and an uncertain future." As B. J. Leonard notes, "Questions of Baptist identity—the church of believers, the community (covenant community), freedom of conscience, biblical hermeneutics, global mission—all this requires careful study, a new examination and even a reformation with the participation of Baptists groups along the entire theological spectrum."[27]

It would seem that post-Soviet Christians now stand at a crossroads. They have a choice either to remain in the isolation of fundamentalism, national pride, historical myopia, and anti-intellectualism, or to restore the interrupted connections, and to join the fragments of the whole through honest reflection and theological education.

The Post-Soviet Context, and Evangelical Identity: From the Past to the Future

In its spiritual significance and social relevance, Christianity is defined not only by its past. Christianity grows from the fabric of history, but it does not remain hostage to it. The horizon of the future is the main backdrop to a self-understanding of Christianity and its interpretations by outside scholars. In our time, there is a marked shift underway from assessments configured from the past to reassessments processed via the future. It is the future that is becoming the point of reference, an eschatological point of departure from which the entire history of Christianity is read, including the present day.

At the Third Lausanne Congress in Cape Town (October 2010), there was much talk about the growth of churches in the regions of the global South, and the once Christian Europe was addressed only in a section tellingly titled, "Is there a Future for Christianity in Europe?" For the post-Soviet space and the rich Christian tradition (and not just the Orthodox space), such a statement of the problem may seem like an exaggeration or a *reductio ad absurdum*, but it is direct questions such as this that highlight the difference between the nominal and real and which disclose the reality of the current predicament. In the same way we can ask directly, "Do post-Soviet evangelical churches have a future?" This is a complicated question that offers no easy answers. Obviously, references to history are not arguments for questions about the future. No matter how rich the past, there are no guarantees about the future.

Nevertheless, there are some projections from the past to the future, projections from experience and memory upon which we can build. The question about the future can be worded as follows: "What is the future

27. Leonard, *Challenge of Being Baptist*, 126.

of the post-Soviet evangelical movement based on the historical path we have already travelled?" Continuing along the already traversed portion of the path may be different, but the dynamics of the future path will be determined by the contradictions that have already been enshrined along the way. We will try to name a few primary issues that are crucial to the history of evangelical Christians and which are promising from a future perspective. These are matters that are fundamental not only to the evangelical movement, but also to Russia and Ukraine themselves as regards both governmental and socio-cultural traditions. These issues raise fundamental questions concerning the Church, the State, and the society in their interrelationship and mutual significance.

Given the historical fact that the evangelical movement arose in a spiritual and social context that had already been formed, its own self-image, its self-identification and its search for a special historical destiny is manifested through its relationship to the prevailing, normative, conventionally accepted triad of Orthodoxy-autocracy-nationalism (i.e., to the relationship of nominal religion, statehood, and society). For Evangelical Christian Baptists the relationship to any ideological concept was negative, be it the triad named above, or the Communist entanglement of atheism-Party-proletariat. If Protestantism were to be placed in the triad, replacing Orthodoxy or atheism, it, too, would be rejected. The very connection of faith with the political system, the integration of faith with the social order, is unacceptable to evangelical churches. Any triad, regardless of the terms, encroaches on freedom of conscience and the fidelity of the church to the gospel message, drawing the Church into the totality of the political.

Rejection of the triad does not mean that churches distance themselves from Orthodoxy, the State and society, or that they adopt an anti-Orthodox, anti-state, anti-social attitude. Rejection of the triad means that the Church is building relationships not on an ideological plane, where the parties in relationships are indistinguishable. Rather, it relates to each subject individually, taking into account their specificity: with Orthodoxy in the context of the history of the Church (and not that of autocratic policies or national chauvinism); with the State through the respect for law, the guarantee of civil rights and the fulfillment of duties and responsibilities (and not spiritual servitude or slavery); with the people (through solidarity with their legitimate aspirations).

Thus, the evangelical Christian consciousness separates what in ideological, totalitarian consciousness is firmly embedded in homogenized indivisibility. The relationship to Orthodoxy becomes deliberately apolitical and depoliticized. The fact that Orthodoxy evolved into part of the political system is seen as a legacy of the old Byzantine-Moscow complex. For believers from evangelical churches, the Orthodox are, first and foremost, brothers and sisters of the one Universal Church, though it be divided. Orthodoxy is not to be seen in the political perspective, but primarily in its ecclesiastical-historical perspective.

If we think of Orthodoxy as the State Church, the titular religion for the country as a whole, the evangelical churches are the reputable opposition, not so much in terms of a conscious antithesis, but by virtue of their own nature, and as a result of being in the position of a religious minority. In this regard, it is noteworthy that self-defined evangelical churches between Western Protestantism and Russian Orthodoxy have evolved not through the selection of one over the other, but by a synthesis of the two traditions. But the approach to the traditions is selective. Moreover, within the traditions, we encounter that which we can neither accept nor reject, but which is worth deepening, developing and supplementing.

It is through selective synthesis, the cleansing of traditions, revising them from an evangelical, apostolic perspective that the doors are thrown open to the evangelical movement of a broad, ecumenical perspective. In a world divided into spheres of religious influences, the evangelical movement can be a place of meetings, dialogue and communication. Such a healthy ecumenism means no more and no less than the acceptance of genuine ecclesiastical diversity, good neighborliness and the preservation of openness to others. As evangelicals we can be loyally and wholeheartedly committed to our own unique tradition without believing that it embodies final and exclusive truth, and without thereby abandoning the hope that there is more to be learned from other traditions.[28]

In the context of de-ideologization, the relationship to the State can also be perceived differently. The attitude to authority is liberated from dangerous sacralization. Such dangerous and discredited ideologies, such as pan-Slavism and Russian exceptionalism have deprived evangelical Christians of their significance, because these religious minorities are not regarded (neither by the Orthodox Church nor the Russian State) as part of the indigenous Christian community. Moreover, the "harmony" between Church and State which appears to the Orthodox Church a sacred archetype, for evangelicals is merely a pragmatic political construct

28. Searle, "Ecumenical Imperative," 5–23.

126

and something human, even "all too human." Evangelicals understand and that in an interdenominational country, human rights are grounded in the Constitution and are not "based on the teachings of the Russian Orthodox Church on Human Dignity, Freedom and Rights." History teaches us only too well about the persecution and discrimination to which "non-historical" denominations and religious minorities are subjected in a context of cozy alliances between the Official Church and the State. Evangelicals have trod a difficult path to legalization of their church in a State governed by the rule of law. Their hopes for the future should be connected with the legal and not the sacred character of the State; with its constitutional responsibilities and not its dangerous ambitions to unite the political and religious institutions into the totality of a single authority. For evangelical Christians, the archetypes of a "God-bearing people," "Holy Russia," and "Orthodox people" are devoid of their customary magical hold. The alliance of Church and State is without biblical justification and is morally bankrupt. The hegemony of the (Russian) Orthodox Church in post-Soviet society has not led to spiritual revival, but has created a thin veneer of Christianity among a people who live in fear of the power of the Church-State. Neither Orthodox monarchism nor atheistic communism, along with their prevailing authoritarianism, is compatible with the freedom of the gospel.

We see the legacy of this unholy alliance between Church and State and the defunct messianic ideology of "Christian" pan-Slavism being played out in the violent Russian incursions into Eastern Ukraine. Notwithstanding all the Russian propaganda about the apparent threat to Russian nationals living in non-Russian territories of the FSU posed by the so-called Maidan fascists, the appellation of "Nazism" and right-wing extremism could be much more accurately applied to the contemporary exponents of Russian-led pan-Slavism. Not only are the leaders of the pitiful so-called Donetsk People's Republic alleged to have criminal backgrounds and links with neo-Nazi fascist groups operating in Russia, but there are also clear parallels between this kind of pan-Slavic ideology and the Nazi ideology of Hitler's Germany. In the same way that pan-Slavists, supported by Putin and the Patriarch Kyrill, claim that Russia has been given a special role by God to save the world from liberals, communists, gays and Jews, etc., so too did Hitler believe that he was engaged in a divine mission to rid the world of such "evil" and "degenerate" influences. In light of this history and a proper understanding of the clear and numerous biblical injunctions against the evils of idolatry and racism, the defunct ideology of neo-Slavic Messianism (the belief that Russia has been appointed by God to save the world) must be exposed as a demonic perversion of the true gospel.

Instead of servile submission to the State and captivity to moribund ideologies, the Church should demonstrate solidarity with the legitimate social and political aspirations of ordinary people, particularly those who are marginalized or who have been excluded from the political process. Seeking to serve their surrounding society, evangelical believers openly decry its social and spiritual wounds. Evangelical Christians possess freedom from the past and a powerful potential for reform. Originating against the backdrop of socio-economic reforms of traditional peasant communities, the evangelical movement reflected aspirations for a new life, for the modernization of a backward society and an overcoming of the oppressive triad of "Orthodoxy-autocracy-nationality." A successful economy, the mechanization of labor, the creation of strong communities, the distribution of books, the promotion of literacy and education and the formation of Christian social movements created a visible social alternative to this traditional triad, which alarmed both the Orthodox monarchists and the Soviet communists.

Although springing up from the people, evangelical communities were not assimilated by the people, partly because of the image of evangelicalism as ascetic, egalitarian and fraternal, and partly because of persecution by the State and the condemnation by the Orthodox hierarchy. Remaining in epicenters for the neglected and disenfranchised people, evangelical Christians retained influence over lower social groups, but were limited to these strata of society. Simply put, our task today is to demarginalize evangelical churches, and restore their full presence in society, in all its spheres and levels. Despite ongoing discrimination and persecution, evangelical communities in many parts of the FSU have succeeded in attaining legalization, but legal status does not guarantee a real place in the social structure. The path from legalization to socialization is long and difficult, and we must begin this journey as soon as possible, and with a clear understanding of what the future promises—namely the transformation of all spheres of society in accordance with the teachings of the gospel.

Through their century and a half of existence in Russia, evangelical Christians have demonstrated the possibility of another way of life, a different stance toward the terms laid down by the triad of Orthodoxy-autocracy-nationalism. Being Russian or Ukrainian does not necessarily mean to be Orthodox, and certainly does not require being a monarchist.

One of the lessons from the history of the evangelical movement in this region is that the future of Christianity is not determined by high ideals—be they expressive, vague, or brilliant—but by strong families, a firmly established morality, a conscious personal faith, and a principled fidelity to the integrity of one's convictions. Evangelical believers have not created their own ideological triads, but their respect for the Orthodox tradition, their civil responsibility to the State, and their service to the surrounding society, is known to all. The evangelical identity implies coexistence with other church traditions, fidelity to one's convictions under any State, and rooted adaptation to any social environment. The presence of evangelical churches enriches both the spiritual and social life of any nation, and the nations of the FSU are no exception.

The centuries-old crystallization of any of the triad signifies a reproduction of the past, and an entrapment in a mythologized antiquity. By maintaining our unity, integrating an understanding of our religious qualities and responsibility for a shared historical destiny, common citizenship and our place in the Kingdom of God, evangelical Christians have lived through two great empires (Imperial Russia and Soviet Communism). Without assimilating and by retaining their otherness, the evangelical churches have defended their freedom and secured their future. Freedom of conscience and the Church, social responsibility, interchurch dialogue—these are the basic prerequisites for the development of evangelical churches, as proven by history. These freedoms remain as relevant and necessary today as at any time in the past. Even in a totalitarian State, when ostracized by the Official Church and living on the outer margins of society, the evangelical church has not only survived, but found opportunities for active service. History has shown that the future of the evangelical movement is connected not with a favorable external environment, but with a firm sense of identity and faith in its God-given mission.

The apocalyptic pages of the New Testament reveal the image of the Church as a persecuted minority, small in numbers, but influential. Such an image places responsibility not so much on a change of circumstances or a struggle for rights and opportunities, but on a clarification of our personal identity. For evangelical Christians, the question of self-identity and our relationship to the world (and to other denominations, the State and society) is more important than the relationship of the world to the Church. Indeed, the question of the future should be transposed into the issue of identity.

Ecumenism and Mission

"Conflicts between Christians," explains Vladimir Fedorov, "do not arise because of denominational motives but out of a clash between two types of mentality: fundamentalist and creative."[29] It is often assumed that the fundamental causes of disunity and division among various churches are primarily matters of doctrinal disagreement on specific issues, such as the sacraments, ordination, apostolic succession, Eucharist and baptism. On closer inspection, however, as H. Richard Niebuhr demonstrated in his 1929 book on the *Social Sources of Denominationalism*, disunity in the Church reflects not doctrinal disagreement, but the institutional church's compliance with divisive socio-economic forces and socio-political ideologies, such as nationalism and racism.[30] In order to overcome such divisions, the ecumenical movement must be sustained by a vision of a transfigured world and the fusion of the entire human community. This vision is expressed in terms of the Kingdom of God, which constitutes a spiritual fellowship without barriers or distinctions of any kind.[31]

The Kingdom of God, rather than any particular model of ecclesial organization or hierarchy, should be both the object and point of departure of evangelical engagement in the ecumenical movement. The Kingdom of God both encompasses and transcends any particular church community. This understanding of the Kingdom of God should engender an element of humility born of the conviction that the full realization of the Kingdom can be compared to an ever-receding horizon that will evade all our efforts to dominate it or to grasp it completely. The conviction that one church group embodies in an exclusive way the true fulfillment of the Kingdom vision is antithetical to the true spirit of ecumenism. Moreover, if a particular church that makes such a claim assumes that this privileged status confers upon it the right to impose its own structures on others, it thereby deviates from the true ecumenical vision of unity in diversity in favor of insipid forms of uniformity and institutional hierarchy.

Anti-ecumenism has been a prominent feature of post-Soviet evangelical theology and spirituality. There is a genuine fear among many post-Soviet evangelicals that participation in ecumenical dialogue constitutes a grievous compromise that will lead to a diminishing of the distinctiveness

29. Fedorov, "Ecumenical Missionary Needs."
30. Niebuhr, *Social Sources*.
31. Bulgakov, *Bride*, xvii.

of their Christian witness. The anti-ecumenical sentiment of some Baptists is often manifested in the fear that the ecumenical movement is paving the way towards a syncretistic liberal church, which subordinates the truth of the gospel to the claims of unity. Much of the post-Soviet evangelical apprehension about ecumenism is attributable to a lack of understanding concerning the meaning and significance of ecumenism and an ignorance about its true aims and the evangelistic missionary zeal to which the modern ecumenical movement traces its origins.

Such concerns, therefore, should not preclude the possibility of developing mutually enriching partnerships with Christians from other traditions, especially with Catholics and Orthodox believers. In engaging with ecumenical partners, post-Soviet evangelicals can rightly insist on the central place of mission and the Kingdom of God as core values and ideas that must be central to any ecumenical vision to which they can contribute as enthusiastic participants. Therefore, notwithstanding the understandable misgivings of many evangelicals, these must be counterbalanced by a recognition of the ways in which disunity among the churches in the FSU has been a major impediment to mission. The current disunity of the Church is lamentable, not merely because division is inherently sinful or deplorable, but because it hinders God's activity in saving and redeeming the world. In other words, the *missio Dei*, rather than unity *per se*, is the ultimate aim or telos of the ecumenical movement. This is the central insight that forms the basis of evangelical participation in ecumenical dialogue.

The disunity of the Church has also been proven to be an impediment to the effectiveness of theological education. The extent to which mission, church unity and theological education are inseparable and mutually reinforcing was made explicit in a report published by the World Council of Churches:

> Without an increased commitment in theological education for ecumenical dialogue and cooperation, the unity of the church, its holistic mission and service in today's world and dialogue with people of other faiths, we might see an increased fragmentation of world Christianity. Growing trends of religious fundamentalism and a severe lack of properly trained Christian leadership in many fast growing churches demand . . . more investments in infrastructure and programs of theological education.[32]

32. WCC, "14 Reasons for Global Solidarity."

Connecting mission, ecumenism and theological education, Vladimir Fedorov explained that

> Theological education today should be mission-minded. Such a development suggests ecumenical co-operation. The word "education" implies not only the academic routine of communicating some knowledge, fostering some skills and training various specialists for various fields of action, but also a strategic task for the whole culture. Education is the dynamics of culture. A broader understanding of the nature of ministry (lay, ordained and collective) is connected with a new understanding of the contemporary mission of the church. It is worth emphasizing that there is a common need to become aware of the fact that theological and general education should be a primary concern of the Church.[33]

Writing in relation to Russia, Fedorov concludes that "a new missionary orientation of theological education is urgently needed today in order to help to realize that in a situation of absence of a culture of tolerance and pluralism, no inter-confessional Christian dialogue, no interfaith dialogue and—what matters most in Russia—no dialogue between believers and unbelievers is ever possible."[34]

What Fedorov said about Russia is just as pertinent for other countries of the FSU, including Ukraine. According to Vasyl Markus (writing in 1995), all of the churches in Ukraine

> have failed to achieve any degree of understanding, compassion, and sense of community of Christian faith that would be needed in order to initiate ecumenical dialogue. In addition, there is much resentment and many counterclaims, leading sometimes to confrontation. No previous ecumenical experience and basic education in ecumenism, which Western churches have been experiencing for at least three decades and now take for granted, are available.[35]

However, there are promising recent developments that seem to signal a new openness towards ecumenical engagement, particularly on the part of the Ukrainian Catholic community. One particularly noteworthy enterprise has been the Master's Program in Ecumenical Studies (MPES) in Lviv. Launched in 2006 at the Ukrainian Catholic University and Lviv National

---

33. Fedorov, "Theological Education," 522.

34. Ibid., 523–24.

35. Markus, "Religious Pluralism," 180.

University, the program has drawn on other successful courses in Ecumenical Studies that have been running in Western Europe since the 1950s. Writing about the aims of MPES, Antoine Arjakovsky explains that, "The programme has as its purpose to acquaint students with the theological foundations of the study of the Christian faith in an ecumenical perspective, to give them the opportunity to deepen their knowledge of inter-confessional theological dialogues, to teach them to comment on and critically explain religious themes and events, to understand the role of Christianity and Christian values in the contemporary world, to provide the necessary pedagogical, methodological, and practical preparation for the teaching of Christian ethics and work in the sphere of religious journalism."[36] At the heart of the program is the aim to cultivate the character and values of the students in order to equip students with a broad understanding of the legitimate variety of Christian tradition and a generous, inclusive hermeneutic which perceives difference not as deviance, but as an enriching and necessary quality of the Church in all its diverse expressions. As long as post-Soviet evangelicals fail to recognize the urgency of the ecumenical imperative, it is inconceivable that a similar program of ecumenical studies could be launched at an evangelical theological seminary in the FSU.

Although there are no sustainable biblical or theological arguments for not participating in ecumenical dialogue, post-Soviet evangelicals can nevertheless raise legitimate concerns about where crucial disagreements remain. One of the hindrances to the progress of ecumenical dialogue has been the conception of the Church as a divinely instituted structure, rather than as a living, organic and spiritual union of believers. As the Bulgarian Baptist theologian, Parush Parushev rightly maintains, "Jesus was more concerned with enactment of the coming of the kingdom rather than the establishment of the institution of a church."[37] In a post-Soviet context in which State-sponsored and institutionally endorsed religion retains considerable power as a key marker not only of religious affiliation but also national identity, the evangelical movement is a vital part of the Church. The evangelical churches, by insisting on the supremacy of Scripture and committing themselves to a disciplined life of faithful witness to the gospel, can guard against the dangers of nominalism and challenge the Church to remain focused on its first calling, which is to participate in the building of the Kingdom of God "on earth as it is in heaven." In this way evan-

36. Arjakovsky, "Theological Education," 527–28.
37. Parushev, "Kingdom of Heaven," 289.

gelicals can make an important contribution to contemporary ecumenical discourse in the post-Soviet space.

However, before post-Soviet evangelicals can be persuaded to engage in ecumenical dialogue, many will need to undergo a process of *metanoia* in order to break through the layers of suspicion, prejudice, distrust and fear of Christians from other traditions and denominations. This is why theological education should be directed towards promoting a more generous vision of evangelicalism that is able to affirm one's commitments while recognizing that there are several different (yet legitimate and complementary) ways of participating in and thinking about the Christian faith. There are many different ways of following the crucified and risen Christ today and of living out our common Christian vocation. We do not need to regard everyone who has a different perspective from us as "deviant," "apostate," "heretical," or "liberal."

We propose some possible components in an interdenominational and Church-public dialogue about freedom in post-Soviet society: a well-informed Christian community; the monitoring of church-society relations; a open and equal dialogue between Christian traditions; solidarity between churches in addressing major social needs; a consolidated Christian position on freedom of conscience and other democratic freedoms; a proper understanding of the transformational nature of the Church's influence on society, and the strengthening and development of civil society in a future of Christian values. The doors of freedom are rapidly closing and can slam shut at any moment. Against this background what is expected from the Church is not criticism of liberty so much as the defense of it. It is precisely the Church that can endow the concept of freedom with new meaning by making it constructive and responsible. Churches can offer society a lesson in unity and reconciliation. The unity of churches with each other and with society is a condition for the rebirth of public life oriented toward democratic and evangelical principles. When the State has a place for such churches, for such a society, that is when freedom will be protected.

Thankfully, recent events in Ukraine have demonstrated the extent to which churches of different backgrounds and traditions can work together for the common good of society. The Revolution of Freedom and Dignity, which began on the streets of Kyiv in November 2013, has generated a new spirit of ecumenical co-operation among the various churches in Ukraine.[38]

---

38. For a lucid, well-informed, and balanced assessment of the impact of the Revolution on the Ukrainian churches, see Lunkin, "The Ukrainian Revlolution and the

The Ukrainian Revolution appears to have revealed that the national divisions run far deeper than confessional divisions. Ukrainian Baptists have demonstrated solidarity with the people, whereas Russian Baptists, on the whole, have chosen to be loyal to the authorities. While Russian Baptists have tended to condemn the Revolution and have given tacit or explicit support to Vladimir Putin, Ukrainian Baptists have (literally) stood alongside Orthodox and Catholic Christians on Maidan, demonstrating the Church's solidarity with the legitimate aspirations of the vast majority Ukrainian for freedom, democracy and accountability. Recent events have demonstrated how Russian evangelicals' allegiances have been closer to the oppressive and corrupt Russian authorities than to their suffering Ukrainian Baptist brethren. Ukrainian Baptists, for their part, have been closer to Ukrainian Catholics and the Kyiv–Patriarchate Ukrainian Orthodox Church in their attitude towards Maidan, political liberty and religious freedom. It is to be hoped that the Revolution of Freedom and Dignity will lead to a long-term reconciliation between various Christian communities and confessions, not only in Ukraine, but throughout the FSU. As Antoine Arjakovsky notes,

> Such a reconciliation of Churches—Orthodox, Catholic and Protestant—in Ukraine would have a double advantage. It would reassure the Orthodox population that Ukraine's membership in Europe does not mean pure and simple entry into a secularized and agnostic world. But it would equally comfort the Ukrainian Greek Catholic population, which hopes that recognition of the primacy of the seat of Rome does not do injury to the life of the local Church. Finally, it would guarantee to Protestants that freedom of conscience would always come first, before what Giorgio Agamben calls the "dictatorial impulses of modern States."[39]

This wish for a large-scale reconciliation between Orthodox, Catholics and Protestants in Ukraine is a worthy aspiration, which would constitute a significant and progressive step in Ukraine's long journey out of the post-Soviet transition. There may even be reconciliation between the Russian and Ukrainian churches. When Russians begin to see a strong Church in Ukraine that enjoys the love and respect of the people, they will come to visit, make friendships, and learn from us. And God will delight in this.[40]

Christian Churches."

39. Arjakovsky, "Role of the Churches."

40. Lunkin, "Ukrainian Revlolution and the Christian Churches," 5.

6

Theological Education and Its Mission

Church Personnel

In topics concerning leadership, church governance structure, and the system for the training of clergy, leadership qualities come to the fore not only in internal church debates, but also on the list of public interests. Recently, interest in the Church has shifted from doctrinal concerns to the theological reflection on interpersonal relations. People outside of the Church are not as concerned about understanding the intricacies of history and doctrine as they are about trusting and respecting those Christians they meet in the course of their everyday lives. Undoubtedly, even within the Church itself, the need for decent, loyal, trustworthy and competent Christian leaders at all levels is felt all the more deeply and sharply. Responsibility for the "lost generation" of failed or rejected young leaders is recognized, as is an understanding of the value of every minister as a unique individual. So it is that society makes high demands and shows a genuine interest in the composition of church leadership; but the Church itself is seriously concerned about shortages in personnel and their quality, realizing that the post-Soviet period is drawing to a close and the new era will require qualitatively new ministers and leaders.

In the following brief points, we want to draw attention to the special aspects of the selection and training of senior ministers in the churches of the Evangelical Christian Baptists (ECB) in the post-Soviet period, and also to identify possible problems and prospects for Christian leadership associated with emerging from the post-Soviet transition and overcoming this extended interim period.

For post-Soviet churches, the very issue of a personnel policy seems strange because in the beginning the notion of a system for the training, selection and promotion of administrative personnel did not manifest itself. This is explained by the "sectarian" (meaning not the self-identification of "sects," but, rather, the "sectarian" conditions in which the Church had to live) history and the corresponding mentality that prevailed in ECB communities. When surviving in extreme conditions and constantly living in the fear that every day might be the last, one does not tend to develop an idea or sense of an order, system, procedures or rules.

The traditions of education and training of members of the post-Soviet churches date back to pre-revolutionary times, when everything was just beginning, when people were dreaming about many things, but were content with little and reassured themselves that, although times were difficult, better days lay ahead of them. There was no personnel policy and most of the leaders of the evangelical movement were individual talents. Each had an interesting biography, but, with rare exceptions, no formal education, or systematic training. Some were able to obtain a theological education abroad. A few received lessons in ministry from foreigners living nearby in the Russian Empire or from evangelical colonists. Still others were able to study rare books and developed independently under their influence. The early history of the evangelical movement was a time of bright, slightly eccentric, charismatic personalities that nobody purposefully selected, but who suddenly appeared on the pages of that history, and shaped it.

Something similar happened in this last twenty years of post-Soviet history. There was a prevailing sense of the transitional character of the era and therefore no one tried to construct a system of "professional" training for clergy and leaders. Christians schools sprang up spontaneously. Many took the initiative and received an education in foreign seminaries. In the sea of newly available literature and educational resources, there were no guidelines, nor were there many restrictions. The opportunities were incomparably greater than at the start of the evangelical movement, but all this wealth was consumed or dissipated by the feeling that "this is temporary," "this won't last long," "who knows what's coming next," and "who knows if this is the right thing or not."

In the post-Soviet period, people liked to recall that the apostles were simple fishermen, that "God chose the foolish things," and that Ryaboshapka and Ratushny became leaders without any education. The national character and the main thrusts of the evangelical movement were disrupted in the expectation that its leaders must necessarily hail from the same native soils, from the same "class." Education, as well as any kind of vocational training, was considered a marker of foreignness. This explains the hitherto existing suspicion and even hostility towards those with a college or university level education (especially in a humanities subject that is not directly connect with the "faith"): these talents can sometimes be *used*, but they must never be *trusted*. Ministerial selection is generally carried out on an ad hoc basis. There are no formal selection procedures designed to identify candidates' discipline, motivation, vocation, personal qualities or their ability to exercise their ministries in difficult conditions and to mobilize resources effectively. Selection is made on the basis of intuitive and situational personnel decisions, which are isolated and inconsistent. As such, it is not clear if the possession of a formal theological education affects the selection and promotion of a leader within the "system." It seems that education is not seen as a social or ecclesiastical advantage, but as a threat to the "system." As a result, the Christian seminary and Church are separated from each other, in what again appears to be a hangover from the Soviet legacy. It seems that the talented graduates of Christian seminaries can only find work in the same educational institutions. In this way, the seminary prepares people to teach in the seminary. The educated are not needed in the Church because they are not the product of the "system"; rather they come out of a free intellectual environment and are seen as promoters of its "liberal" values. A Christian education could make up for a personnel shortage, but graduates either do not want to work in an outdated "system," or they are rejected by it.

A post-Soviet "system" thus reproduces itself. The State no longer requires external filters, but the "system" continues to work in the same mode, transitioning to self-imposed filters and self-censorship. The emergence of a new wave of leaders who think differently, who profess the values not of the sovietized system, but of the evangelical movement are looked upon as "treasonous," "deviant," and "liberal." By closing off the influx of new leaders, the "system" is forced to work with internal resources that are inevitably aging and declining. The first leaders complain about the absence of worthy, bright leaders, but the existing "system" is unable to produce them. Those promoted inside the "system" are "insiders" and often servile functionaries of the "system," but they are not respected; on the other hand, the educated newcomers, who come from the outside and who shake up the "system" are respected but not promoted. The "system" seems incapable of reforming itself. Being closed, it appears condemned to personnel shortages and progressive self-destruction.

Hope for renewal will therefore arrive from outside. Along with the emergence from the post-Soviet transition, the ineffectiveness of the old administrative methods of command and control becomes evident. Archaic, nepotistic relationships, the lack of democratic procedures and the absence of proper transparency and viable structures of accountability all vitiate the life and vitality of the faith community. The renewal of evangelical communities requires new standards of pastoral and missional competence. Education and self-education are not additional points in the assessment of competence, but the basic, the most essential conditions for effective ministry and leadership. In the very near future, what will be required is not an *education that confirms* competence ("authority," "reliability") with an attractive diploma, but an *education that transforms*, develops, and invigorates.

The emergence of new networks, communities, competing with vertically integrated systems, activates other types of leadership, authority, and control. The time is coming for communities united by ideas and values, communities that trust each other and are coming together to develop their vision of the future. The demand is surfacing for new reformers, for committed innovators and principled leaders. The time has come for bold, yet responsible, evangelical entrepreneurs who are willing to take risks for the sake of the gospel. Like orchids that can grow in a greenhouse or in a nature reserve, leaders do not all emerge from the same source. This is why one must know not only the Church, but also the related spheres of activity that can produce potential leaders.

Post-Sovietism was a transitional state in which society and the Church was mired for a long time. Throughout this time, Soviet mechanisms, resources, and approaches still retained some operative power, but with each passing year they became increasingly less reliable in their ability to function. The uncertainty of the future is unsettling, and the "system" is not able to conceptualize itself as absent or altered, and so it is constantly looking back to past experience, returning to exhausted management models, selecting the kinds of leaders with which it is familiar.

To exit from the post-Soviet transition, we must unlearn the habit of looking at the Church as a "system"; it is preferable to speak about an organic movement of people. It is impossible to reform a "system"; one can only endeavor to subsume it within a movement, and include it in the broader context of spiritual reforms within the evangelical community. It is difficult to imagine the possibility of building a self-sufficient system for the training and selection of personnel for a separated union of Evangelical Christians-Baptists. There is unlikely to be sufficient internal dynamics, ideas and resources of their own for self-renewal and self-development. Yet if the focus of our reforming efforts is not the union of the ECB, but the broader evangelical movement, there are opportunities to learn from each other, to facilitate co-operation between training institutions, to pool resources, and to experiment with different models of church structure and missional leadership.

In the near future we can expect to address issues that are beyond the abilities of one tradition or one church union. Looking to the future we need to develop not only ways of running church organizations; we also need to change the ways of selecting and appointing those who lead. We need to allow leaders the space to be innovative and independent. We need to find ways of connecting spiritual devotion with managerial competence, and organizational efficiency with emotional intelligence. A new model of selection based on accountable and transparent procedures must be developed as an alternative to the administrative-command system of the communism years and the populist, dictatorial, corrupted or force-oriented models of authoritarian leadership that dominated Soviet power structures. The evangelical community needs to find a model of leadership that is recognized and respected not only by the closed church community, but also by the outside world.

The evangelical community stands on the threshold of a new era, much like the beginning of the evangelical movement in the Russian Empire. The sense of the impending reformation, of a great spiritual movement that transcends the traditional boundaries of the system is gaining momentum. There is a powerful call both from within the Church and from society for a renewal of leadership, for a cleansing of the ranks, for new types of leaders, for people with ideas, vision and courage. This reformation will be pioneered by those for whom the concept of the "system," of a career, power and authority, will not be of paramount importance. This positive challenge to the Church is also a critical test of the Church's ability to recognize and nurture those leaders with the necessary gifts and vision.

Education and Science as Tools of Mission

The topic of Church relations, education and science is one of the most pressing in the evolving evangelical theology of post-Soviet churches and refers to several of its areas of interest: social theology, the theology of culture, missiology, the history of the Church; as well as one of the key contemporary debates about the specifics of what is "Christian," about the "Christian world," "Christian education," "Christian philosophy," "Christian intellectuals," and so on. Today, the Church is not only present and attests internally to the public significance of education and science; it also creates its own education and develops its own science in order to meet the internal needs of theology and for external missional objectives. The urgency of the topic for post-Soviet churches is determined by the opportunities and challenges of "freedom after atheism"—not only the inner freedom of conscience or narrowly defined religious meetings, but also the freedom to express one's faith in the public sphere, including in discussions about the scientific world and the content of education, and the freedom to found schools, to plant churches and to publicly declare one's theological position. The Church's attitude to education and science is defined by biblical and theological principles, but also by key elements taken from our religious, political, cultural history. While professing the Lordship of Jesus Christ as the Incarnate God in all spheres of life (spiritual, material, social, cultural and intellectual), Christians can affirm education and science as instruments for learning about God's world and for growing in wisdom and knowledge.

For the evangelical Church in the Russian Empire and the Soviet Union the spheres of education and science were closed. Christians were deprived not only of the opportunity to receive academic awards, but even simple attendance at academic institutions was forbidden. The violent marginalization of the Church left its indelible mark first of all on the social image of evangelical Christianity. The perception that formed of evangelical believers depicts them as worker-peasants, sects, and an illiterate mass of ignorant obscurantists. Secondly, this forced exclusion left its mark on their theology. Their sectarian tendencies and their lack of access to education and science eventually led to a pervasive anti-intellectualism among evangelical believers, many of whom came to regard education and science as irrelevant and harmful. However, under *perestroika* the evangelical Church began to orientate itself more favorably towards science and education. After the collapse of the Soviet Union, the scientific and educational sectors were regarded as newly opened mission fields, as well as channels for the demarginalization of the Church. Engagement in scientific research and commitment to education became means of overcoming the Church's alienation from public life.

In the history of the evangelical movement in Russia and the Soviet Union there have appeared many educated persons of note who were recognized even by those outside the evangelical community. These include Vasily Pavlov, Ivan Prokhanov, Ivan Kargel, Vladimir Martsinkovsky, Yuri Grachev, Alexander Karev, Evgeny Pushkov, Georgy Vins, and Oswald Tyarek. Their presence in the marginalized evangelical community had the significant effect of opening up the areas of science and education to the marginalized evangelical community. Their example also demonstrated to the Church and the world new opportunities offered by science and education for Christian testimony and intellectual creativity and how these could be applied for the benefit of the Church and society.

Against the backdrop of the information society and the ongoing scientific and technological revolution, the relevance of an organic theology and system for Christian education is gaining momentum. The task confronting Christian education after the post-Soviet transition is not only to improve internal church theological literacy, but also to overcome fabricated dichotomies, such as Bible vs. science, religious emotions vs. scholarly application of the mind, learning vs. inspiration, and spiritual revelation vs. worldly knowledge.

Among the most controversial and, at the same time, long-term issues in the relationship of contemporary post-Soviet evangelical churches to education and science, the following are worthy of special consideration: the meaning and significance of postmodernism as a cultural and philosophical phenomenon; critical assessment of the ongoing scientific and technological revolution and its implications for the Church and society; the issue of humanism in its secular and Christian manifestations, and the related issues of transhumanism and human nature; the prospects for teaching Christian ethics in schools; the institutionalization of theology as an academic and scientific discipline; the consolidation of teachers and scholars in Christian professional associations and Christian intellectuals as a social group; the development of partnerships between Christian, public and private educational institutions; the formation of a social position and missionary strategy for evangelical churches corresponding to education and science as spheres of public life. The future of evangelical churches in post-Soviet society largely depends on the extent to which Christians can facilitate the theological development of education and science as mission fields, as territories of the Kingdom, as languages of culture, and as instruments of learning and creativity.

Theology as a Science

Without the development of an appropriate theology, a theological conceptualization of education and science as means of exerting public influence is not possible. In recent years theology has become a familiar word, but it tends to evoke apprehension both in the Church and in the University. In response to fears and criticism, it is necessary to set forth a few points regarding theology as a science. Theology is the conscious faith of the Church, the experience of knowledge about God expressed in words—our words in response to the Word of God and towards the creative elucidation of the Word. Theology arose in the Church as the result of the inclusive experience of faith. Of course, religious experience can be individualized and outside the Church and it can engender insights and reflection, but Christian theology is an expression of faith by the Church, and, as such, is under no compulsion to become a science.

Theology, aspiring to becoming one of the sciences, enters the scientific community, where there are rules, ethos, categories and criteria of rationality. It must be ready to confirm its scientific claims in the appropriate language and to demonstrate its explanatory power. A dual accountability is required from the theologian as a scholar—to the university in terms of scientific competence, and to the Church in terms of knowledge and loyalty to the faith experience obtained within the Church. A theologian as a scientist must confirm her status by demonstrating professional knowledge and skills. At the same time the theologian is also responsible to the Church and must be able to represent her traditions to the scientific world, articulating the experience of faith in the form of theoretical knowledge that is understandable and useful to the other sciences. Our time provides another choice, another fork in the road: to remain preoccupied in the internal affairs of the Church, or to step into the world of universities and academies, responding to them and transforming them with a Christian presence.

Christianity in the Post-Soviet University

Not only the Church, but also the post-Soviet university fears the Christian presence in education. Adherents of the old Soviet system as well as some Orthodox officials continue to utter phrases taken from the Council of People's Commissars about the separation of Church from the State and school. The "Decree on the Separation of the Church from the State and the Schools from the Church" was adopted in 1918 and to this day it remains in effect, as if the Soviets remained in power and were still in control of the education system.

We may highlight some interesting points in this decree. The first provision stipulates that the Church must be separate from the secular State. The second provision asserts that restraints of any kind on the freedom of conscience or which would grant special rights or privileges on the basis of the religious affiliation of citizens is forbidden. The seventh provision expressly forbids the teaching of religion in school. Citizens should teach and be taught religion only in private. The document is contradictory: on the one hand, it promotes democratic principles of freedom, equal opportunity and a ban on privilege. On the other hand, prohibitions and sanctions apply only to the Church and the teaching of religion. Soviet-style freedom is freedom from religion, and for the protection of that kind of freedom restrictions had to be imposed on the freedom of the "sects" and their "dangerous" teachings. The complete freedom of atheism deprives everyone else not only of freedom, but also of very tangible rights. According to provisions 9 and 10, all church and religious associations were deprived of property on behalf of the people, and did not have the rights of a legal entity. Despite the downfall of the USSR the whole system of education, from kindergarten to university, remains solely under the control of the State. By suppressing dissent and banning alternative approaches, regardless of the ideological choice of students and their parents, the system of education in the countries of the FSU continues to reproduce an atheistic matrix of consciousness. The conveyor belt of the post-Soviet education factory continues to work and churn out *homo sovieticus.*

Post-Soviet education remains one of the last citadels of the Soviet culture and atheism. Throughout Europe, including in Western Europe, the State hegemony of atheist ideology is morphing into a monopoly of secularism and omnivorous tolerance. Under such conditions everything is permitted except faith. Post-Soviet Christians are called upon to dispute these seemingly "natural" hegemonic assumptions and to uncover the unnatural essence of any monopoly, including those that profess to be Christian.

The challenges of secularism (as in the post-Soviet context) or of constraints on the public activity of believers (as in the European context) should be taken as a call for creativity. Appeals to historical merits and attempting to occupy a position of authority in the universities on the basis of the Christian provenance of the modern university will not be sufficient (even though the universities were, in fact, founded and developed by Christians); it is also futile to demand preferential treatment on the basis of ideological content or educational philosophy. What is truly essential is the readiness and ability to compete in a professional environment, to present arguments in defense of one's convictions, and finally, to demonstrate those same Christian qualities of character that have always signified more than logical proofs. To be a person of integrity, to be a diligent student or a wise teacher, to be self-critical and broadminded, to respect other approaches and at the same time to have the courage to follow one's principles—in today's university, this personal "courage to be" is more important and persuasive than political or clerical battles over spheres of influence. There are no decrees—neither of the Soviet nor of the European variety—that have the power to deprive us of these kinds of possibilities.

Church Structures and Missional Movements in the FSU

Already in the late Soviet period, which witnessed a real expansion in religious freedom, our longstanding dream of being free to preach the gospel openly and establish our own theological schools began to become a reality. In Ukraine, the first national mission, Light of the Gospel, was founded in 1989, and initially relied solely on local resources. This initiative was directed at developing new mission fields in the Volga region, Siberia, and the Far East. The central office of the mission was in Rivne and there were also offices in Makeyevka, Yakutsk, and Kazan. In addition to establishing new churches and launching humanitarian projects, publishing initiatives, and educational programs, the mission established a significant missionary school, Donetsk Bible College, later renamed Donetsk Christian University. In the late 1990s, the Light of the Gospel mission was reconfigured as an association, and today its projects and ministry have expanded in scope and are fully independent.

The years of active mission and the missionary boom were a time of peak demand for education—both theological and missionary in orientation. Schools sprang up one after the other, almost spontaneously, without much long-term planning or collaboration with other institutions. In 1989, in Odessa, the first training program opened, which later gave birth to the Odessa Theological Seminary. In the same year the Logos Institute opened its doors, and subsequently evolved into St. Petersburg Christian University. The following two years saw the appearance of Christian universities in Donetsk and Kyiv. In 1993, the Moscow Theological Seminary was founded and an association of evangelical institutions from the former USSR was initiated, which led, in 1997, to the establishment of the Euro-Asian Accrediting Association of Evangelical Schools (EAAA), which at that time united 37 organizations.

Today, the EAAA includes fifty-five educational institutions from various evangelical churches (twenty-four Evangelical Christian Baptist schools, twenty-one Christians of Evangelical Faith schools, and ten schools belonging to other evangelical denominations). The EAAA has enabled newly created schools to gain access to resources and partnerships, and has facilitated their adaption to unified educational standards. Only after coming together were these institutions able to produce a flagship journal of serious academic merit, entitled, *Bogoslovskiye razmyshlenia* (*Theological Reflections*). As well as facilitating the research development of post-Soviet evangelical scholarship, the EAAA has also helped to establish training programs for teachers and school administrators and has enabled them to integrate themselves into international organizations and associations, and to attract financial support for grant proposals. Additionally, the EAAA has provided counseling to schools in crisis situations, and has assisted schools in dealing with the visits of commissions and independent experts.

After 2011, the EAAA restructured its management, and now the executive management operates in a collective format. A research center has been established with a department of education and a department of accreditation, each of which has its own director. Accreditation issues and common academic standards are becoming less viable—the simplified requirements are clearly inadequate for the development of the schools, but it would place a heavy burden on the weaker schools if standards were to be raised. Most schools cannot afford to maintain well-qualified teaching staff and attract high-caliber students, so the requirements of accreditation commissions are deliberately lowered. In conditions such as these, the

EAAA works primarily to coordinate research projects and partnerships between schools, contributing to the development of their human resources and academic-theological potential. Looking to the future, an important focus of EAAA and other structures that unite education and Christian organizations will be mediation between missions, schools and churches, establishing an effective interaction that results not only in enhanced education, but also in greater missional engagement.

In the FSU, most mission organizations continue to prefer a more traditional, "evangelization" format in how they operate. Among the most well known are the Renaissance Christian Center (a branch of the Billy Graham Evangelistic Association); Licht im Osten (the oldest German mission to the Slavs); the Slavic Gospel Association (the largest mission organization, which works mainly with conservative Baptist groups); the Biblical Mission; the Bible League; and Heart to Heart.

Recognizing the limitations of traditional models of evangelization, there is a new demand among many post-Soviet evangelicals for integrative approaches to the mission, in which the issues of education, culture, ideology, social responsibility, and professional calling all occupy an important place. New approaches to missional engagement are beginning to emerge in the ministries of the Fellowship of Christian Students, the Association for Spiritual Renewal (Russian Ministries), the Alliance of Professional Christian Organizations, the Christian Science and Apologetics Center, the Crimean Christian Centre for Science and Apologetics, and the REALIS Centre.

The main problem with most Christian missions and schools is a narrow understanding of the missionary vocation of Christian education and church-oriented religious interests. A church is ready to support a school or a mission only when it regards it as its own, with ownership rights and when it is under no obligation to share these rights with others. Most interchurch projects are developing slowly. Most church leaders have no concept of the Kingdom, the symbol of which is the local church, and because of this, the parochial interests of local churches are not just the top priority, but also shut our everything else, including: the aspirations of the Christian community as a whole; the vision of God's Kingdom; prospects for the transformation of society; and opportunities for interchurch cooperation.

Still another challenge faced by Christian institutions is their inability to respond to the unique missional challenges and opportunities of their times. Schools and missions arose and developed in the 1990s as though the era of unprecedented opportunities and religious euphoria would last forever. The limitations to these organizations were thus embedded in their very foundations. Now, when post-Soviet society, the attitude of the State, global trends, church dynamics, religious needs and financial opportunities have all changed beyond recognition, difficult questions emerge about how to bring the institutions and organizations that were created in a different era into line with the requirements of our time, and whether their reform, restructuring and readjustment is even possible. As our recent history has demonstrated, one of the lessons of the Soviet *perestroika* (in English, "restructuring") was that some structures cannot withstand restructuring without collapsing.

The analogy with *perestroika* is no coincidence. Not only Soviet society, but also the Soviet and post-Soviet churches as part of that society, turned out to be limited by their times. As is well known, they were not able to restructure the Soviet Union and Soviet society—everything Soviet was, in principle, unreformable, because ideology was considered most important—more important than effectiveness, competence or even relevance. Society itself was closed, self-sufficient, and oriented towards inward evaluation and criteria. Moreover this closed society was holistic, homogenous and highly centralized. It was easier to replace it completely than to change an individual detail. Moreover, freedom and creativity were limited by total government regulation. The rigid structure made movement impossible.

Unfortunately, post-Soviet society still depends on Soviet structures (political, economic, educational, religious) and organizes itself around them. Despite their extremely low effectiveness, they remain a factor of stability, because there are few who see the possibility of something else and even fewer who are capable of taking responsibility for developing more liberating alternatives. The Church, too, seems unable to take a leading role in envisioning new structures that would encourage the development of humanity, compassion, creativity and justice in post-Soviet society. Christian churches, missions, and educational institutions founded in the years of the fall of the USSR (1989–91) are steadily losing their relevance in the face of new circumstances in society and church life.

There is only one way of extending the life of organizations and projects in states of constant change and that is to make them open, accepting, and responsive to these changes, and thereby to make them into movements. A movement means constant building and rebuilding (*perestroika*). A movement is goal-oriented rather than structure-oriented; innovation and informed risk-taking are valued more than stability and security. A movement cherishes freedom, imagination and creativity, whereas an institution is more concerned about maintaining order.

One example of how a project can become a movement is the School Without Walls (SWW) initiative.[1] The first SWW groups were founded in 2004 in Ukraine and then spread to Russia. These groups prepared young leaders for service in the Church and in missions. They had no formal structures or signs, and therefore raised lots of questions, "Who are these people? What is this project for? Who gave permission for this? Who controls this?" Answering these questions was not easy, because the model of SWW worked according to a completely different logic. The Association for Spiritual Renewal/Russia Ministries was the initiator, while local churches were partners, although the students and their teachers played the main role. They planned their classes and practical activities, focusing on what was most important and most useful. They were the owners of the "project"—or rather, they were active participants in a major movement. The name itself indicated that SWW was a movement, which began in the church, mobilized its young leaders, and then directed them to ministry outside of its walls. Thus, School Without Walls became a ministry without walls. To be fair we have to admit that the potential of SWW is much greater than its practical results. Not many are capable of taking initiative without instructions from above and a stable budget to support them. Additionally, the "familiar walls" of churches and organizations give comfort, and at first the prospect of a movement "without walls" can be frightening and disorienting for those who are familiar with tight church structures and hierarchical models of leadership. But, as the author of *perestroika*, Mikhail Gorbachev, famously said, "the process has started." Now there is not just School Without Walls, but also Churches Without Walls, and a Festival Without Walls. A new generation of leaders has grown up with this idea. When this generation comes of age, we will witness a major transformation in the practice of mission and ministry in the FSU.

1. To learn more about the School Without Walls model and how it responds to the needs of local churches, missions, and schools, see the following article: Cherenkov, "School Without Walls," 16–25.

It is worth noting that various evangelical churches and independent Christian organizations are part of what local historians and theologians call the "evangelical movement" of Eurasia. And the main subject of Christian history in the region are not Baptists or Pentecostals or individual missions organizations or schools, but the "evangelical movement" as a whole. Such unity does not exclude diversity, but rather actually demands it. A movement's dynamic is only possible given the autonomy of individual parts, inner creativity and diversity. Moreover, what is needed are openness and a high degree of integration into the world evangelical movement and global trends. For instance, such integration assumes the readiness of theological schools to integrate into the general educational sphere, submit to high academic standards, treat the experience of others as its own, find and take a humble place without claims to more, and acknowledge the priority of international standards and principles. A degree of submission is also expected of churches and missions—transforming from a passive recipient to a full-scale partner of all, giving to those in greatest need, developing national theology in international and interchurch dialogue, to combine local and global dimensions of missiology.

The Euro-Asian Accrediting Association in its current format[2] serves as an example of such integration. Its board of directors includes representatives of Pentecostal, Baptist, and Presbyterian churches, which serve a community of theological schools of various traditions and denominations, offering not only unifying projects and establishing common standards, but also providing a common vision and even a common Statement of Faith. Another precedent is the "evangelical movement" and "evangelical conventions," which began in Moscow in 2010 and include a variety of Protestant communities of Russia and Ukraine: Lutheran, Pentecostal, Charismatic, and Baptist. These "conventions" unite not only groups of believers but also spheres of ministry into a single yet diverse movement.[3]

2. See the EAAA website: www.e-aaa.info.

3. Information about theological conferences of the "Evangelical movement" can be accessed online at http://evangelicals.ru/.

7

A Vision for Theological Education as Mission[1]

Introduction to Chapter 7

The aim of this chapter is to outline the contours of a holistic vision of theological education that goes beyond both worldview formation and practical training in church activities. It is argued that the development of a contextual missional paradigm that could be used to invigorate evangelical theological education and mission in the FSU is one of the most urgent tasks of evangelical theology in Slavic contexts today.

In his thought-provoking article in a recent issue of the *European Journal of Theology*, Johannes Reimer laments the lack of an "appropriate Evangelical missiology for the Slavic world."[2] Reimer argues convincingly that such a missiology must arise out of "a continuous conversation between Scripture, a discerning community of believers and the socio-political context in which mission is being done."[3] He calls upon evangelicals to engage in dialogue with Orthodox believers to develop a transformative missiology appropriate to the post-Soviet context.[4] Following a well-trodden path

---

1. This chapter is based on an article published in the *European Journal of Theology*, under the title "From Christian Worldview to Kingdom Formation."
2. Reimer, "Recovering the Missionary Memory," 137–48.
3. Ibid., 138.
4. Ibid., 145.

in recent scholarship, Reimer decries what he calls the "mixed blessing of Western assistance"[5] and claims that the dominance of Western thinking and practices has left the evangelical churches in the region ill-equipped to face the missiological challenges of post-Soviet society.[6] Reimer makes a crucial point that the churches in this region urgently need a contextual theology that connects with the spiritual, social and economic realities of the communities within which evangelicals live and work. If they are to develop a contextually appropriate missiological paradigm, then Slavic evangelicals must not uncritically adopt the categories and concepts that have dominated missiological discourse in Western European or North American settings. Rather, as Reimer rightly insists, Russian and Eastern European evangelicalism will need to "collect its own mission-historical memory"[7] to engage with Scripture and develop a post-Soviet missiological paradigm that will invigorate the missional practice of the Slavic evangelical churches. This chapter is thus offered as a contribution to an ongoing conversation concerning the characteristics of an appropriate missiology for post-Soviet evangelicals.

The Need for a Contextual Missiology

Contextual theology teaches that shifts in theological paradigms invariably occur against a background of broader cultural change. Contextual theological engagement occurs not when theologians posit theories from their armchairs, but when communities of believers ask the question, "What would be a meaningful and empowering gospel message for the particular people in this specific culture that God has called us to serve in this particular region?" One of the most persistent themes of scholarship on mission in nations of the FSU has been the lament over the lack of contextualization of theological curricula and missional practices and methodologies.[8] Surveying the recent literature produced by Slavic evangelicals themselves on this issue, one of the most common themes that one finds to prevail in these

5. This term was also used in Elliott, "Theological Education after Communism," 67.

6. Reimer thus echoes the lament of Mykhailo Cherenkov, who has likewise called for a renewal of evangelical mission and theological education along the lines of a theologically robust and contextually relevant post-Soviet missiological paradigm. See Cherenkov, "Postsovetskiye yevangel'skiye tserkvi v poiskakh," 7–16.

7. Reimer, "Recovering the Missionary Memory," 139.

8. Sawatsky, "Visions in Conflict," 13, 20.

writings is that of "crisis."[9] On the way towards mapping the contours of a transformative contextual missional paradigm that could overcome this crisis, this chapter will draw on archetypes from the history of the FSU in order to illustrate the transformative potential of an integrated vision of "theological education as mission."[10]

The development of a holistic vision of theological education is particularly pertinent to Eastern Europe and the FSU, where the notion of compartmentalization tends to be alien to the Eastern Slavic mindset, which distinguished commentators from Berdyaev to Zernov have noted, inclines more towards integration, rather than atomization of segments and components.[11] Moreover, the contextualization of mission and theological education will necessitate a radical overhaul of the individualist modes of evangelization that were exported to Eastern Europe, Russia and Central Asia by Western missionaries following the demise of the USSR, but which were so unsuited to the communitarian context of the post-Soviet society.[12]

The Formational Imperative: Creating Agents of the Kingdom for the Transformation of Post-Soviet Society

Another unfortunate aspect of the importation of North American educational approaches to Eastern Europe and the FSU since the early 1990s has been an overemphasis on the concept of "worldview" and a concomitant neglect of the integrated formation of character that determines one's pre-critical orientation to the world.[13] Conservative evangelicals from North America have defined "worldview" as "a tapestry of interdependent ideas, principles and metaphysical claims that are derived from the Hebrew-Christian Scriptures."[14] It has further been argued that, "If the

---

9. See, for example, Cherenkov, *Baptizm bez kavychek*; Zhybryk, *Boh pod arestom*; Khoruzhyy, *Kryzys evropeyskoho cheloveka*, 41–49.

10. The notion of "theological education *as* mission" in the European context is developed from a variety of perspectives in Penner, *Theological Education*.

11. This point is helpfully illustrated in Parushev, "East and West," 31–44. See also Pilli, "Toward a Holistic View," 171–84.

12. Chapman, "Collectivism in the Russian World View."

13. Smith, *Imagining the Kingdom*, 13. The emphasis on "Christian worldview" as the aim of theological education has been particularly prevalent in conservative evangelical or fundamentalist literature. For example, see Dockery and Thornbury, *Shaping a Christian Worldview*.

14. Beckwith et al., *To Everyone an Answer*, 14; quoted in Smith, *Desiring the Kingdom*,

Christian worldview can be restored to a place of prominence and respect at the university, it will have a leavening effect throughout society."[15] The task of theological education was thus said to consist in forming students in "*the* Christian worldview" through the teaching of abstract principles pertaining to Christian ethical norms and metaphysical postulates, supposedly derived from Scripture. According to this conception, theological education is concerned not primarily with transforming students' material interaction with the world, but with changing students' beliefs about the world.

The basic problem with an educational approach which has as its primary goal the induction of students into a Christian worldview is that it is possible for learners to obtain intellectual cognition of Christian concepts in a way that does not shape their pre-critical orientation to life as embodied beings in the world. An overreliance on "worldview" can lead to a reductive presentation of Christian faith as a system of propositional truth claims, rather than as a comprehensive mode of being that radically alters one's material participation in the world.[16] Theological education must be concerned not only with the "life of the mind,"[17] but also with the formation of hopes and passions and the transfiguration of the imagination in ways that correspond to the Kingdom values of the gospel and which "evoke a radically transformed life of loving enemies, giving away worldly goods, and standing up against injustice."[18] Furthermore, the need to avoid reductive notions of Christian faith as a belief system of dogmatic propositional claims is accentuated by the degenerative process through which words have become meaningless in a culture that became accustomed to the lies and deceit of Soviet propaganda. In a post-communist society words have become devalued, first by Soviet propaganda and now by Western-style advertising, which has cheapened and degraded language and has led to the impoverishment of everyday vocabulary.

This is not to suggest that "worldview" is not an important aspect of formation or that the intellect, like the imagination, does not need to be transformed. Nevertheless, as James Smith rightly maintains, "human

31.

15. Moreland and Craig, *Philosophical Foundations*, 2.

16. Rollins refers to Christianity as "a radical transformation that alters one's mode of being in the world" (*Fidelity of Betrayal*, 95).

17. Smith, *Desiring the Kingdom*, 18.

18. Rollins, *Fidelity of Betrayal*, 100.

beings are not primarily 'thinking things' and cognitive machines."[19] Ernst Bloch claimed that to be human is to hope and that volition is determined primarily not by intellectual abstraction, but by vision and hope and an underlying "passion for the possible."[20] If we accept that, "behind every pedagogy is a philosophical anthropology,"[21] and that to be human is to hope, then it follows that theological education must go beyond inducting students into a Christian worldview through the impartation of facts and concepts and should take seriously the role of dreams, visions and the imagination as basic realities governing human volition.[22]

The need for an integrated transformative conception of theological education is even more critical in relation to post-Soviet society. The idea of an armchair theologian engaging in detached academic speculation is alien to the philosophical orientations and historical experience of the post-Soviet peoples. There has historically been a bias towards "practical philosophy" to the extent that, "Pure philosophy, in the sense of exclusively theoretical inquiry, never flourished in Russia."[23] Berdyaev explained that for those living in the shadow of Marx-Leninist ideology, which asserted "an indissoluble union between theory and practice," the ultimate sin was the attempt to distinguish between "philosophy and politics, between speculation and social building."[24] He castigated the "limitless social day dreaming, with no connection with actual reality," which he found in the intellectual life of parts of Europe.[25]

The Soviet system likewise inherited this long-established disdain for abstract theorizing and the aims of Soviet philosophies of education went far beyond inducting students into the worldview of Marx-Leninism. This becomes immediately apparent when one reads the atheist textbooks for

19. Smith, *Desiring the Kingdom*, 28.

20. Bloch, "Zur Ontologie," 41. The phrase "passion for the possible" (*eine Leidenschaft für das Mögliche*) is found in Moltmann, *Theologie*, 15. This phrase is attributed originally to Søren Kierkegaard. See Ricoeur, "Freiheit im Licht," 205.

21. Smith, *Desiring the Kingdom*, 27.

22. Macquarrie, *In Search of Humanity*, 3–4.

23. Copleston, *Philosophy in Russia*, 5.

24. Berdyaev, *End of Our Time*, 216.

25. Berdyaev, *Origin of Russian Communism*, 25. Although Berdyaev can be accused of overstating his case, many Western observers have likewise noted that since at least the beginning of the nineteenth century, Western theology has been characterized by rational, historical investigation. See Kirk, "Re-envisioning the Theological Curriculum."

students and teachers from the Soviet era.[26] Examples of such works include a dense textbook, titled *The Cultivation of an Active Atheist Position among Young Students*, published by the Soviet authorities in 1982:

> The Communist Workers Party regards education as an important front in the struggle for communism. One of the objectives of its program is the holistic formation of the individual and the development of the whole character, subject to the conditions and requirements of the communist society, and the ability to make use of all communism's material and spiritual benefits . . . Organizing the construction of a new society and purposefully carrying out this process, the Communist Party of the Soviet Union has created a coherent system of communist education for all workers, covering all social strata and groups, and using every form of economic, political, and, above all, ideological influence on the masses.[27]

As well as its repeated use of the term *vsestoroniy* ("holistic" or "comprehensive"; literally, "all-sided") in its description of the educational task, the book consistently argues for the need for active engagement in communist practices that will change the way that people habitually participate in the concrete reality of their material world. Another Soviet tract, titled *Atheistic Education in Higher Learning*, published in 1982, elucidated the main aims of communist education in terms of inculcating active and comprehensive participation in the building of socialist values: "through a system of higher education in our country many millions of Soviet youth representatives and new generations of educators are being trained through active labor and political activities to become the creators of new cultural values."[28] The Soviet system of education was concerned not merely to change students' worldviews, but aimed additionally at the development of "socially active, spiritually rich, harmoniously developed character[s]" through the comprehensive transformation of people's material practice.[29] The "most distinctive single feature" of communist education in the Soviet Union, according to one commentator, was that it encompassed "all educational aims and concerns." He continued, noting that "the shaping of the future through the training of children is a commitment which extends far beyond the class-

---

26. Many of these have been preserved in the Keston Archive. There are several illustrated textbooks that were clearly aimed at young children.

27. Tancher, *Vospytanye aktyvnoy ateystycheskoy pozytsyy*, 2.

28. Pashkov, *Ateystycheskoe vospytanye*, 3.

29. Konforovych, *Ateystycheskoe vospytanye*, 3.

room and the workshop into society, and indeed into the ways of thinking and perceiving human relationships of every kind."[30] Education had to be concerned, therefore, not merely with forming students' worldviews but with facilitating revolutionary activity that would transform the productive forces of the material structure of society. According to one Marxist philosopher of education, "The distinguishing element in the educational process of mankind is the social-productive involvement of man, which alters his environment."[31] The Soviet ideologues thus seem to have taken heed of Marx's critical observation in his *Thesen über Feuerbach* (1845) that, "Philosophers have only interpreted the world in various ways; but the real task is to alter it."

Although the Soviet Union no longer exists as a political entity, the Soviet aversion to abstract theorizing remains an important characteristic of post-Soviet intellectual life. That being the case, evangelical theological education should relinquish its fixation with questions of knowledge and worldview and should instead be conceived as a holistic and integrated task that is directed towards the transformation of those "material practices that shape the imaginative core of our being-in-the-world."[32] The efforts of Christian institutions of higher learning in the post-Soviet society should, accordingly, be directed towards not merely producing thinkers with a Christian worldview, but forming agents with a Kingdom mission. As Smith notes, "the end (*telos*) of Christian education is *action*: the Christian university is a place from which students are *sent* as ambassadors of the coming Kingdom of God."[33]

The crucial point is that the centralized Soviet education system recognized what one commentator calls "the supremacy of experience over purely theoretical constructions."[34] Education was directed not so much towards forming people in a Marx-Leninist worldview, but rather was aimed at equipping them to participate actively and energetically in the building of a utopian communist society in ways that were concrete, tangible and materially transformative. As one Soviet theorist put it: "The problem of philosophy and the problem of developing the consciousness stand in the

---

30. King, "Concept of Ideology," 1.

31. Suchodolski, *Grundlagen*, 408–9.

32. Smith, *Imagining the Kingdom*, 12, 15.

33. Ibid., 15.

34. Khoruzhyy, *Delo khrystyanskoho prosveshchenyya*, 31.

closest connection with the problem of transforming social life."[35] Berdyaev maintains that the communists' search for "a synthetic philosophical system wherein all theory and practice shall be indissolubly unified" was "admirable in many respects." Tellingly, Berdyaev argues that, Christians *"must do the same*—but in quite another name." Just as the Communists aimed to produce "a new man [*noviy chelovek*], a new psychic entity," so too, according to Berdyaev, should Christians put their hopes in "the birth of a new man."[36] The term "new man" was promoted by Marx-Leninist ideology in the form of the "new Soviet man" (*noviy sovetskiy chelovek*).[37] This concept was developed by Soviet propagandists to promulgate the idea of a new generation of people who would be endowed with Soviet virtues of discipline, selflessness, hard work and intelligence as a result of being nurtured in a Soviet culture and formed according to the material practices of Marx-Leninism.[38] Ironically, as noted in chapter 2, this term has subsequently been lampooned by some post-Soviet commentators as depicting a new type of degraded, servile human being,[39] known as *homo sovieticus*.[40]

Considering this book's vigorous and extensive critique of the Soviet system, it may seem perverse even to suggest that Christians in post-Soviet countries today could learn from the methodologies of Soviet ideologues from the communist past. However, like a rebel army that captures the weapons of an tyrannical oppressor and uses them against him, post-Soviet Christians might also be able to adapt some of the educational philosophies of the Soviet Union in order to understand the importance not only of changing students' worldviews, but of transforming their material practices in ways that serve the building of the Kingdom of God, rather than the Marx-Leninist utopian society. Therefore, although the atheist-materialistic ideological content of the Soviet education was gravely flawed, the methodologies pursued by Soviet pedagogues were remarkably effective in so far as they were directed towards people's material practices, rather than merely focusing on abstract "worldviews." The Soviet authorities aimed to

---

35. Suchodolski, *Grundlagen*, 24.

36. Berdyaev, *End of Our Time*, 256.

37. The notion of transfigured humanity is also a key theme of Eastern Orthodox theology; see Lossky, *Mystical Theology*, 220–35.

38. Berdyaev, *Sud'ba Rossyy*, 196.

39. There are obvious allusions here to Eph 4:24, which reads, "And that ye put on the new man, which after God is created in righteousness and true holiness" (KJV).

40. This term was invented by the prominent social critic Aleksandr Zinovyev in his book of the same title. See Zinoviev, *Homo Sovieticus*.

inculcate not intellectual acquiescence to an ideological system, but proactive conformity to an applied social philosophy that would transform the material reality of all those living under the system.[41]

As long as theological education was confined to the formation of a "Christian worldview," the Soviet authorities perceived little threat to their ideological hegemony. It is therefore understandable why permission was granted to the All-Union Council of Evangelical Christians-Baptists (AUCECB) in the 1960s to run a part-time theological correspondence course for trainee evangelical pastors. Topics included in the first curriculum were Christian Doctrine, Exegesis, Introduction to the Bible, Preaching, Pastoral Care, History of the ECB, and the Constitution of the USSR.[42] When one looks in more detail at the lecture notes for these courses offered by the AUCECB, the abstract theoretical content soon becomes apparent.[43] Apart from brief appendices containing summary biographies of Tolstoy and Dostoevsky, no attempt is made to connect the material to the Russian or Eurasian context. It is possible that these lecture notes, which were used for these courses, were in fact Russian translations of a work previously published in English, although it is not clear (at least not to us) what the original source might have been. The lack of contextualization of the topics covered in these courses may also be attributable to the strict state censorship on all material used by the AUCECB under the Soviet system, but it nevertheless underlies the point that some evangelical theological programmes, even before the collapse of the USSR, were largely focused on the formation of a "Christian worldview."

This is not to say, however, that all the Baptist training programmes were concerned solely with the issue of worldview. The courses appear to have been clearly focused on church practices, most of all on preaching. Alexander Popov, a young Baptist theologian who teaches at Moscow Theological Seminary, states that Baptist theological education in the USSR was "first of all focused on training preachers and, secondly, it addressed certain specific questions about particular ministries in the church."[44] Furthermore, Heinrich Klassen claims that the courses offered by the AUCECB in

41. Tancher, *Vospytanye aktyvnoy ateystycheskoy pozytsyy*; Belov, *Soderzhanye y metody*; Duranov, *Ateystycheskoe vospytanye*.

42. *Bratskyy Vestnyk*, 77.

43. These notes can be found under the heading "Nravstvennoye bogosloviye," in file <SU/Ort.15/18> in the Keston Archive.

44. Popov, "Evangelical Christians-Baptists," 164.

the time of the USSR were mainly concerned with mission (or witness).[45] Referring to Soviet Baptists, Klassen maintains that "Christianity effected [sic] the daily life of members in Christian churches and presented [in] this way a danger for socialism."[46] However, if this was the case, then judging by the content of the material for the AUCECB training programmes, this was in spite of—rather than because of—the training that Baptist leaders received from the Correspondence Course. Whether these initiatives were concerned with shaping students' worldviews or whether they aimed at improving competence in the performance of certain church practices, neither of these objectives translated into subversive social transformation for the sake of the Kingdom of God. They posed no great risk to the authorities and were thus to some extent tolerated by the Soviet system.

Although these kinds of evangelical educational initiatives were tolerated by the authorities and even began to flourish,[47] those learning communities that went beyond the notion of "worldview" or training in specific church practices and which aimed to instigate a transformation of the material reality of contemporary society through the development of a radical Christian anthropology were mercilessly—and often brutally—suppressed by the KGB. One such initiative was the Christian Seminar, which represented a contextual utopian vision that drew deeply from the wells of the Slavic literature, theology and philosophy.

Building a Utopian Community through Education: The Christian Seminar

As a learning community that represented an attempt to embody "God's truth in the language and culture of a people"[48], the Christian Seminar offers some important lessons from which leaders of all churches and seminaries (evangelical and Orthodox) in post-Soviet society could learn. The

---

45. Klassen, *Mission*.

46. Klassen, "Mission as Bearing Witness," 170.

47. According to one source (in file <SU Ort 15/18> of the Keston Archive), Leningrad Bible College, led by Ivan Prokhanov, helped to graduate more than six hundred preachers and pastors before the Soviet authorities closed the college down in 1927. Between 1968 and 1980, the Keston Institute reported that 207 students had graduated from the theological correspondence course run by the AUCECB.

48. Stamoolis, *Eastern Orthodox Mission Theology*, 61.

Christian Seminar was founded by young Orthodox intellectuals in 1974.[49] Explaining the founding of the Christian Seminar, one of the key early leaders remarked that, "As we were dissatisfied with the mere performance of a religious cult, had had no opportunity to receive a religious education and needed to establish brotherly Christian relations, we began in October 1974 to hold a religious and philosophical seminar."[50] Concerning its ultimate goals, the Christian Seminar aimed to become part of a mass youth movement that would culminate in "a new type of human community." A document dating back to 1979 expresses the utopian aspirations of those who founded the Seminar:

> We are all in need of a deeper and warmer type of communication: the force of active love must transfigure the world around us . . . It has become impossible to go on living in falsehood. An unbearably aimless existence in a frenzied world, dull attendance at useless jobs, meaningless debilitating disputes, faceless socialist culture, newspaper pathos and lies, lies, lies. Corrosive, destructive, humiliating lying motivated by fear, which some justify as caution, others as inevitability, others as wisdom . . . From the moment we are born, socialist culture presents us with a complete, total, and absolutely false image of the world. This world, excluding tragedy, compassion and in effect all Christian values from life, sets the pattern of one's life from birth to death with the dreary inevitability of fate.[51]

This vivid and lucid critique of life under Soviet communism can be applied just as pertinently to contemporary life in post-Soviet society. The eschatological language employed by the participants in the Christian Seminar has a profound resonance with some key themes in Slavic history and philosophy and the indebtedness of the Seminar's leaders to figures,

49. Ellis, "USSR," 92–101. Michael Bourdeaux quotes the vivid impressions of one participant concerning the setting and content of the meetings of the Christian Seminar. See Bourdeaux, *Risen Indeed*, 35.

50. Ogorodnikov, quoted in Bourdeaux, *Risen Indeed*, 30.

51. Letter written by five members of the Christian Seminar to sympathizers in North America (November/December 1979). Keston Archive <Ort 21/1/80>.

such as Berdyaev, Dostoevsky, Soloviev and Kavelin is apparent from their *samizdat*[52] publications.[53]

Despite their deeply pessimistic appraisal of their situation, the leaders of the Christian Seminar looked to the Christian faith, in particular to the peculiar synthesis of Christian eschatology and nationalistic messianism that was expressed in the so-called Russian Idea, associated with Dostoevsky and Soloviev:

> We feel that we are that living material out of which Christ will make all things new: a new community, a new culture, a new family, a new kind of man and a new kind of woman. Essentially, he is creating a new people out of us. But at the same time this is a return to the primal roots of the Russian national soul, which is trustingly thrown open to receive God's world and all the nations which live in it.[54]

Particularly noteworthy was the Christian Seminar's reliance on eschatological themes, which related to key elements of the literary and philosophical heritage of the Slavic peoples. Berdyaev wrote that, "there are two dominant myths which can become dynamic in the life of a people—the myth about origins and the myth about the end. For Russians it has been the second myth, the eschatological one, that has dominated." Berdyaev thus described Russians as "a people of the end" (*narod kontsa*).[55] Sergei Bulgakov likewise spoke of "apocalypse" as the defining aspect of the "sociology of our time."[56] The Christian Seminar was thus able to contextualize its message and connect it with deep themes in Russian history. The literature produced by the Christian Seminar testifies to the philosophical sophistication and theological erudition of its authors. It is perhaps owing

52. *Samizdat*, from the Russian word meaning "to self-publish," referred to a miscellaneous variety of uncensored work on various religious, literary and journalistic topics and current affairs as well as some creative work such as poems and novels. *Samizdat* was written by dissidents in the USSR and often appeared in typed or mimeographed form. *Samizdat* was circulated clandestinely throughout the Soviet Union.

53. The second issue of the Seminar's *samizdat* journal, *Obshschina*, contained articles with such titles as "The Ontological Problems of Russian Sophiology" and "Konstantin Kavelin on Nihilism."

54. Letter written by five members of the Christian Seminar to sympathizers in North America (November/December 1979). Keston Archive <Ort 21/1/80>.

55. Berdyaev, quoted in Bethea, *Shape of Apocalypse*, 12.

56. Bulgakov, quoted in Bortnes, "Religion," 125.

to the sophistication and complexity of its academic content that the Christian Seminar never became a mass movement.

The Christian Seminar, however, represented a lucid critique not only of the Marx-Leninist worldview, but also of the mundane material practices on which the continued existence of the whole Soviet system depended.[57] This critique drew heavily on the resources of Christian theology, particularly eschatology and utopia, and can serve as a model and inspiration for contemporary faith-based critiques of post-Soviet society. The essence of the social critique consisted in the indictment of Soviet society's neglect of human values that had been articulated by Russia's great literary and philosophical figures, such as Dostoevsky, Soloviev and Berdyaev and which were encapsulated in such concepts as *mir* (peace or world),[58] *obschschina* (community)[59] and, above all, *sobornost* (universal brotherhood).[60] Bringing these concepts into material reality would result in a "transvaluation of values" (*pereotsenka tsennostei*)—a Nietzschean term used by the members of the Christian Seminar to depict a wholesale transformation of society that would undermine all the tacit assumptions and material practices upon which the continued existence of the Soviet system depended.[61] Perhaps recognizing the grave threat to their ideological hegemony posed by these cultural critiques, the Soviet authorities suppressed these informal educational initiatives with disproportionate brutality that involved the detainment, torture, and forced confinement to psychological correction institutions of their leaders.[62]

---

57. For a helpful recent account of the activities of the seminar that focuses on the biography of one of its leaders, see Wolf, *Dissident for Life*.

58. Gustav Wetter writes that "it was only in the Russian people and their peasant institutions, the *Mir* and *Obshchina*, that the collectivist principles of an inbred solidarity were deployed to fullest effect" (*Dialectical Materialism*, 64).

59. "*Obshchina*," often translated into English as "community," can more accurately be rendered as "the inborn spirit of collectivism."

60. The term *sobornost* is more accurately translated by Boris Jakim as "the authentic spirit of community." See Berdyaev, *End of Our Time*, 216.

61. The term *pereotsenka tsennostei* was a translation from the German "Umwertung aller Werte," which Nietzsche used in his *Also sprach Zarathustra*. One of the leaders of the Christian Seminar, Ogorodnikov, used the term in his essay "Sovremennaya russkaya kul'tura."

62. Alexander Ogorodnikov, one of the main leaders of the Christian Seminar, was only twenty-eight years old when he was arrested in November 1978. He was sentenced to a forced labor camp for six years, followed by five years' exile. Another founding member of the seminar, Tatyana Shchipkova, was likewise arrested in 1980, charged with

Christian institutions of higher education in post-Soviet society today that are looking to go beyond the "worldview" model of theological formation could learn from the example of the Christian Seminar. Future evangelical initiatives in theological education should be based not on Western models of evangelism that emphasize the imperative of individual conversions and which promote pre-packaged versions of Christianity that are designed to sell to mass audiences on an open consumer market. In order to avoid the problem of a lack of integration of educational methods and local cultural contexts, Christian institutions of higher education in the FSU should recognize "the cultural dependency of all forms of gospel witness."[63] Accordingly, in terms of mission and theological education in post-Soviet society, the emphasis should be placed on the concepts of *mir*, *obschschina*, and *sobornost*. In particular these concepts can be used to connect the message of the gospel with the realities of contemporary culture in regions throughout the post-Soviet space. Any initiative that were to be built on such a foundation would not merely be more relevant and applicable to the history and traditions of Eastern European Slavic cultures, but would arguably be much more faithful to the message of the gospel—a gospel which is concerned not solely with individual conversions, but also with the creation of redeemed communities of men and women inspired with a vision to transform the wider world for the sake of the Kingdom of God.

The Limits of Contextualization

It may be objected that this chapter's allusion to generalized terms such as "Slavic missional paradigm" and "Eastern Slavic mindset" contradicts the main argument concerning the necessity of developing contextualized models of mission and theological education that are appropriate to post-Soviet society. While acknowledging the obvious diversity between the various independent nation states, many of which have their own distinctive cultures, histories and languages, there is also much more that they have in common. The cultural and linguistic differences between, for instance, Russia and Belarus or between Ukraine and Bulgaria, are relatively minor compared to the differences between any of these countries and the United Kingdom or the United States. Therefore, even if a "Slavic missional paradigm" cannot be applied uniformly to every context of theological

"malicious hooliganism," and sentenced to three years in a labor camp.

63. Curtis Freeman, Introduction to McClendon, *Witness*, xxxii–xxxiii.

education in the FSU, if such a model were applied in this way, it would still be immeasurably more in tune with the local context than a model imported from the UK or the USA.

Learning from the Past to Reimagine the Future

In order to chart the course for theological education in the FSU, it is necessary for evangelicals to situate themselves historically within the context of broader trends of their regional histories. The leaders of evangelical seminaries would gain considerable insight and wisdom from reading about the history, not only of their predecessors in the Baptist movement, but also of educational initiatives that originated out of different traditions, such as the Christian Seminar. Unlike the Bible Correspondence Course of the AUCECB—and in contrast to other previous short-lived evangelical theological residential courses established in the early years of the USSR[64] whose educational aims were limited to the training of pastors and preachers—the Christian Seminar offered a more comprehensive vision of holistic theological education. It is important that the vision of the Christian Seminar should be revived and contextualized for the contemporary setting, because its social critique and profound connection to the history and spiritual reality of Russia and Eastern Europe, are as relevant and necessary today as the were at the height of Soviet power.

Nevertheless, a valid criticism can be made that the Christian Seminar was too idealistic and utopian in its outlook and that its aims. Its goal of building "a new community, a new culture, a new family, a new kind of man and a new kind of woman" would have been unfeasible, even in the most auspicious social and political conditions, and utterly impossible in the adverse context of Soviet censorship and suppression. The evangelical leaders of the AUCECB may have set out fairly limited educational aims (i.e., training pastors and preachers for ministry to local congregations),[65] but they were at least achievable, even in the unfavorable circumstances created by the Soviet regime. The challenge for the next generation of evangelical leaders in the education sector working in the FSU is to learn from the example of groups such as the Christian Seminar and the AUCECB and to develop new and creative programmes of theological education that will equip people with the conceptual resources to engage in cogent philosophi-

---

64. These initiatives are summarized in Popov, "Evangelical Christians-Baptists," 162.

65. Ibid., 164.

cal critiques of culture (i.e., in the tradition of the Christian Seminar), while still attending to the immediate pastoral and missional needs of churches (i.e., as the AUCECB sought to do).

The salient question that arises from the foregoing reflections is a simple one: Would it be possible to combine the following elements: (1) the idealism and passion of the Christian Seminar and (2) the attention to the immediate pastoral and missional needs of local churches demonstrated by the AUCECB with (3) the focus on the transformative dimensions of material practice evinced by the Soviet educational philosophies? In engaging with this question, the aim is not uncritically to adopt the methods of the past, but to re-envision them from the perspective of the Kingdom of God in order to invigorate mission and theological education in the post-Soviet society today.

A Dream and a Vision: "Eastern European Christian University"

Since leaving Donetsk Christian University, both authors have been dreaming about the creation of a major center of Christian education in Eastern Europe that would become a beacon of hope for the whole region. This dream, at its heart, is a vision of unity. This center of learning would unite all the various divided, crisis-ridden, struggling and ineffectual Bible schools and academies that currently exist in this region. We like to call this integrated community of learning, the "Eastern European Christian University," but so far it exists only in our imagination and in the hopes of a few like-minded friends in Ukraine, Belarus and Russia. This learning community would be generously evangelical in its theological outlook and would welcome Christians of other faith traditions to contribute to the development of the university's ethos and values.

In our increasingly interconnected and globalized world, strategic partnerships, built on relationships of trust and respect, will play an ever more crucial role in university-level education. One of the major tasks of Christian academic leadership today is therefore to identify points of convergence where visions and values meet and to initiate and nurture the kind of transformative relationships that will help us to surmount the challenges that we face. It is our hope that these relationships would flourish and develop in such a way as to lay a path towards the eventual merger of several Christian institutions in this region in order to form a single community of learning. This is the conviction that lies behind the vision of a new united center of Christian learning in Eastern Europe. The Eastern European Christian University would manifest the presence and hope of the Kingdom of God and the values of freedom, integrity and humanity to a region that continues to bear the scars of the Soviet legacy.

A recurring thesis of this book has been that the main aim of theological education should not simply be to train future pastors in the skills of practical church ministry, but to liberate people to become effective change agents of society and to bring their Christian faith to bear in every sphere of their professional lives. This university would thus be a hub of Christian academic excellence from which the Kingdom values of hope, hospitality, humanity, compassion and generosity would be disseminated not only into churches, but also into the wider society. The university would thereby become a prototype of the heavenly city in which diverse peoples from a multitude of nations are unified and reconciled through the compassionate and gentle, yet inexorable, workings of divine grace.

Moreover, the research and teaching practices of this university would be rooted in the vision of the Kingdom of God in which the values of mutual respect, humanity and servanthood would determine the coordinates of communal life. The faculty chairs would be occupied by women and men of integrity, warmth and compassion who would seek only to serve the other members of their community, rather than their own careers and interests. These faculties would be occupied by people who would recognize that there is no greater crown for their labors than the reward of seeing their students thriving and flourishing and growing in faith and knowledge and thereby becoming more effective laborers in the great vineyard of God's Kingdom. Instead of jostling for position in crude power games that destroy trust and undermine personal integrity, the members of the faculties of this university would be people for whom career and promotion were less important than serving the collective interests of the community of students and fellow teachers and administrative colleagues. When tenures were to be granted or promotions were to occur, they would be used not for self-promotion purposes, but would be received joyfully and humbly as an opportunity to increase one's capacity to serve.

Instead of being an industry of investigative ferment driven by powerful vested interests, the *research* of this university would be directed toward the pursuit of a kind of knowledge that would provide a solid basis for action and which would be orientated towards practical wisdom.[66] The university would gratefully acknowledge the tremendous contributions of science to modern life, but would nevertheless recognize that many of the issues that most concern human life cannot become subjects of scientific methodologies and that the empirical sciences do not have a monopoly on knowledge and truth.[67]

There is so much more that could be said about this dream, but our aim here is not to write a separate treatise or to anticipate every possible objection or criticism. Doubtless this dream is naive; perhaps it is unfeasibly utopian and abstract. Nevertheless, we will continue to cherish the hope that with God all things are possible and that we and those who share this vision might yet live to witness the opening of the "Eastern European Christian University."

66. Willard, "Bible, the University and the God," 17–39.
67. Ibid., 27.

Conclusion

The Story Continues: Predictions and Recommendations

"Post-Soviet evangelical Christianity" is released from captivity precisely to the extent that it ceases to be post-Soviet (i.e., although "post," but still Soviet in that we bear the scars of the tragic experience of the Soviet repression, marginalization and exclusion). In Ukraine, the prolongation of the Soviet transition was interrupted by Maidan. In Russia, judging by the current trends, the restoration of Sovietism is possible, and with it, a corresponding clampdown on evangelical churches. Backslides into a Soviet ethos are possible anywhere at anytime, but the mainstay for the development of evangelical churches remains a simple and open Christianity that is free, humble, generous, hospitable, full of grace, and ready to listen, learn and serve.

After Maidan, the evangelical movement in post-Soviet society has an unprecedented opportunity to become a shining example of a "Church without walls," serving not itself, but the whole of society, representing the Kingdom of God in all spheres of life. In the coming years we will see a flowering of evangelical ecumenism in action. Christian solidarity will flourish and will overflow denominational boundaries and parochial vested interests. Suddenly, we shall encounter the long-awaited Christian unity, but not in the Church institution, not in dogma, but outside the walls of the Church: in the missionary "field" and in the midst of society.

Another place where we will witness and experience the manifestations of the revived spirit of the Christian community will be in the Christian university or seminary. It is here that a holistic vision of spiritual growth is made possible. Theological education can combine devotion to the writings of the early Fathers, commitment to catholic social teaching, and fidelity to the spirit of the Reformation. All of these can be taught in one and the same evangelical Protestant seminary. The kind of understanding and mutual respect that promotes Christian unity is the fruit born in work and study, not in church disputes and interdenominational polemics. In the coming years we will see a new generation of young leaders who may not become pastors of churches, but will nonetheless be authoritative and influential. We will see the displacement of the centers of influence from the church offices to educational institutions, theological think tanks, and the media. We will witness, in other words, the emergence of a "Church without walls."

The experience of the Ukrainian Greek Catholic Church demonstrates that the development of the Church does not necessarily launch a movement simultaneously on all fronts of the current issues. At the start, it is sufficient to create a powerful intellectual center, the Ukrainian Catholic University (UCU). UCU has become not only an educational resource for the UGCC, but also a center of transformative education for the whole country, a place that attracts thinkers among the youth, the politicians, businessmen and journalists alike. This is a notable example of the realization in a single project of purely theological and missionary objectives, a combination of the interests of the Church and those of society.[1] Interestingly, back in 1908, a prominent leader of the Russian Baptists, Vasily Pavlov, suggested creating a unified educational center in Ukraine: "I am of the opinion that for all nationalities in Russia we should introduce a single provisional seminary . . . As for its location, then I suggest . . . in Odessa near many Russian and German communities."[2]

In the coming years we will see many surprises: new ecclesiastical forms, an inter-denominational theological movement, a rediscovery of the

1. Among the successful initiatives for building a Protestant Christian University, LCC International University in Klaipeda, Lithuania, is worth noting. Its non-denominational status offers many advantages for the development of educational programs, but its theological influence and contacts with churches are rather limited. In addition, with the accession of Lithuania to the EU, LCC is now outside the post-Soviet space, and therefore inaccessible to many due to cultural, financial, and visa policies.

2. Pavlov, *Načalo, razvitie i nastojašee položenie*, 94.

main Christian truths, a re-envisioning of communality, a genuine spiritual hunger and powerful awakening, the transforming vitality of the Holy Spirit in action, including the gift of the tongues and the power of prophetic testimony. But all this will require, and, in fact, requires right now our readiness to abandon "business as usual," and to move out of the shadow of the Soviet past and away from formulaic responses. We need to shun easy answers and to turn away from the familiar system of coordinates, which we have uncritically adopted from previous generations.

Our hope and our future are directly connected with this freedom to move forward. The evangelical community should live not in nostalgia for the Soviet past and a desire to return to "the good old days." Rather, in joyful fulfillment of God's perfect will, we should demonstrate a gracious acceptance of new circumstances and the ability to discern in them the miraculous providential plan of the "God of incalculable surprises."[3] Our emergence from the post-Soviet transition does not mark an end; rather it is a promising continuation of the major history of evangelical renewal in Eurasia. We do not choose the era or society in which we are destined to live, but we can accept all that we encounter as opportunities to fulfill the Great Commission handed down to us by God: "'For I know the plans I have for you,' declares the LORD, 'plans to prosper you and not to harm you, plans to give you a future and a hope'" (Jer 29:11).

We foresee a time in which post-Soviet theology will come of age as Christians embrace the opportunities that God is offering to churches in this pivotal region. Maidan and the revolutionary events that followed can be interpreted in the providence of God as a divine summons to all Christians living in post-Soviet society, but particularly to evangelicals, to repent of their fear-induced social inertia and pietistic withdrawal from the world. Maidan may prove to be God's gracious call to Christians in this region to engage proactively in the transformation of social structures, to demonstrate solidarity with those fighting for freedom and justice and thereby to become salt and light to their society. Ukraine has blazed a new trail out of the post-Soviet captivity of the Church, which other countries in the region may now follow. Perhaps, whenever Putin and his Kremlin apparatchiks are finally forced to release their stranglehold on Russian public opinion and when the Church in Russia rediscovers its true prophetic voice, even Russia itself will have its own "Maidan" on Red Square. As *homo sovieticus* gradually gives way to *homo maidanus*, this may be followed by similar

---

3. McClendon, *Ethics*, 265.

revolutions in Minsk and Astana and perhaps even in Bishkek, Tashkent, Dushanbe and Ashgabat.

Whatever might happen in the political sphere, we can predict a movement toward the Church's radical openness to the world and a concomitant transformative theological development, which will lead to a distancing from defunct models of ministry and mission. An exit from the post-Soviet transition will require a renewal of our social position and missional practice, as well as theological revaluations, a new hermeneutics of the biblical text and Church tradition, and a reevaluated understanding of our social and political responsibilities. We will need to reimagine the meaning and significance of basic terms, such as "power," "the world," and "culture," in the light of the gospel witness. We will need to overcome dichotomies between the spiritual and the intellectual, between revelation and science, and wisdom and knowledge. We will need to properly demarcate between the spheres of legitimate influence of the Church, the State and society, by rediscovering our responsibilities as citizens of our nations and of God's Kingdom. We also need to learn to avoid the extremes of national exclusivism and naive Westernism.

In light of these challenges, we can recommend a series of practical steps aimed at ushering the Church, and its mission, theology and education, toward an open vision characterized by maturity, competence, integrity, and transparency:

- The creation of unified cultural and educational center to be shared by evangelical churches in the post-Soviet space. Such a center will bring together the best of humanist intellectuals, theologians, missiologists and clergy.

- The construction of a multi-tiered system of continuing education for leaders and members of churches. This would range from informal leadership training as outlined in "School Without Walls"[4] for potential ministers to doctoral programs for the development of the best existing clergy.

- An ad hoc association of professional Christians, which is able to offer the Church and society timely, qualitative analytics, the monitoring of religious freedom, and annual reports on trends in religious life, theological education, and Church-society relations.

---

4. Cherenkov, "School Without Walls," 16–25.

- Preparation for the leading evangelical denominations of fundamental theological documents. These documents would provide clarity on issues including: principles of faith, social teachings, missions and missiology, the place and role in the history of the country and the region, and the Christian presence in education and science.

- The organization of a series of international consultations on the identity of post-Soviet evangelical Protestantism in its relationship with Western Protestantism and Russian Orthodoxy.

- A resumption of the work of the Theological Society of Eurasia (which operated in 2000–2003) or the establishment of a national theological society (similar to the "Bible Societies").

- An intensification of publishing activities to help teacher-theologians and clergy, focusing on three key areas: Western Protestant theology (the "high" theology of the "Global North"), national evangelical authors,[5] and non-Western theology (the national theology of the "Global South").

- The establishment of interfaith relations in the areas of social theology and theological education with the dominant historical denominations with the aim of consolidating positions and collaborating in securing protection in the public sphere.

- The launch of a series of briefings for journalists and experts containing theological assessments of events and annual summaries for the Church and the world would also signify transparency and accountability on the part of the Church and would consolidate the service of the theological community to society.

- The creation of an ecclesiastical and national endowment for theology and theological education.

- In collaboration with professional sociologists and missiologists, the conduction of a large-scale sociological study that produces realistic results of missionary activity and church growth, and the impact of theological education[6] and a picture of theological orientations.

---

5. The series National Evangelical Authors is published by the Association for Spiritual Renewal. The specialized publishing house Colloquium (Cherkassy, Ukraine) gives priority to national authors. Several domestic scholars have been published by the Orthodox publisher Biblical Theological Institute (Moscow).

6. For a precedent, see EAAA, "Effectiveness of Theological Education," 192.

- The organization of a series of consultations[7] by leaders of theological schools, missions and church alliances with the aim of reaching agreement on positions and working out a strategy for the development of effective forms of theological education to render aid to churches and missions.

- The conclusion of an agreement on cooperation between Christian, public and private universities, the outlining of plans for joint consultations, projects and events to integrate theology and theological education in the scientific community.

- The inclusion of the topic of education as a form of mission in the program of missionary consultations and conferences.

These recommendations are dictated by the logical development of evangelical churches in the post-Soviet space. They aim to put into practice what was proposed by the great leaders of the evangelical movement, Ivan Prokhanov, Vladimir Martsinkovsky and Vasily Pavlov. Pavlov defined the immediate tasks as follows: "The first and most important task is to preach the gospel. To achieve this, we need to have people capable of this. To this day, we have only had preachers without the benefit of an education . . . We need to give our preachers, and if possible, the best education so that they can meet the challenges of the times. This need points us to our second problem, namely, we must build a theological seminary."[8] The list of steps to be taken goes on: the production and distribution of Christian literature, a foundation to help churches and preachers, the construction of a missionary home in St. Petersburg.

Thus, not only the challenges of our time, not only the anticipation of the future, but also the traditions of the past demand from today's post-Soviet churches the restoration of the broken connections between the Church, mission, theology and education. Therefore, the forthcoming labor of collecting these broken fragments and reconstructing in its entirety the missiological picture should begin not with invention and innovation, but with a recollection, consolidation and continuation of what has already been started. In the end, our future and hope are not the product of our inventions nor the fruit of our labor, at least not at first. Above all, we must remember that our future and our hope are embedded in history and given

7. See an interesting and completely representative study by Dyatlik, "What Expectations Do Pastors and Local Churches," 97–119.

8. Pavlov, *Načalo, razvitie i nastojašee položenie*, 95.

to us by God as a promise and as a gift. According to this providential view of history, hope is a dynamic force that sustains and nurtures the future of the evangelical churches, including those in the gloomy post-Soviet era. This era signifies nothing more than a transition to a different condition, which will be more authentically Christian than an atheist or nominally Orthodox past. The painful travails of the post-Soviet transition are like birth pangs that presage the beginning of a new era of hope and renewal. Thus evangelicals in the former USSR have every reason to look to the future with hope as they understand their mission in the light of God's great plan for the redemption of the nations and the reconciliation of all things.

Afterword

While reading this work by Mykhailo Cherenkov and Joshua Searle, two of my closest colleagues, I could not help but be optimistic about the future of the evangelical movement and its mission in Eurasia. These two bright young scholars are the products of two very different upbringings and worldviews: Dr Searle was raised and educated in the post-Christian West, where his father had a leading position among the British Baptists; Dr Cherenkov, by contrast, was raised in the underground church behind the Iron Curtain, where his father had been imprisoned for his faith. While these men hail from sharply contrasting backgrounds, they are now both leaders of a new missional movement focused on spiritual transformation through the Next Generation.

This is a miracle from God, since I believe that something significant has happened to the evangelical movement during the past twenty five years, following the fall of the Iron Curtain. The dynamic church growth that took place during the early 1990s has now been replaced by visible stagnation. However, the impassioned words of these two young scholars give me reason to hope, because they are committed to searching for new strategies and applying new concepts that will help equip the Church to transform their communities through the Next Generation. I am confident that these new concepts in leadership education and missional strategies can help to overcome the manifold crises that confront the Church and society in this part of the world.

During the past twenty five years, through the efforts of many different churches and para-church organizations, thousands of church leaders have been trained; hundreds of missionaries have moved to remote areas to plant new churches and hundreds of Christian educators have begun teaching at new Bible schools and seminaries. However, there seems to be little cohesion or connection among these various initiatives. In this work, Dr Searle and Dr Cherenkov encourage an ongoing reformation of mission and ministry in the FSU. The vision that they set out will bring cohesion and united endeavor in working towards the reformation of the Church and the transformation of post-Soviet society through the dynamic engagement of the emerging generation of young scholars and church leaders.

The crisis that emerged between Russia and Ukraine in early 2014 presents an enormous challenge that may trigger unrest throughout the entire Eurasian region or even have a global historical significance. However, I would like to suggest that this crisis can and should be used as an opportunity to advance the gospel. I wholeheartedly agree with Dr Searle and Dr Cherenkov that the future of these countries, even during this time of crisis, is in the hands of the Next Generation. I also believe that this Next Generation must be open to the moving of the Holy Spirit through new strategies and outreach models that will facilitate the renewal and transformation of churches, communities, and whole nations.

The Next Generation has great opportunities to advance the gospel, but it also bears great responsibilities to the Church and to the wider society. In these times of crisis and increased persecution, especially in parts of Russia and Central Asia, it is imperative that the Church does not retreat again behind its walls, as it did during the Soviet years. The Next Generation must help the post-Soviet Church to become part of the global evangelical movement by gaining fresh experiences and initiating new dialogues.

As Dr Cherenkov and Dr Searle discuss in this important work, it is my desire that the Next Generation not only pursue educational opportunities, but that they are strategically mobilized and prepared for effective leadership roles that will bring dynamic transformation through the Church to the whole of post-Soviet society. After reading this hope-filled work, I am confident that the light at the end of the long and dark post-Soviet tunnel is finally approaching.

Dr Sergey Rakhuba
President, Russian Ministries

Bibliography

Anderson, Ray S. *The Shape of Practical Theology: Empowering Ministry with Theological Praxis*. Downers Grove: InterVarsity, 2001.

Andreyev, L. and K. Elbakian. "Is the Law of God from God?" *Independent Military Review* 07 (2012). http://nvo.ng.ru/history/2012-03-07/7_zakon.html.

Arjakovsky, Antoine. "The Role of the Churches in the Ukrainian Revolution." *ABC Religion and Ethics*, 6 March 2014. http://www.abc.net.au/religion/articles/2014/03/06/3958163.htm.

―――. "Theological Education in the Ukraine: The Case of the Master of Ecumenics Program in Lviv." In *Handbook of Theological Education in World Christianity: Theological Perspectives, Ecumenical Trends, Religious Surveys*, edited by Dietrich Werner et al., 527–28. Oxford: Regnum, 2010.

Åslund, Anders. *How Ukraine Became a Market Economy and Democracy*. Washington, DC: Peter G. Peterson Institute for International Economics, 2009.

Åslund, Anders, and Michael McFaul. *Revolution in Orange: The Origins of Ukraine's Democratic Breakthrough*. Washington, DC: Carnegie Endowment for International Peace, 2006.

Bauman, Zygmunt, and Leonidas Donskis. *Moral Blindness: The Loss of Sensitivity in Liquid Modernity*. Cambridge: Polity, 2013.

Beckwith, Francis, et al., ed. *To Everyone an Answer: A Case for the Christian Worldview*. Downers Grove, IL: InterVarsity, 2004.

Belov, A. V. *Soderzhanye y metody ateystycheskoho vospytanyya shkol'nykov*. Moscow: Pedahohyka, 1984.

Berdyaev, Nikolai. *The Divine and the Human*. London: Geoffrey Bles, 1969.

―――. *The End of Our Time*. New York: Sheed and Ward, 1933.

―――. *The End of Our Time*. Translated by Boris Jakim. San Rafael: Semantron, 2009.

―――. *The Origin of Russian Communism*. Translated by R. M. French. London: Geoffrey Bles, 1937.

―――. *Sud'ba Rossyy: Opyty po psykholohyy voyny y natsyonal'nosty*. 2nd ed. Moscow: Mysl', 1990.

―――. *Ystoky y smysl russkoho kommunyzma*. Paris: YMCA, 1955.

Bethea, D. *The Shape of Apocalypse in Modern Russian Fiction*. Princeton: Princeton University Press, 1989.

Bevans, Stephen B. *Models of Contextual Theology*. Maryknoll, NY: Orbis, 2004.

Bevans, Stephen B., and Roger P. Schroeder. *Constants in Context: A Theology of Mission for Today*. Maryknoll, NY: Orbis, 2004.

Bincarovs'kij, Dmytro. "Protestantizm bez Reformacii." *Filosofs'ka Dumka* 4 (2013) 212–29.

Bloch, Ernst. "Zur Ontologie des Noch-Nicht-Seins." In *Auswahl aus seinem Schriften*, edited by Ernst Bloch, 41. Hamburg: Fischer, 1967.

Bociurkiw, Bohdan R. "The Rise of the Ukrainian Autocephalous Orthodox Church, 1919–22." In *Church, Nation and State in Russia and Ukraine*, edited by Geoffrey A. Hosking, 228–49. London: Macmillan, 1991.

Bonhoeffer, Dietrich. *Ethics.* Moscow: BBI, 2013.

Bonnett, Alastair. *Left in the Past: Radicalism and the Politics of Nostalgia.* New York: Continuum, 2010.

Bortnes, Jostein. "Religion." In *The Cambridge Companion to the Classic Russian Novel*, edited by Malcolm V. Jones and Robin Feuer Miller, 125. Cambridge: Cambridge University Press, 1998.

Bosch, David J. *Transforming Mission: Paradigm Shifts in Theology of Mission.* Maryknoll: Orbis, 1991.

Bourdeaux, Michael. *Gorbachev, Glasnost and the Gospel.* London: Hodder and Stoughton, 1990.

———. *Risen Indeed: Lessons in Faith from the USSR.* London: Darton, Longman and Todd, 1983.

Bratskyy Vestnyk 4 (1968) 77.

Bremer, Thomas. *Kreuz und Kreml: Kleine Geschichte der orthodoxen Kirche in Russland.* Freiburg: Herder, 2007.

Bromet, E. J., et al. "The State of Mental Health and Alcoholism in Ukraine." In *The WHO World Mental Health Surveys: Global Perspectives on the Epidemiology of Mental Disorders*, edited by Ronald C. Kessler and T. Bedirhan Ustun. New York: Cambridge University Press, 2008.

Brown, Cheryl, and Wes Brown. "Progress and Challenge in Theological Education in Central and Eastern Europe." *Transformation* 20 (2003) 1–12.

Bulgakov, Sergei. *The Bride of the Lamb.* Translated by B. Jakim. Grand Rapids: Eerdmans, 2002.

———. *Karl Marx as a Religious Type: His Relation to the Religion of Anthropotheism of L. Feuerbach.* Translated by Luba Barna. Belmont: Nordland, 1979.

———. *Unfading Light: Contemplations and Speculations.* Grand Rapids: Eerdmans, 2012.

Buttrick, David. *Preaching Jesus Christ: An Exercise in Homiletic Theology.* Philadelphia: Fortress, 1988.

Center for the Study of Global Christianity. "Christianity in Its Global Context, 1970–2020: Society, Religion, and Mission." http://www.gordonconwell.edu/resources// Global-Context-of-Christianity.cfm.

Chapman, Steven R. "Collectivism in the Russian World View and Its Implications for Christian Ministry." *East-West Church and Ministry Report* 6 (1998) 12–14.

Cherenkov, Mykhailo N. *Baptizm bez kavychek. Ocherki i materialy k diskussii o budushchem yevangel'skikh tserkvey.* Cherkassy: Kollokvium, 2012.

———. "Evangelical Christians and the Orthodox Church." http//www.risu.org.ua/en/ index/expert_thought/open_theme/40240.

———. "Postsovetskiye yevangel'skiye tserkvi v poiskakh podkhodyashchey missiologii: Global'nyye tendentsii i mestnyye realii." *Bogoslovskiye razmyshleniya* 12 (2011) 7–16.

———. "Post-Soviet Churches Struggle to Identify their Strategic Missiology."

———. "School Without Walls and the Local Church: A Model of Informal Leadership Training in Post-Soviet Countries." *Common Ground Journal* 8 (2011) 16–25. http://www.commongroundjournal.org.

———. "The Theology of Post-Soviet Evangelical Churches in the Intellectual Context of Postmodernity: From Historical Reconstructions to Future Projects."

———. "Toward a Relevant Missiology for Post-Soviet Evangelicals." *Theological Reflections* 12 (2011) 49–58.

Comaroff, Jean, and John L. Comaroff. "Millennial Capitalism: First Thoughts on a Second Coming." In *Millennial Capitalism and the Culture of Neoliberalism*, edited by Jean Comaroff and John L. Comaroff, 1–56. Durham: Duke University Press, 2001.

Copleston, Frederick C. *Philosophy in Russia: From Herzen to Lenin and Berdyaev*. Tunbridge Wells: Search, 1986.

Cottrell, Stephen. *From the Abundance of the Heart*. London: Longman, Darnton and Todd, 2006.

Cox, Gary. "Making Mission Possible." *Frontier*, July/August 1990, 7–8.

Crossman, R. H., ed. *The God That Failed: Six Studies in Communism*. New York: Columbia University Press, 2001.

Dmitrenko, O. *Vid ponedilka do p'jatnici*. Kyiv: Patronat, 2011.

Dockery, D. S., and G. A. Thornbury. *Shaping a Christian Worldview: The Foundations of Christian Higher Education*. Nashville: Broadman and Holman, 2002.

Dostoevsky, Fyodor Mikhailovich. *The Brothers Karamazov*. Translated by Constance Garnett. Hazleton: An Electronic Classics Series, 2013.

Drane, John. *Faith in a Changing Culture: Creating Churches for the Next Century*. London: Marshall Pickering, 1997.

———. *The McDonaldization of the Church: Spirituality, Creativity and the Future of the Church*. London: DLT, 2000.

Dubrovskij, A. "Fundamentalizm kak tormozjashhij faktor v razvitii evangel''skih cerkvej postsovetskogo perioda." *Forum* 20 (2011) 27–45.

Dudar N. P., and L. I. Shanhina. *Vira y relihiya v zhytti ukrayintsiv*. Kyiv: Tsentr Razumkova, 2001.

Duranov, M. E. *Ateystycheskoe vospytanye shkol'nykov: Voprosy teoryy y praktyky*. Moscow: Pedahohyka, 1986.

Durkot, Juri. "Zwanzig Jahre danach. Der mühsame gesellschaftliche Wandel in der Ukraine." In *Religion und Wende in Ostmittel- und Südosteuropa, 1989–2009*, edited by Johann Marte et al., 219. Innsbruck: Tyrolia-Verlag, 2010.

Dyatlik, Taras. "What Expectations Do Pastors and Local Churches in the FSU Have of Higher Theological Education at the Beginning of the 21st Century?" *Theological Reflections* 10 (2009) 97–119.

EAAA. "The Effectiveness of Theological Education in Ukraine: A Research Project." *Theological Reflections* 7 (2006) 178–205.

The Economist (10 December, 2011).

Edgar, Scott D. "Faculty Development for Post-Soviet Protestant Seminaries: With Special Reference to Ukraine." *East-West Church and Ministry Report* 17 (2009) 5–7.

Elliott, Mark R. "The Current Crisis in Protestant Theological Education in the FSU." *East-West Church and Ministry Report* 18 (2010) 15–16.

———. "The Current Crisis in Protestant Theological Education in the FSU." In *History and Mission in Europe*, edited by Mary Raber and Peter F. Penner, 213–36. Schwarzenfeld: Neufeld, 2011.

————. "Post-Soviet Theological Education: Highlights of Two Doctoral Dissertations." *East-West Church and Ministry Report* 8 (2000) 9–10.

————. "Theological Education after Communism: The Mixed Blessing of Western Assistance." *Asbury Theological Journal* 50 (1995) 67–73.

————. "Theological Education after Communism: The Mixed Blessing of Western Assistance." *East-West Church and Ministry Report* 3 (1995) 11–12.

Ellis, Jane. "USSR: The Christian Seminar." *Religion in Communist Lands* 8 (1980) 92–101.

Epstein, Mikhail. "Post-Atheism, or Minimal Religion." *Oktiabr* 9 (1996) 158–65.

Erlanger, Steven. "Ukrainian Leader's Defeat Worries Kiev Bureaucrats." *New York Times*, 13 July 1994. http://www.nytimes.com/1994/07/13/world/ukrainian-leader-s-defeat-worries-kiev-bureaucrats.html.

Erlikman, Vadim. *Poteri narodonaseleniia v XX veke*. Moscow: Spravochnik, 2004.

Evangelical Alliance Commission on Unity and Truth among Evangelicals. *Evangelicalism and the Orthodox Church*. Carlisle: Paternoster, 2001.

Fairbairn, Donald. *Eastern Orthodoxy Through Western Eyes*. Louisville: John Knox, 2002.

————. *Inymi glazami. Vzglyad evangelsrogo khristianina na vostochnoye pravoslavie*. St. Petersburg: Byblyya dlya vsekh, 2008.

Fedorov, Vladimir, "Ecumenical Missionary Needs and Perspectives in Eastern and Central Europe Today: Theological Education with an Accent on Mission as a First Priority in Our Religious Rebirth." *International Review of Mission* 92 (2003) 66–83.

————. "Orthodox View on Theological Education as Mission." In *Theological Education as Mission*, edited by Peter F. Penner, 69–101. Schwarzenfeld: Neufeld, 2005.

————. "Theological Education in the Russian Orthodox Church (in Russia, Ukraine, Belarus)." In *Handbook of Theological Education in World Christianity: Theological Perspectives, Ecumenical Trends, Religious Surveys*, Dietrich Werner et al., 522. Oxford: Regnum, 2010.

Feuerbach, Ludwig. *Das Wesen des Christentums*. Berlin: Akademie-Verlag, 1956.

Filaret, Patriarch. "We Think That Russia Has Taken the Path of Lies." *RISU*.org, 14 March 2014. http://risu.org.ua/en/index/all_news/orthodox/uoc_kp/55711/.

Finger, Thomas. "Anabaptism and Eastern Orthodoxy: Some Unexpected Similarities?" *Journal of Ecumenical Studies* 31–32 (1994) 67–91.

Flett, John G. *The Witness of God: The Trinity, Missio Dei, Karl Barth and the Nature of Christian Community*. Grand Rapids, Eerdmans, 2010.

Florovsky, Georges. *Ways of Russian Theology*. Translated by R. L. Nichols. Belmont: Nordland, 1979.

Frei, Hans W. *The Eclipse of Biblical Narrative: A Study in Eighteenth and Nineteenth Century Hermeneutics*. New Haven: Yale University Press, 1974.

Froese, Paul. *The Plot to Kill God: Findings From the Soviet Experiment in Secularization*. Berkeley: University of California Press, 2008.

Fromm, Eric. *Marx's Concept of Man*. New York: Continuum, 2003.

Frost, Michael. *Exiles: Living Missionally in a Post-Christian Culture*. Peabody, MA: Hendrickson, 2006.

Frost, Michael, and Alan Hirsch. *The Shaping of Things to Come: Innovation and Mission for the 21st-Century Church*. Peabody, MA: Hendrickson, 2003.

Fukuyama, Francis. *Trust: The Social Virtues and the Creation of Prosperity*. New York: Free, 1995.

Gadamer, Hans-Georg. *Wahrheit und Methode*. Berlin: Akademie-Verlag, 2007.

Garadzha, V. Y. "Pereosmyslenye." *Nauka y Relyhyya* 1 (1989) 2.

BIBLIOGRAPHY

————. "Religion in an Age of Scientific-Technological Revolution." *Izvestia*, 27 January, 1972, 5.

Gerlich, Fritz. *Der Kommunismus als Lehre vom Tausendjährigen Reich*. München: Bruckmann, 1920.

Gorder, Andrew Christian van. "Post-Soviet Protestant Missions in Central Asia." *East-West Church and Ministry Report* 17 (2009) 3–4.

Graves, Jack L. "Plugging the Theological Brain Drain—Churches, Mission Agencies and Seminaries All Have a Part to Play in Avoiding Failures in Our Training Investments." *Evangelical Missions Quarterly* 28 (1992) 154–61.

Grenz, Stanley J. *Theology for the Community of God*. Grand Rapids: Eerdmans, 2000.

Gronemeyer, Marianne. *Die Macht der Bedürfnisse. Überfluss und Knappheit*. Darmstadt: WBG, 2002.

Gundersen, P. *Pavel Nikolai from Monrepo: A European Unlike the Rest*. Moscow: BBI, 2004.

Hanouz, Margareta Drzeniek, and Thierry Geiger, eds. *The Ukraine Competitiveness Report 2008: Towards Sustained Growth and Development*. Geneva: World Economic Forum, 2008.

Haymes, Brian, et al. *On Being the Church: Revisioning Baptist Identity*. Carlisle: Paternoster, 2004.

Hilberath, Bernd Jochen. *Der dreieinige Gott und die Gemeinschaft der Menschen*. Mainz: Grünewald, 1990.

Hirsch, Alan. *The Forgotten Ways: Reactivating the Missional Church*. Ada, Michigan: Brazos, 2009.

Hoffmann, Lutz, and Felicitas Möllers, eds. *Ukraine on the Road to Europe*. Heidelberg: Physica, 2001.

Holovakah, Evhen I. "Popular Social and Political Attitudes in Ukraine." In *Ukraine: The Search for a National Identity*, edited by Sharon L. Wolchik, 203. Oxford: Rowman and Littlefield, 2000.

Holovaty, Nicholas. "An Ideal Theological Education: The Vision of Moscow's Protestant Leaders." *East-West Church and Ministry Report* 8 (2000) 6–7.

Huntington, Samuel P. "The Clash of Civilizations?" *Foreign Affairs* 72 (1993) 22–49.

————. *The Clash of Civilizations and the Remaking of World Order*. New York: Simon and Schuster, 1996.

Ivakhiv, Adrian. "In Search of Deeper Identities: Paganism and Native Faith in Contemporary Ukraine." *Nova Religio* 8 (2005) 7–38.

————. "The Revival of Ukrainian Native Faith." In *Modern Paganism in World Cultures*, edited by Michael Strmiska, 209–39. Santa Barbara, CA: ABC-CLIO, 2005.

Jameson, Fredric, and Masao Miyoshi, eds. *The Cultures of Globalization*. Durham: Duke University Press, 1998.

Jones, Keith G. "Leading a Theological Institution in (Central) Europe Today." In *Theological Education as Mission*, edited by Peter F. Penner, 289–308. Schwarzenfeld: Neufeld, 2005.

Kenworthy, Scott M. "To Save the World or to Renounce it: Modes of Moral Action in Russian Orthodoxy." In *Religion, Morality and Community in Post-Soviet Societies*, edited by Catherine Wanner and Mark Steinberg, 21–54. Bloomington: Indiana University Press, 2008.

Keston News Service 98 (15 May, 1980).

Key, Alistair. "Marx's Messianic Faith." In *Messianism Through History*, edited by W. Beuken, S. Freyne, and A. Weiler, 101–13. London: SCM, 1993.

Khoruzhyy, Serhey. *Delo khrystyanskoho prosveshchenyya y paradyhmy russkoy kul'tury*. Saint Petersburg: VRFSH, 2000.

———. *Kryzys evropeyskoho cheloveka y resursy khrystyanskoy antropolohyy*. Moscow: Kul'turnyy tsentr, 2006.

King, Edmund. "The Concept of Ideology in Communist Education." In *Communist Education*, edited by Edmund King, 1. London: Methuen, 1963.

Kirk, J. Andrew. "Re-envisioning the Theological Curriculum as if the Missio Dei Mattered." In *Theological Education as Mission*, edited by Peter F. Penner, 22–37. Schwarzenfeld: Neufeld, 2005.

———. *What Is Mission? Some Theological Explorations*. London: DLT, 1999.

Klassen, Heinrich. *Mission als Zeugnis: zur missionarischen Existenz in der Sowjetunion nach dem Zweiten Weltkrieg*. Berlin: Logos-Verlag, 2003.

———. "Mission as Bearing Witness—Immigrant Witness in Germany." *Mission Focus* 14 (2006) 170.

Knox, Zoe. *Russian Society and the Orthodox Church*. London: RoutledgeCurzon, 2005.

Koch, K. *Khrisiyani v Evropi. Novi shlyakhi peredayyiyaviri*. Kyiv: DUKH I LITERA, 2013.

Komarov, Victor. *Byt' mudrym bez Boga!* Moscow: Moskovskiy Rabochiy, 1986.

Konforovych, A. H. *Ateystycheskoe vospytanye v protsesse prepozhavanyya matematyky*. Moscow: Radyans'ka shkola, 1980.

Kool, Anne-Marie, and Peter F. Penner. "Theological Education in Eastern and Central Europe: Major Developments and Challenges since 1910." In *History and Mission in Europe*, edited by Peter F. Penner and Mary Raber, 83–106. Schwarzfeld: Neufeld, 2011.

Kotaleichuk, Anna. "Yes, We Can." *New Eastern Europe* 3 (2014) 61.

Kovalenko, Georiy. "Politiki pryeoovyelichivayoot znachyeniye gyeopolitichyeskoy intyegratsii." http://www.pravmir.ru/prot-georgij-kovalenko-politiki-preuvelichivayut-znachenie-geopoliticheskoj-integracii/.

Krindatch, Alexei D. "Ukraine: The Re-awakening of Greek Catholicism, Orthodox Cleavages and the Rise of Islam." In *The Changing Religious Landscape of Europe*, edited by Hans Knippenberg, 164–88. Amsterdam: Het Spinhuis, 2005.

Kuzio, Taras. "Oligarchs Wield Power in Ukrainian Politics." *Eurasia Daily Monitor*, 1 July 2008. http://www.jamestown.org/programs/edm/single/?tx_ttnews%5Btt_news%5D=33765&tx_ttnews%5BbackPid%5D=166&no_cache=1#.VH-B94vF9OE.

Kuzio, Taras, and Paul J. D'Anier, eds. *Dilemmas of State-Led Nation Building in Ukraine*. Westport, CT: Praeger, 2002.

Lelich, Milan. "Victims of Russian Propaganda." *New Eastern Europe*, July/August 2014, 75–80.

Lenin, V. I. *On Religion*. Moscow: Progress, 1965.

Leonard, B. J. *The Challenge of Being Baptist: Owning a Scandalous Past and an Uncertain Future*. Waco: Baylor University Press, 2010.

Lewis, David C. "A Sobering Critique of Russian Protestant Church Growth." *East-West Church and Ministry Report* 9 (2001) 5–8.

Lossky, Vladimir. *The Mystical Theology of the Eastern Church*. Cambridge: James Clarke, 1968.

Lukács, Georg. *The Process of Democratization*. Translated by Susanne Bernhardt and Norman Levine. Albany: State University of New York Press, 1991.

Lukes, Steven. *Marxism and Morality*. Oxford: Oxford University Press, 1987.

Lunacharsky, A. V. *Bezbozhnik* (25 December, 1923).

Lunkin, R. "The Ukrainian Revolution and Christian Churches." *East-West Church and Ministry Report* 22 (2014) 1–5.

Lyubaschenko, V. "Protestantizm v Ukraïni: tvorennja stereotipiv trivae." *Ï* 22 (2001). http://risu.org.ua/ua/index/monitoring/religious_digest/16446/.

MacArthur, John. *Terrorism, Jihad, and the Bible: A Response to the Terrorist Attacks*. Nashville: W Publishing Group, 2001.

MacIntyre, Alasdair. "Epistemological Crises, Narrative and the Philosophy of Science." In *Why Narrative: Readings in Narrative Theology*, edited by Stanley Hauerwas and L. Gregory Jones, 139. Grand Rapids: Eerdmans, 1989.

Macquarrie, John. *In Search of Humanity*. London: SCM, 1982.

Manzhul, Victor. "Verit, chtoby znat." Kyiv, 2013.

Marinovich, Miroslav. "The Authenticity of Eastern Christianity Can Enrich Western Europe." http://risu.org.ua/ru/index/expert_thought/interview/54232/.

Markus, Vasyl. "Politics and Religion in Ukraine: In Search of a New Pluralistic Dimension." In *The Politics of Religion in Russia and the New States of Eurasia*, edited by Michael Bourdeaux, 171. London: M. E. Sharpe, 1995.

———. "Religious Pluralism in Ukraine." In *The Politics of Religion in Russia and the New States of Eurasia*, edited by Michael Bourdeaux. London: M. E. Sharpe, 1995.

Marsh, Christopher. *Religion and the State in Russia and China: Suppression, Survival, and Revival*. New York: Continuum, 2011.

Martsinkovskii, V. "Khristos gryadushchii." *Vestnik spaseniya* 20 (1967) 12–16.

———. "Pervaiia lyubov.'" *Vestnyk istiny* 63 (1976).

Marx, Karl. *Zur Kritik der Hegelschen Rechtsphilosophie*. Marx-Engles-Werke 1. Berlin: Institut für Marxismus-Leninismus, 1956.

———. *Zur Kritik der Nationalökonomie—Ökonomisch-philosophische Manuskripte*. Stuttgart: Kröner, 1970.

McClendon, James Wm. *Systematic Theology: Volume I: Ethics*. Nashville: Abingdon, 1986.

———. *Systematic Theology: Volume II: Doctrine*. Nashville: Abingdon, 1994.

———. *Systematic Theology: Volume III: Witness*. Nashville: Abingdon, 2000.

McCullagh, Francis. *The Bolshevik Persecution of Christianity*. London: John Murray, 1924.

Melnichuk, Alexei. "Keys to Re-energizing Our Outreach." *East-West Church and Ministry Report* 17 (2009) 2–3.

Merkle, Judith A. *Being Faithful: Christian Commitment in Modern Society*. London: T. & T. Clark, 2010.

Meyendorff, John. "From Byzantium to Russia: Religious and cultural legacy." In *Tausend Jahre Christentum in Rußland: Zum Millennium der Taufe der Kiever Rus'*, edited by Wolfgang Heller, 86. Göttingen: Vandenhoeck and Ruprecht, 1988.

Millar, James R., and Sharon L. Wolchik, eds. *The Social Legacy of. Communism*. Cambridge: Woodrow Wilson Center and Cambridge University Press, 1994.

Mitrokhin, L. "Baptism o smisle zhizny." *Nauka i Relygiya* 4 (1967) 24–29.

Moltmann, Jürgen. *The Church in the Power of the Spirit: A Contribution to Messianic Ecclesiology*. Translated by Margaret Kohl London: SCM, 1977.

———. *Theologie der Hoffnung*. München: Kaiser, 1964.

———. *Trinität und Reich Gottes: Zur Gotteslehre*. München: Kaiser, 1980.

Moreland, J. P., and William Lane Craig. *Philosophical Foundations for a Christian Worldview*. Downers Grove: InterVarsity, 2003.

Murzin, Andrey. *Dialogue with the Orthodox Church.* Kyiv, 2013.

Myklushchak, Pavel. "Chelovek kak transendentnoe sushchestvo: Bohopodobye s dohmatyko-antropolycheskoy tochky zrenyya." In *Znachenye khrystyanskoy antropolohyy pered lytsom sovremennykh obshchestvennykh zadach y problem,* edited by Andrei Lorgus, 143. Moscow: Yndryk, 2003.

Negrov, Alexander I., and Miriam Charter. "Why Is There No Russian 'Protestant' Theology in Russia? A Personal Outcry." *Religion in Eastern Europe* 17 (1997) 30–41.

Nesmeyanov, A. *Nauka i Relyhyya* 1 (1959) 3.

Newbigin, Lesslie. *Foolishness to the Greeks: The Gospel and Western Culture.* Grand Rapids: Eerdmans, 1986.

———. *The Gospel in a Pluralist Society.* Grand Rapids: Eerdmans, 1989.

———. *The Open Secret: An Introduction to the Theology of Mission.* London: SPCK, 1995.

———. *Proper Confidence: Faith, Doubt, and Certainty in Christian Discipleship.* Grand Rapids: Eerdmans, 1995.

———. *Truth to Tell: The Gospel and Public Truth.* Grand Rapids: Eerdmans, 1991.

Newman, John Henry. *The Idea of a University.* London: Putnam's, 1891.

Nichols, Gregory L. *The Development of Russian Evangelical Spirituality: A Study of Ivan V. Kargel (1849–1937).* Eugene, OR: Pickwick, 2011.

———. "Reflections on Twenty Years of Ministry: From Odessa to Prague." *East-West Church and Ministry Report* 19 (2011) 3–5.

Niebuhr, H. Richard. *Social Sources of Denominationalism.* New York: Henry Holt, 1929.

Nietzsche, Friedrich Wilhelm. *Also sprach Zarathustra: Ein Buch für Alle und Keinen (1883–1885).* Berlin: de Gruyter, 1968.

———. *The Will to Power.* Translated by Walter Kaufmann and R. J. Hollingdale. Edited by Walter Kaufmann. New York: Vintage, 1968.

Ogorodnikov, Alexander. "Sovremennaya russkaya kul'tura." *Keston Archive* (August, 1976) <SU / Ort 12>.

Parashchevin, M. *Relihiya ta relihiynist' v Ukrayini.* Kyiv: Instytut polityky and Instytut sotsiolohiyi NAN Ukrayiny, 2009.

Parushev, Parush R. "East and West: A Theological Conversation." *Journal of European Baptist Studies* 1 (2000) 31–44.

———. "East-West: A Theological Conversation." *Common Ground E-Journal: Perspectives on the Church in the 21st Century* 1 (2004) 11–21.

———. "Kingdom of Heaven." In *A Dictionary of European Baptist Life and Thought,* edited by J. H. Y. Briggs at al., 289. Milton Keynes: Paternoster, 2009.

———. "Towards Convictional Theological Education: Facing Challenges of Contextualization, Credibility and Relevance." In *Theological Education as Mission,* edited by Peter F. Penner, 185–208. Schwarzenfeld: Neufeld, 2005.

———. "Walking in the Dawn of the Light: On the Salvation Ethics of the Ecclesial Communities in the Orthodox Tradition from a Radical Reformation Perspective." PhD diss., Fuller Theological Seminary, 2006.

Parusinksi, Jakub. "Poroshenko's Historic Opportunity." *New Eastern Europe,* July/August 2014, 81–86.

Pashkov, N. A. *Ateystycheskoe vospytanye v vysshey shkole.* Moscow: Yzdatel'stvo Moskovskoho Unyversyteta, 1982.

Pavlov, V. "Načalo, razvitie i nastojašee položenie baptizma sredi russkih." In *Baptisty: cerkov" i gosudarstvo,* edited by V. Pavlov, 85. Moscow, 2004.

Penner, Peter F. "Case Study: EEST/CEETE." In *Theological Education as Mission*, edited by Peter F. Penner, 254. Schwarzenfeld: Neufeld, 2005.

———. "Critical Evaluation of Recent Developments in the CIS." In *Mission in the Former Soviet Union*, edited by Walter W. Sawatsky and Peter F. Penner, 120–64. Schwarzenfeld: Neufeld, 2005.

———. "Scripture, Community, and Context in God's Mission in the FSU." In *Mission in the Former Soviet Union*, edited by Walter W. Sawatsky and Peter F. Penner, 22. Schwarzenfeld: Neufeld, 2005.

Petrenko, Viktor. *Bogoslovie ikon. Protestantskaya tochka zreniya*. St. Petersburg: Byblyya dlya vsekh, 2000.

Petrenko, Vytalyy. *Vlast' v tserkvy. Razvytye kontseptsyy vlasty v Russkoy pravoslavnoy tserkvy*. Cherkassy: Kollokvyum, 2012.

Pilli, Einike. "Toward a Holistic View of Theological Education." In *Theological Education as Mission*, edited by Peter F. Penner, 171–84. Schwarzenfeld: Neufeld, 2005.

Pleines, Heiko. "The Political Role of the Oligarchs." In *Ukraine on Its Way to Europe: Interim Results of the Orange Revolution*, edited by Juliane Besters-Dilger, 103–19. Frankfurt: Peter Lang, 2009.

Popov, Alexander. "The Evangelical Christians-Baptists in the Soviet Union as a Hermeneutical Community." PhD diss., University of Wales, 2010.

Poresh, Vladimir. "Faith and Lack of Faith in Russia." *Religion in Communist Lands* 19 (1991) 75.

Pospielovsky, Dmitry V. *A History of Marxist-Leninist Atheism and Soviet Anti-Religious Policies*. New York: St. Martin's, 1987.

"Programma—nezavisimost." *Vestnik istiny* 3 (2011) 33.

Prokhanov, Ivan Stepanovich. "A Brief Note about the Origin, Development and Current State of the Evangelical Movement in Russia." *A New, or Evangelical Life* 5 (2009) 24.

Proshak, Vitaliy. "Paganism in Ukraine: Its Beliefs, Encounter with Christianity and Survival." *Theological Reflections* 7 (2006) 141–48.

Puglisi, Rosaria. "The Rise of the Ukrainian Oligarchs." *Democratization* 10 (2003) 99–123.

Raber, Mary. "Expectation and Reality: Theological Education among Baptists in Ukraine." *Religion in Eastern Europe* 17 (1997) 33–37.

Rajchinec, F. *Svoeobrazie baptizma: chetyre hrupkih svobody. 400-letie baptizma i princip svobody sovesti*. Erlangen, 2010.

Rauschenbusch, Walter. *Christianity and the Social Crisis*. 1907. Reprint, Louisville: Westminster John Knox, 1991.

Reimer, Johannes. "Mission in Post-Perestroika Russia." *East-West Church and Ministry Report* 4 (1996) 8–9.

———. "Mission in Post-Perestroika Russia." *Missionalia* 24 (1996) 16–39.

———. "Recovering the Missionary Memory: Russian Evangelicals in Search of an Appropriate Missiology." *European Journal of Theology* 22 (2013) 137–48.

———. *Transformation of Society*. Kyiv: KML, 2007.

"Relihiya i vlada v Ukrayini: problem y vzayemovidnosyn." Informacijni materialy do Kruhloho stolu na temu: "Derzhavno-konfesijni vidnosyny v Ukrayini stanom na 2013 rik: rux do partnerstva derzhavy i Cerkvy chy do kryzy vzayemyn?" 22 kvitniya 2013. Kyiv: 2013.

Riabchuk, Mykalo. "A Blessing in Disguise." *New Eastern Europe* 3 (2014) 67.

Richters, Katja. *The Post-Soviet Russian Orthodox Church: Politics, Culture and Greater Russia*. London: Routledge, 2012.

Ricoeur, Paul. "Freiheit im Licht der Hoffnung." In *Hermeneutik und Strukturalismus: Der Konflikt der Interpretationen I*, translated by Johannes Rütsch, 205. München: Kösel, 1973.

Rollins, Peter. *The Fidelity of Betrayal: Towards a Church Beyond Belief*. London: SPCK, 2008.

———. *How (Not) to Speak of God*. London: SPCK, 2006.

Rosenthal, James M., and Susan T. Erdey, eds. *Living Communion: Anglican Consultative Council XIII*. London: Anglican Communion Office, 2006.

Sawatsky, Walter W. "Return of Mission and Evangelization in the CIS (1980s–Present): An Assessment." In *Mission in the Former Soviet Union*, edited by Walter W. Sawatsky and Peter F. Penner, 94–119. Schwarzenfeld: Neufeld, 2005.

———. "Visions in Conflict: Starting Anew Through the Prism of Leadership Training Efforts." In *Religion after Communism in Eastern Europe*, edited by Niels Nielsen, 13, 20. Boulder: Westview, 1994.

———. "Without God We Cannot, Without Us God Won't: Thoughts on God's Mission within the CIS in the Future" In *Mission in the Former Soviet Union*, edited by Walter W. Sawatsky and Peter F. Penner, 258. Schwarzenfeld: Neufeld, 2005.

Schreiter, Robert J. *Constructing Local Theologies*. Maryknoll, NY: Orbis, 2002.

Searle, Joshua T. "The Ecumenical Imperative and the Kingdom of God: Towards a Baptistic Perspective on Church Unity." *Journal of European Baptist Studies* 14 (2013) 5–23.

———. "From Christian Worldview to Kingdom Formation: Theological Education as Mission in the Former Soviet Union." *European Journal of Theology* 23 (2014) 104–15.

———. "Learning from the Past to Reimagine the Future: Theological Education in the (Former) Soviet Union." *Keston Newsletter* 19 (2014) 10–21.

———. *The Scarlet Woman and the Red Hand: Apocalyptic Belief in the Northern Ireland Troubles*. Eugene: Wipf and Stock, 2014.

———. "Tserkov' bez sten." http://dcu.org.ua/ru/proektyi.html.

Shamgunov, Insur. "Listening to the Voice of the Graduate: An Analysis of Professional Practice and Training for Ministry in Central Asia." PhD diss., Oxford University, 2009.

———. "Protestant Theological Education in Central Asia: Embattled but Resilient." *East-West Church and Ministry Report* 18 (2010) 10–13.

Shapovalova, Natalia. "Ukraine: A New Partnership." In *The European Union and Democracy Promotion: A Critical Global Assessment*, edited by Richard Youngs, 65–66. Baltimore: Johns Hopkins University Press, 2010.

Shenk, Wilbert R. *Changing Frontiers of Mission*. Maryknoll, NY: Orbis, 1999.

Shurden, Walter. *The Baptist Identity: Four Fragile Freedoms*. Macon: Smyth and Helwys, 1997.

"Skorochuyetsya chyselnist baptystiv v Ukrayini." http://www.religion.in.ua.

Smith, Christian. *The Bible Made Impossible: Why Biblicism Is Not a Truly Evangelical Reading of Scripture*. Grand Rapids: Brazos, 2011.

Smith, James K. A. *The Church and Postmodernism*. Colloquium, 2012.

———. *Desiring the Kingdom: Worship, Worldview and Cultural Formation*. Grand Rapids: Baker, 2009.

———. *Imagining the Kingdom: How Worship Works.* Grand Rapids: Baker, 2013.

Stamoolis, James J. *Eastern Orthodox Mission Theology Today.* American Society of Missiology Series 10. Maryknoll, NY: Orbis, 1986.

Stassen, Glen H., and David P. Gushee. *Kingdom Ethics: Following Jesus in Contemporary Context.* Downers Grove, IL: InterVarsity, 2003.

Stearns, Peter N. *Consumerism in World History: The Global Transformation of Desire.* London: Routledge, 2001.

Stoner-Weiss, Kathryn. "Whither the Central State? The Regional Sources of Russia's Stalled Reforms." In *After the Collapse of Communism: Comparative Lessons of Transition,* edited by Michael McFaul and Kathryn Stoner-Weiss, 130–72. New York: Cambridge University Press, 2005.

Suchodolski, Bogdan. *Grundlagen der marxistischen Erziehungstheorie.* Warsaw: VEB, 1961.

Tancher, V. K. *Vospytanye aktyvnoy ateystycheskoy pozytsyy studencheskoy molodezhy.* Kyiv: Holovnoe yzdatel'stvo, 1982.

Taylor, Charles. *A Secular Age.* Cambridge: Harvard University Press, 2007.

Theodorovich, Nadezhda. *Religion und Atheismus in der UdSSR.* Translated by I. Stoldt and P. J. Braun. Munich: Claudius Verlag, 1970.

Thistleton, Anthony. *The Two Horizons: New Testament Hermeneutics and Philosophical Description.* Grand Rapids: Eerdmans, 1980.

Tillich, Paul. *The Courage to Be.* New Haven: Yale University Press, 1952.

Tomka, Miklós, and Paul M. Zulehner. *Religion in den Reformländern Ost(Mittel)Europas.* Schwabenverlag: Ostfildern, 1999.

Tomlinson, John. *Globalization and Identity: Dialectics of Flow and Closure. Globalization and Culture.* Cambridge: Polity, 1999.

Turij, Oleg. "Das religiöse Leben und die zwischenkonfessionellen Verhältnisse in der Ukraine seit der Wende." In *Vom Umbruch zum Aufbruch? Kirchliche und gesellschaftliche Entwicklungen in Ostmitteleuropa nach dem Zerfall des Kommunismus,* edited by Dietmar W. Winkler, 258–94. Vienna: Tyrolia-Verlag, 2010.

———. "Kirchen in der Ukraine. Zwischen gesellschaftlicher Wende und verwundeter Gesellschaft." In *Religion und Wende in Ostmittel- und Südosteuropa, 1989–2009,* edited by J. Marte et al., 196–217. Vienna: Tyrolia-Verlag, 2010.

"Universal Priesthood." *Philosophic and Religious Notebook* 7 (2013) 84.

Ushakova, Tanya. "There Is No Sex in the USSR!" *Frontier,* March-April 1991, 1.

Uzlaner, D. "The Pussy Riot Case and Peculiarities of Russian Post-Secularism." *State, Religion, Church* 2 (2013) 93–133.

Volf, Miroslav. *After Our Likeness: The Church as the Image of the Trinity.* Grand Rapids: Eerdmans, 1998.

———. *A Public Faith: How Followers of Christ Should Serve the Common Good.* Grand Rapids: Baker Academic, 2011.

Walters, A. *Renewed Creation: Basics of a Biblical Worldview.* Kyiv, 2013.

Wanner, Catherine. *Communities of the Converted: Ukrainians and Global Evangelism.* Ithaca: Cornell University Press, 2007.

———. "Evangelicalism and the Resurgence of Religion in Ukraine." *NCEEER,* February 2006, 1–21.

Wardin, Albert. "How Indigenous was the Baptist Movement in the Russian Empire?" *Journal of European Baptist Studies* 9 (2009) 29–37.

World Council of Churches. "14 Reasons for Global Solidarity in Ecumenical Theological Education." http://www.oikoumene.org/en/folder/documents-pdf/Communication_Leaflet_for_ETE.pdf.

Wenz, Gunther. "Episkope im Dienst der Apostolizität der Kirche. Eine thematische Skizze im Lichte des lutherisch-anglikanischen Dialogs zum Bischofsamt." In *Das kirchliche Amt in apostolischer Nachfolge. I. Grundlagen und Grundfragen*, edited by Th. Schneider and Gunther Wenz, 38–67. Freiburg: Herder, 2004.

Wetter, Gustav. *Dialectical Materialism: A Historical and Systematic Survey of Philosophy in the Soviet Union*. Translated by Peter Heath. London: Routledge and Kegan Paul, 1964.

Willard, Dallas. "The Bible, the University and the God Who Hides." In *The Bible and the University*, edited by David Lyle Jeffrey and C. Stephen Evans, 17–39. Grand Rapids: Zondervan, 2007.

———. *The Great Omission: Reclaiming Jesus's Essential Teachings on Discipleship*. San Francisco: Harper, 2006.

Wilson, Andrew. "The Communist Party of Ukraine: From Soviet Brotherhood to East Slavic Man." In *The Left Transformed: Social Democrats and Neo-Leninists in East-Central Europe, Russia, and Ukraine*, edited by Jane Leftwich Curry and Joan Barth Urban, 221–25. Lanham, MD: Rowman and Littlefield, 2003.

Wink, Walter. *The Powers That Be: Theology for a New Millennium*. New York: Doubleday, 1998.

Wolf, Koenraad de. *Dissident for Life: Alexander Ogorodnikov and the Struggle for Religious Freedom in Russia*. Grand Rapids: Eerdmans, 2013.

Wright, Nigel Goring. *A Theology of the Dark Side: Putting the Power of Evil in Its Place*. Downers Grove, IL: InterVarsity, 2003.

Wunderink, Susan. "Faith and Hope in Ukraine." *Christianity Today*, 17 October 2008. http://www.christianitytoday.com/ct/2008/october/25.70.html?start=1.

Yannoulatos, Anastasios. "The Purpose and Motive of Mission from an Orthodox Theological Point of View." *Porefthendes* 9 (1967) 5.

Yekelchyk, Serhy. *Ukraine: Birth of a Modern Nation*. New York: Oxford University Press, 2007.

Zernov, Nicholas. *The Russian Religious Renaissance of the Twentieth Century*. London: Darton, Longman and Todd, 1963.

Zhybryk, Aleksandr. *Boh pod arestom*. Kyiv: Knyhonosha, 2012.

Zinoviev, Aleksandr. *Homo Sovieticus*. Translated by Charles Janson. New York: Atlantic, 1986.